DATE DUE

GAYLORD   PRINTED IN U.S.A.

GAYLORD
FG

John Churchill, first duke of Marlborough, was one of the two greatest military commanders in British history and the first subject to achieve and exercise a dominating influence in European affairs. With Wellington and Nelson he is the nearest that Britain has had to a national hero, yet today his reputation has faded. Few, apart from specialists in military history, have any appreciation of the extent of his achievements.

This new study sets Marlborough's career in its contexts: the royal Court of the last Stuart monarchs, the desperate struggle against French attempts to establish hegemony in western Europe and the bitter political strife in Britain between the Whig and the Tory parties. It examines the opportunistic ways in which John Churchill rose from obscurity and poverty to wealth and greatness, his decisive role in the Revolution of 1688 and the circumstances and reasons for his dramatic fall.

BRITISH LIVES

Marlborough

BRITISH LIVES

Edited by Maurice Cowling
Fellow of Peterhouse, Cambridge
and John Vincent
Professor of History, University of Bristol

This is a series of short, biographical studies which will address the lives of major figures from the early medieval period to modern times. Each figure will be of political, intellectual or religious significance in British or British imperial history. A major aim of the series is to seek out and scrutinise figures whose current interpretation has become stale or conventional, and to establish a lively interaction between author and subject in an attempt to place each historical figure in a new light.

Titles in the series

Pitt the Elder
JEREMY BLACK

William Temple
JOHN KENT

Marlborough
J. R. JONES

Other titles are in preparation

Marlborough

J. R. JONES

Emeritus Professor of History, University
of East Anglia

CAMBRIDGE
UNIVERSITY PRESS

Published by the Press Syndicate of the University of Cambridge
The Pitt Building, Trumpington Street, Cambridge CB2 1RP
40 West 20th Street, New York, NY10011–4211, USA
10 Stamford Road, Oakleigh, Victoria 3166, Australia

First published 1993

Printed in Great Britain at the University Press, Cambridge

A catalogue record for this book is available from the British Library

Library of Congress cataloguing in publication data
Jones, J. R. (James Rees), 1925–
Marlborough / J. R. Jones.
p.   cm. – (British Lives)
Includes bibliographical references and index.
ISBN 0 521 37571 1. – ISBN 0 521 37593 2 (pbk.)
1. Marlborough, John Churchill, Duke of, 1650–1722.   2. Great
Britain – History – Stuarts, 1603–1714 – Biography.   3. Great Britain –
Court and courtiers – Biography.   4. Statesmen – Great Britain –
Biography.   5. Generals – Great Britain – Biography.   I. Title.
II. Series.
DA462.M3J66   1993
941.06′9′092 – dc20
[B]   93-31672   CIP

ISBN 0 521 37571 1 hardback
ISBN 0 521 37593 2 paperback

Contents

Maps

Note on dates

All dates given for events, or correspondence originating, in England are Old Style; for those in Europe New Style. In the seventeenth century the Old Style were ten days behind New Style, adjusted in the eighteenth century to eleven. The years given all begin on 1 January.

Biographical note

The following works are cited in abbreviated form in the footnotes.

Murray   George Murray, *The Letters and Dispatches of John Churchill, First Duke of Marlborough, from 1702 to 1712* (5 vols., 1845)

Snyder   Henry L. Snyder, *The Marlborough–Godolphin Correspondence* (3 vols., Oxford, 1975)

T'Hoff   B. Van T'Hoff, *The Correspondence 1701–1711 of John Churchill, First Duke of Marlborough, and Anthonie Heinsius Grand Pensionary of Holland* (The Hague, 1951)

Vault and Pelet   F. E. de Vault and J. J. G. Pelet, *Mémoires militaires relatifs à la succession d'Espagne sous Louis XIV* (11 vols., Paris, 1835–62)

Place of publication is London unless otherwise stated.

Introduction

Marlborough's earliest biographers were concerned to vindicate his reputation from the libels of hostile politicians and journalists. Both Francis Hare, whose *Life and Glorious History* appeared in 1705, and Thomas Lediard, who published a full *Life* in 1736, had served Marlborough personally, Hare as his chaplain, Lediard as an attaché during his mission to Altranstadt.[1] The latter based his work on wide manuscript materials and so has served as a quarry for later historians. This is also the case with William Coxe's *Memoirs of John, Duke of Marlborough* (1818–19) and the relevant portions of Onno Klopp's *Der Fall des Hauses Stuart* (Vienna, 1880–5). The latter is historiographically interesting because it reflects the ambivalence of contemporary Habsburg attitudes to Marlborough – unease at their unfortunately unavoidable dependence on him and predominantly Protestant allies, disgust at his betrayal of legitimist principles in 1688 and social contempt for an upstart who saw himself as the equal of hereditary princes.

In the second half of the eighteenth century three Scottish

---

[1] [Francis Hare], *The Life and Glorious History of John, Duke and Earl of Marlborough* (1705; 2nd edn 1707). See Robert D. Horn, 'Marlborough's first biographer: Dr Francis Hare', *Huntington Library Quarterly*, 20 (1957), 145–6. Thomas Lediard, *The Life of John, Duke of Marlborough* (1736; 2nd edn 1743).

exponents of the new Toryism produced new criticisms of Marlborough. David Hume in leading the rehabilitation of the Stuarts excoriated his behaviour in 1688. Sir John Dalrymple and James Macpherson published documents from the French and Jacobite archives compromising him as a traitor after as well as in 1688.[2] But it was the classical Whig historians of the nineteenth century who set out with effect to demolish his reputation. First Henry Hallam presented a ferocious indictment on moral grounds in his *History* (1827). Hallam found in his political career 'nothing but ambition and rapacity in his motives, nothing but treachery and intrigue in his means'. This moral line was continued by T.B. Macaulay in his most magisterial manner. In his essay on Hallam's *History* (1828) he depicted Marlborough as the product of an essentially corrupt Court: 'in no other age could the path to power and glory have been thrown open to the manifold infamies of Churchill'.[3]

Macaulay's hostile interpretation embodied not only early Victorian moral values but also the political principles and expectations of progressive, liberal Whigs. Unlike Hallam who doubted the wisdom of the 1832 Reform Act, Macaulay had no doubts about progressive development. For him Marlborough as a courtier and patronage broker belonged to an evil system, the Old Corruption whose remains liberal Whigs were eradicating. As a soldier-politician Marlborough disquietingly resembled Wellington, the arch-reactionary, and it was contrary to the principles of reformed representative government for the entire destiny of the nation to lie in

---

[2] David Hume, *The History of Great Britain* (2 vols., Edinburgh and London, 1754–7): this ended in 1688 with continuation volumes by Tobias Smollett. Sir John Dalrymple, *Memoirs of Great Britain and Ireland* (2 vols., 1771–3). James Macpherson, *Original Papers Containing the Secret History of Great Britain* (2 vols., 1775).

[3] Henry Hallam, *The Constitutional History of England* (3 vols., 1872), vol. III, p. 124–5. The first edition was in 1827, review by T. B. Macaulay, *Edinburgh Review*, September 1828.

the hands of a single man, and particularly a soldier. Marlborough had been concerned with high politics – diplomacy on a continental scale, the subsidisation of allies, the internal policies of allied states, policies that depended on armed force or its threat for their implementation – not with reforms and the improvement of conditions of life.

However the main reason for Macaulay's harsh treatment of Marlborough is that he needed him as a villain to sustain the particular interpretation which he had formed. He discarded the stock condemnation of James II as a tyrant because this had been exploited by anti-Catholic demagogues to create prejudices that had obstructed Catholic emancipation and were still a potent force. Macaulay installed Marlborough as the replacement villain guilty of a succession of betrayals, particularly in 'revealing' the plans for an attack on Brest in the Camaret Bay letter. James in contrast was seen as foolish and gullible. Macaulay emulated Tacitus and Clarendon in inserting carefully crafted character sketches in his narrative, and these tended to be in stark tones of black and white: he unsparingly caricatured Marlborough as an odious careerist driven by ambition, avarice and an unbalanced wife who manipulated Anne without mercy.

Macaulay's artful selection of evidence to fit his case was exposed in devastating detail by John Paget, but the fully documented refutation came in Winston Churchill's four-volume biography published between 1933 and 1938.[4] He expanded Paget's condemnation of Macaulay's covert use of dubious sources, his unfailing readiness to attribute base motives and to accept unfavourable contemporary judge-

---

[4] John Paget, *The New Examen* (1861); essays previously published in *Blackwood's Magazine*. Winston S. Churchill, *Marlborough: His Life and Times* (4 vols., 1933–8). See also C. H. Firth, *A Commentary on Macaulay* (1938). T. B. Macaulay, *The History of England from the Accession of James II* (6 vols., 1849–61); best edition is by C. H. Firth, 1913–15.

ments. However Churchill had a wider purpose than just rehabilitating the reputation of his ancestor (as he had tried to do for his father): the biography was designed to warn his readers about the reappearance in Europe of a power even more intent than the France of Louis XIV on dominating all its neighbours. By the time of the publication of the third volume in 1936 the message became entirely explicit. Churchill wrote, 'the tale is rich in suggestion and instruction for the present day'. When he added in the Preface to the last volume, on 13 August 1938 not long before Munich, 'happy the state or sovereign who finds such a servant in years of danger', he was not so much celebrating Marlborough as hopefully anticipating his own return to power, given the blindness (as he saw it) of both the Chamberlain administration and the leaders of the Labour opposition.

There are two principal aspects of Churchill's work which are historiographically significant. First but unsurprisingly his interpretation reflected Churchill's own characteristics. He praised Marlborough for a major similarity with himself in not being a committed party man and his emphasis on the duke as the devoted servant of Anne reflected his own respect for the sovereign, quixotic in the case of Edward VIII, chivalrous towards Elizabeth II. Negatively Churchill failed to recognise Marlborough's declining physical and mental powers, as he was to refuse to acknowledge his own decline as he clung on to the premiership. Secondly the work which Churchill put into the examination of Marlborough's military and diplomatic leadership of the Grand Alliance proved to be an invaluable education for his own direction of Britain's war-effort in 1940–5. First and foremost it taught him that allied unity must be established and maintained if a predominant power was to be checked and defeated. In the 1930s Churchill was one of the very few (Belloc, also a student of Marlborough's career, was another) who saw how far British security depended on the French army: once this collapsed he saw the United States as the only reliable alternative. He knew from his researches that only intensive personal diplomacy, and constant correspondence, could produce the necessary understanding. Consequently, he risked his life in the dangerous flights to Tours and Briare in the desperate days of 1940, and his health by repeated journeys to talk to Roosevelt and Stalin, in the same fashion as Marlborough with his gruelling journeys (mostly in winter) to Vienna, Berlin, Hanover and Altranstadt.

Paradoxically Churchill found himself in 1941–5 occupying the same position of junior allied partner, with limited resources, as the Dutch Republic whose generals and field deputies he had bitterly criticised for obstructing Marlborough: his contribution to the partnership established with the United States owed much to his earlier appreciation of Marlborough's efforts to mitigate or remove friction between Britain and the Dutch.

Ironically Churchill's study of Marlborough did nothing to prepare him for a repetition of national 'ingratitude' in discarding the author of victory almost as soon as it was achieved. One of the architects of Churchill's defeat in the 1945 elections, Michael Foot, in his admiring study of Jonathan Swift (though a Tory), identified the common reason. By their journalistic polemics Swift and Foot changed public attitudes: each deployed the same arguments, that 'great men' are not indispensable, that the talents needed in waging war may be inappropriate in peacetime and that military men should always be subject to civil authority.[5]

Many military men, historians and even poets have concentrated their attention on Marlborough's military

---

[5] Michael Foot, *The Pen and the Sword* (1958).

campaigns. Robert Southey, during his extremely brief revolutionary and anti-war phase, asserted that Blenheim was a sterile and wicked if famous victory.[6] Napoleon acknowledged Marlborough's talents (though an Englishman) but declined to include him in his list of the top seven generals with Turenne and Eugène (French after all by birth). In recent years military historians have extended the scope of their studies from the actual campaigns to examine the advances in the science of war for which Marlborough, more than any other man in his generation, was responsible and to show how he took full advantage of them. In a Whiggish fashion some have also related his career to the foundation of the British military tradition.[7]

The main emphasis in this study must be on the late flowering of Marlborough's military and diplomatic genius for the simple reason that he altered the history of Europe and Britain by his achievements during the War of the Spanish Succession. Anything else would be perverse and unbalanced. Marlborough followed the example of the French in regarding diplomacy and warfare as co-equal instruments of policy to be used alternatively or concurrently as circumstances demanded. Consequently his diplomatic activities receive considerable attention. As de facto head of a heterogeneous coalition of states he had constantly to reconcile the many differences between allies, to meet the grievances and interests of sovereigns and princes on whose armed contingents he absolutely depended and to prevent the repetition of breaches of undertakings. Similarly he had to try to reconcile the interests of allies with those of Britain,

---

[6] Robert Southey, 'After Blenheim', in Francis Palgrave (ed.), The Golden Treasury (Oxford, 1935), pp. 213–15.

[7] David Chandler, Marlborough as Military Commander (1973). Correlli Barnett, Marlborough (1974). I. F. Burton, The Captain-General (1968). G. M. Thomson, The First Churchill (1979).

to keep a constant eye on the course of domestic politics and to give much-needed reassurance to his colleague lord treasurer Godolphin. And he bore all these tasks and coped with the stresses which they produced, which victories did not reduce or simplify, for a decade. Marlborough carried a crushing and multiple burden of responsibilities and work far greater and far more prolonged than has any other leader in British history: in a wider perspective only Napoleon surpassed him.

Napoleon, the devotee of Ossian, lived in an age which craved for and idolised heroes. By contrast in the Augustan period popular heroes were not yet in vogue, nor had media been developed specifically to project spectacular images of heroes. Hack poets produced routine panegyrics likening Marlborough to Scipio: tapestries and paintings decorated the walls of Blenheim Palace.[8] But public rituals of celebration, with the victorious general returning to the capital at the head of his troops, marching through purpose-built triumphal arches to the sound of martial music, were later inventions of the Romantic age. Popularity in Marlborough's time was suspect anyhow – the most popular man in Anne's reign was the contemptible high-flying cleric, Dr Sacheverell. Marlborough once commented to his wife that nobody in any great station of life could expect to be liked.

One main thesis in this study is that Marlborough's formative experience was as a courtier. He retained courtly characteristics throughout his life, notably the practice of the art of dissimulation. By iron self-control he invariably succeeded in concealing his inner feelings. Despite constant stress and frequent provocations he maintained a courteous and affable manner. His charm, generally remarked on by

[8] Robert D. Horn, *Marlborough: A Survey Panegyrics, Satires and Biographical Writings* (Folkestone, 1975). Alan Wace, *The Marlborough Tapestries at Blenheim Palace* (1968).

contemporaries, became increasingly impressive as his greatness grew: for the most influential and successful man in Europe to be free from arrogance and overbearing pride came as a surprise. Marlborough could achieve this extraordinary modesty of demeanour only by his practice of frequently retiring into privacy. Conventional acquaintances criticised him for not entertaining lavishly at army headquarters and for living simply and inexpensively with a few assistant colleagues. Psychologically such withdrawals from constant scrutiny and lobbying were necessary if he was to maintain an outward appearance of calm, confidence and self-possession. But his smooth, emollient exterior, the detached dignity which he sustained on the battlefield and in the council chamber, make it difficult for historians to get at the man himself, to explore his feelings as well as his thoughts, for the latter can be read and evaluated in his copious correspondence.

The opportunities which came to Marlborough after 1702 were largely due to his, and his wife's, attachment to Anne during the reign of 'Caliban', William III. But Sarah's importance in the partnership which subsequently developed between Anne, the duke and duchess and Godolphin, should not be overstated. From as early as 1704–5 her friendship with Anne began to disintegrate, and after 1706 the relationship became damagingly negative. Sarah's freely revealed Whig opinions and prejudices influenced Godolphin and compromised Marlborough. Her manner was the opposite to that of her husband: she was open, passionate and obstinate, restlessly busy and indiscreet. Although they were much in love to the end, Sarah cannot have been an easy person to be married to, but in her different and at times complementary way – encouraging and soothing him – she was as much a unique phenomenon in that age as her husband. Her spirit and abilities were, despite an inadequate education, more than a match for almost all her male contemporaries. No other wife of a leading British statesman, let alone a soldier, has ever had such a high profile or given so much well-intended support to her husband's career.[9]

---

[9] Frances Harris, *A Passion for Government: The Life of Sarah Duchess of Marlborough* (Oxford, 1991): an excellent new study. Iris Butler, *Rule of Three: Sarah, Duchess of Marlborough and her Companions in Power* (1967).

⁕ Chapter 1 ⁕

The rise to greatness

John Churchill came from an obscure family of minor provincial gentry impoverished by the Civil Wars.[1] Its only real asset were social connections which enabled John's father Sir Winston to find places for his children at Court; thereafter everything depended on their using their opportunities to advance themselves. In the first decades after the Restoration the ruling class had not yet narrowed into an oligarchy, and ministers and leading politicians who originated in the gentry (although mostly from families more substantial than the Churchills) outnumbered those from established aristocratic and Court families and connections. Several upward routes existed for the politically and socially ambitious, of which the commonest way was through leadership in Parliament combined with patronage management, direction of royal finances or the execution of other major administrative and legal functions. But with the exception of Monck and possibly Sandwich, and both earned their distinction by bringing about the Restoration, nobody rose to the very top through military or naval service.

Certainly John Churchill did not. He owed his rise to prominence and great influence to his skills as a courtier, not

---

[1] For the Churchill family see A. L. Rowse, *The Early Churchills* (1956), and Winston S. Churchill, *Marlborough: His Life and Times* (4 vols., 1933–8), vol. I.

a soldier. It was as an adept courtier that he obtained a succession of opportunities, all of which he turned to maximum advantage and which culminated in his command of the allied armies in the Low Countries in 1702–11. Marlborough's great achievements during those years as a general have totally overshadowed his earlier career in the service of Charles II and James II and (with his wife Sarah) in the household of princess Anne. But if he had not been able to develop and deploy his courtly skills he would never have had the opportunity to rise above the rank of a regimental officer, and would certainly never have been able to influence the whole course of history in England and Europe. These skills also contributed significantly to his successes during his decade of greatness, when Marlborough spent almost as much time on diplomatic as on military duties. He used them to great effect on behalf of his country and the 'common cause' in his negotiations and dealings with allied sovereigns, ministers and generals: his affability and seeming openness, unfailing patience, persuasiveness and readiness to listen, his control and concealment of the anger and indignation that he often felt but reserved for his private correspondence, and above all his ability to establish a personal rapport even with strangers – for example crucially with Karl XII in 1707.

These were behavioural traits not associated with the standard military man of that period. Yet the celebrated personal charm and persuasiveness which all contemporaries, even his worst detractors, acknowledged in Marlborough served him well in his military career also. As a young officer he attracted the personal attention of Turenne and even Louis XIV. He did not behave arrogantly and imperiously towards inferiors at any stage of his career. He showed chivalrous respect for defeated opponents during the Spanish Succession War. His personal examples of bravery and readiness to share the hardships of his men, and generally his personal

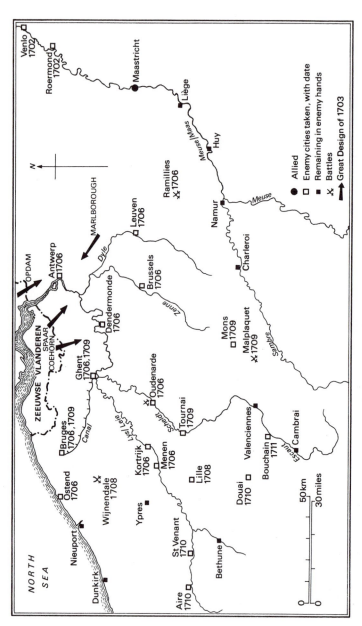

Map 1 The Low Countries during Marlborough's campaigns

Legend:
- ● Allied
- □ Enemy cities taken, with date
- ■ Remaining in enemy hands
- ✗ Battles
- ➤ Great Design of 1703

Venlo 1702
Roermond 1702
Maastricht
Liège
Huy
Namur
Meuse / Maas
Meuse
Charleroi
Ramillies ✗ 1706
Leuven 1706
Brussels 1706
Dyle
MARLBOROUGH
OPDAM
Antwerp 1706
ZEEUWSE VLANDEREN
SPAAR
COEHORN
Dendermonde 1706
Zenne
Mons 1709
Malplaquet ✗ 1709
Sambre
Ghent 1706, 1709
Bruges 1706, 1709
Canal
Oudenaarde 1706
Tournai 1709
Scheldt
Valenciennes
Cambrai
Escaut
Bouchain 1711
Ostend 1706
Kortrijk 1706
Menen 1706
Lys / Leie
Lille 1708
Douai 1710
Wijnendale 1708
Ypres
Nieuport
St Venant 1710
Bethune
Dunkirk
Aire 1710
NORTH SEA
N

50 km
30 miles

magnetism, bonded a relationship of mutual trust and respect between himself and his regimental officers and men such as few generals have achieved. This is all the more remarkable for a general who repeatedly engaged his army in costly set-piece battles; the nearest parallel would seem to be Robert E. Lee.

There was an ironic symmetry between the beginning and the end of Marlborough's career. As he owed his first upward steps to greatness to his skills as a young courtier, so it was as a discarded courtier, not an unsuccessful general, that he lost his offices and was forced into exile in 1712. He could no longer depend on his wife obtaining for him the queen's protection against ministers and bitterly hostile MPs. Furthermore his very success as a courtier was now used to discredit him with the public: his career could be caricatured as that of a favourite, traditionally the target for abusive denigration once his or her influence waned, who had enriched himself inordinately out of the public purse. In an officially male political world he could also be damagingly portrayed as owing his rise to feminine influences – first his sister Arabella's influence over James as his mistress, then through money extracted in return for sex from Charles's mistress the duchess of Cleveland and finally his wife Sarah's ascendancy over Anne.[2]

John Churchill's father, Sir Winston, cut an unimpressive figure throughout a rather chequered life. Ruined by the parliamentarian victory and the composition fines he had to pay as a royalist, he could not maintain an independent household until 1659, when John was nine, but he and his

---

[2] Many other women exerted considerable influence in the fifty years after 1660 (more than ever before, or until the mid-twentieth century) though none as much as Sarah; a few among them were her sister Frances, countess of Tyrconnel, lady Rachel Russell, lady Eleanor Oglethorpe, lady Elizabeth Harvey, the duchess of Somerset, Elizabeth Villiers and Abigail Masham.

growing family had to live as dependants in the house of lady Drake, his mother-in-law and a parliamentarian and puritan. After 1660 he received a knighthood and in 1664 a minor job as compensation for his losses. But unlike most of his greedy colleagues he seems to have profited little from his opportunities as a commissioner to administer the Irish act of (land) Settlement: in 1677 John had to surrender his interest in the family estate so that his father could realise assets to clear his accumulated debts. The one thing Sir Winston could do for his children was to use his connections. These enabled him to place the two eldest in the household of James, duke of York: Arabella as maid of honour to the (first) duchess, John as a page to James. Both gained approval. Arabella became James's acknowledged mistress sometime in 1667, while John placed his feet on the military ladder in September with a commission as ensign in the King's Own Company in the First (later Grenadier) Guards.

Throughout his career Churchill showed great initiative in taking every opportunity to gain experience and improve his career prospects. In 1668 he went out with reinforcements for Tangier, the African outpost where continuous warfare offered the hardest and most dangerous kind of military education: comparable to the North-West Frontier province of British India it provided an incomparable training ground for those soldiers who survived service there, and a totally military atmosphere. It gave him the lasting comradeship of the Tangerines, a generation of young officers who for long retained the esprit de corps they acquired there. In March 1670 Churchill became attached to the Mediterranean fleet, experienced a savage fight with the Algerines and returned to England in the autumn. His liaison with Barbara Castlemaine began shortly afterwards.

In 1672, the first year of the third Dutch War, he again served at sea. First he took part in the unsuccessful attack on the Dutch Smyrna convoy mounted by another of James's protégés, Holmes, and then he was at the battle of Sole Bay in James's flagship, the *Prince*, which took heavy casualties and narrowly survived a ferocious battering. In recognition of his contribution James granted him a captaincy in the Marine regiment, over the heads of longer-serving officers. In these years 1668–72 Churchill not only proved himself as an army officer but also made a most spectacular impact on the royal Court. The role of Barbara's lover – she became duchess of Cleveland in August 1670 at about the time Charles disentangled himself from her – carried with it fame (or notoriety) and envy, but it was not an easy one. Barbara was the most sexually aggressive and voracious of all Charles's many mistresses, unlike most of the others who were passive sex objects or bimbos who allowed Charles to do what he liked with their bodies. Contemporaries thought her old at thirty in 1670, and their male chauvinist prejudices led them to ridicule her continuing and naked need for active sex, which lasted into her sixties. By contrast Charles was approvingly celebrated as the super-stud Old Rowley, named after a famous stallion, although by his late forties he does not seem to have been capable of successful intercourse without considerable manual stimulation – the duchess of Portsmouth's speciality.

More seriously for her young lover Cleveland had a tempestuous personality, which she made little effort to subdue – an ungovernable temper and capricious moods had made Charles tired of her. The task of keeping her satisfied cannot have been an easy one for a young but almost penniless courtier. But it can be seen as an invaluable education preparing him for life with another equally stormy and demanding woman, his wife Sarah, whom he married at some time in 1677 and with whom he established a married partnership that more than any other made an impact on

British history. Sarah was always faithful, but like Barbara she was subject to strong passions and could never be taken for granted. Her husband had to accommodate himself to her moods and damagingly he could not argue her out of her prejudices once these had formed.

Churchill's military experience was greatly widened when his Marine regiment was sent to join the French army at the end of 1672. Instead of being marooned with the bulk of the army at Great Yarmouth for an invasion of Zeeland that could not be attempted, he seized the dangerous opportunities that service in the main theatres of war gave him of distinguishing himself for courage and initiative, and for observing the generalship of the greatest soldier of the age, Turenne. Active service with the French army provided a real trial by fire. British troops though inexperienced and raw were seen as brave and expendable. French generals repeatedly used them as assault forces and they invariably suffered disproportionately heavy casualties. Churchill consciously incurred extraordinary risks in his pursuit of experience and distinction. He volunteered to take part in the siege of Maastricht, where his outstanding courage in desperate and costly attacks earned the personal commendation of Louis who observed it (from a safe distance). In 1674, although he had received a French commission to command a composite regiment of English troops, he left it temporarily to serve with Turenne as a volunteer, but by October he was at the head of his regiment at the battle of Enzheim, where his conduct earned Turenne's praise.

It is now impossible to discover what he learnt from Turenne. However it is revealing that the young officer of twenty-four, in his second set-piece battle and the first in which he commanded a regiment, felt himself qualified to offer strong criticisms of his renowned general for failing to concentrate his forces, leaving some units to bear the brunt of the action and incur unnecessarily severe casualties. However he must have profited from his participation in the winter march across the Vosges which enabled Turenne to achieve a strategic surprise and save Alsace for France by his victory at Turckheim (January 1675): forced marches and the careful organisation that their success necessitated were to be a feature of his own later campaigns.

After Turckheim Churchill returned to England via Versailles, where he had an audience with Louis. On his return he was promoted to lieutenant-colonel of James's Marine regiment: more promisingly James took him into his personal service as gentleman of the bedchamber and master of the robes. Churchill had to pay a substantial sum to the outgoing master; this came from Cleveland, the contemporary story had it that she got the money by prostituting herself to a wealthy eccentric for one night. It was in the nature of a farewell present since Churchill's liaison with her seems to have ended in the summer of 1675, when he probably served his last campaign in the French service. He was wise to leave it at this time. He had possibly learnt all that he could. High personal risks as the French recklessly squandered English and Scottish manpower could make continued service literally a dead end.

By continuing in the French service Churchill would also have incurred considerable political odium. Parliamentary and public opinion had forced Charles to make peace with the Dutch in February 1674 and in the following year MPs demanded the recall of all British troops from France and the criminalisation of all who stayed. Sir Winston was provoked to defend his sons, explaining their service as educational, 'to see such campaigns as never were before'. However Churchill's departure from the French service was not entirely voluntary; in some way he earned the enmity of Louvois the French war minister who vetoed a proposal to give him the command of Monmouth's Royal English regiment.[3]

Churchill was to run very considerable political risks during the new phase of his career. He became identified as one of James's confidential servants, not just as an official in his household, in a period when opinion became increasingly (and vocally) hostile to the now Catholic heir-presumptive who had married a French protégée in 1673, was known to be an admirer of Louis's governmental methods and powers and was seen to be in constant close contact with the French ambassador in London. Presumably it was indeed the distinction which Churchill had earned in the French service, and the contacts he had then made, that led James to employ him in political as well as household duties.

There was a hidden danger in Churchill's new role. James was maintaining two sets of confidential servants and advisers because he was constantly following two alternative lines of possible policy, and indeed these were to prove (in 1687–8) to be incompatible. As well as those who like Churchill served him openly and possessed 'characters', that is James avowed them and would stand by them, there also existed a collection of clandestine political operators, working on a much longer leash, and engaged in activities that if exposed would provoke violent public reactions, and threaten to compromise James's public servants. These operators were Catholics, concerned to enlist French support for the advancement of their religion throughout the British Isles via the strengthening of royal authority. Some were Irish with the particular aim of securing a revision of the Irish land settlement. Eventually they and other members of the so-called camarilla were to take the

[3] Anchitell Grey, *Debates of the House of Commons* (10 vols., 1769), vol. III, pp. 104, 117, 123–4, 128–9, 291, 334–5, 350–4; vol. IV, pp. 97–8, 131–2.

direction of James's policies in 1687–8, but earlier, although Churchill cannot have been unaware of their existence, he would have known nothing of their projects.[4]

Curiously when Churchill carried out his first major politico-military mission in the spring of 1678 the circumstances, and James's political stance, had undergone a sudden and complete alteration. First Charles, and then James, came to appreciate the need to distance themselves from France, in order to take the sting out of the very real antagonism to Louis that was building up as he seemed to be becoming predominant through his series of victories in Flanders. Charles authorised William's marriage to James's daughter Mary, and James found that his acceptance (although privately he had been reluctant to give his consent) made him less unpopular. While Charles continued to follow a double policy James characteristically gave genuine – if short-lived – support to the policy of entering the war against France which had been formulated by lord treasurer Danby.

In order to retain this support from James it was logical for Danby to give Churchill key military tasks. In the expansion of the army Churchill became colonel of one of the new regiments, and in March he was sent to Bruges as advance man to arrange for the arrival of the army. This gave him useful experience of working with allies and in military administration. In April, having quickly concluded an agreement with the hard-pressed Governor of the Spanish Netherlands, Churchill was sent to the Hague to negotiate a convention with William on the deployment of the English army. He did this in company with another of James's associates, and his own future ministerial colleague, Sidney

---

[4] Sarah's sister Frances married James's leading Catholic associate, Richard Talbot, in 1679; others were his brother Peter, Sir Richard Bellings, Edward Coleman, Robert Brent, father Petre, lady Oglethorpe, Sir Nicholas Butler, the earl of Peterborough.

Godolphin who had responsibility for arranging the political details of Anglo-Dutch cooperation.[5]

It would be tempting to agree with Winston Churchill in seeing these negotiations with William, whom Churchill was meeting for the first time, as establishing the basis of his future relationship. In reality, however, these negotiations were a sham. Churchill and Godolphin, as well as William, were being duped in the most cynical fashion imaginable. Both Danby and James had to realise that Charles had no intention of entering the war. James had gone so far as to expect quite unrealistically that he would be given the command of the English army in Flanders, arguing that the limitations imposed by the Test act, which excluded Catholics from offices, did not apply outside the realm. But when he saw that Charles's public statements of his intention to enter the war were really aimed at extracting new subsidies from Louis as the price of not doing so, James quickly switched back to a French orientation. However in public he continued to call for war, and gained some credibility from the despatch of Churchill and Godolphin to the Hague, and an army brigade to Ostend and Bruges.

In career terms Churchill profited from this pretence. In May he became a brigadier general, and senior brigadier in September. But he and the troops in Charles's service had no war to fight. The Englishmen who gained credit with William were the officers and men of the Anglo-Scots regiments in Dutch service, and the volunteers who with them fought in William's last-ditch campaign to keep the war alight. Churchill merely had to watch, inactive. The States General concluded a separate peace with France, leaving their allies to make what terms they could with a dominant France. As the

[5] Andrew Browning, *Thomas Osborne, Earl of Danby* (3 vols., Glasgow, 1944–51), vol. I, pp. 254–65, 269–72, 277–8; vol. II, pp. 425–32. Churchill, *Marlborough*, vol. I, pp. 148–51.

war spluttered out Churchill had to arrange the repatriation of the English forces, a task that occupied him until February 1679.

By the time Churchill returned James was coming under pressure from all sides. Danby lost control of the Commons after the discovery of the secret correspondence of Edward Coleman, secretary to the duchess of York and one of James's clandestine operators. This appeared to implicate James in a design to dissolve Parliament and secure French assistance for the establishment of Catholicism and royal absolutism. Ralph Montague publicly revealed the administration's duplicity over the intended war. Consequently Parliament had to be dissolved. Although the elections went heavily against the Court Churchill was returned for Newtown, Isle of Wight, through the patronage of the Governor Holmes, another member of James's entourage. But before Parliament met, and to James's utter consternation, Charles ordered him into exile outside his realms, albeit with a letter promising to uphold his right to the succession – a pledge that was universally regarded as insincere and worthless.[6]

Churchill accompanied James and his household to Brussels. Throughout the early summer he was busy acting as confidential courier on missions from James to Charles, calling on him to adhere to a firm line and dissolve Parliament rather than allow a bill excluding James from the succession to make progress, and to Louis, apologising for having advocated war the previous year and promising never again to depart from a pro-French line of policy. These missions show how greatly James trusted him. Significantly he was not sent to make similar appeals to William.

Fortune favoured Churchill during the Exclusion Crisis. He happened to be in England when Charles fell dangerously ill

---

[6] Basil D. Henning (ed.), *The House of Commons 1660–1690* (3 vols., 1983), vol. II, p. 69.

in August. After hurried consultations with Halifax and other leading ministers he sped back to Brussels, and brought James over, in disguise as one of his attendants. By the time they arrived Charles had recovered both his health and his determination not to give way to Whig pressure. In order to strengthen his position he approved a proposal by James to despatch Churchill on a secret mission to ask Louis for a subsidy to make the king independent of Parliament. He gave Churchill discretionary powers to negotiate, but at this stage Louis was not prepared to intervene in English affairs. It was not Churchill's fault that he returned empty-handed, via Brussels from where he accompanied James's household on its transfer to Edinburgh.[7]

Although unsuccessful this mission showed that Churchill was now regarded by James as a trusted adviser, not a mere courier. He insisted that Churchill should remain by his side during the rest of the crisis period, making it explicit that he would let him go only to a post of first-class importance in the king's service, where he would be able to uphold James's interest and rights. By this he meant as Charles's diplomatic representative at either Paris, where the incumbent was brother to Halifax whom James distrusted, or at the Hague, where he would replace Henry Sidney whom James rightly suspected of giving William too many Whig notions. It is clear that James was right to place absolute trust in Churchill, who constantly adhered throughout the crisis to the uncommon view that, provided that Charles retained his confidence and determination, he must prevail over all Whig attempts to alter the succession. This unfailing loyalty during the Exclusion Crisis, when most politicians and foreign diplomats expected Charles eventually to abandon James, must be taken into account

[7] Dalrymple, Memoirs, vol. II, appendix part I, pp. 218, 238–9, 240, 292–4, 298.

when considering the latter's reluctance to think that Churchill would turn traitor in 1688.[8]

However Churchill still occupied a political position of secondary importance. It was not he but Laurence Hyde who successfully negotiated the subsidy treaty of March 1681 with the French ambassador that enabled Charles to dissolve the Oxford Parliament, and defeat the Whigs. Churchill served James, not the king, and as the crisis eased his influence diminished. Characteristically James took his loyalty for granted and turned increasingly for advice to Sunderland (despite his earlier support for Exclusion) and to the Catholic associates of the duchess. The consequence was that during 1683 John and Sarah Churchill made what looks like a conscious decision to stake their future on the fortunes of James's younger daughter Anne. These might have turned out to be very limited, although they could (as was to happen) have brought them everything they wanted. But it was also possible that James's second wife, or his elder daughter Mary, would give birth to healthy children, so that Anne would always remain only a princess, or that she might die in child-bed – and she was to have seventeen difficult pregnancies. In 1683 it is unlikely that Churchill had even half-formed ambitions to rise to the very top, to the highest positions of power, influence and wealth. He was only a Scottish peer (1682), unlike his colleague and competitor George Legge who became an English baron that year. Certainly Churchill could not compare his position with that of the rivals Sunderland and Rochester who were both engaged in the balancing act of serving Charles in high offices while also retaining or regaining James's favour.

Consequently the entry of the Churchills into Anne's service did not imply any break with James, still less the

---

[8] H. C. Foxcroft, *The Life and Letters of Sir George Savile First Marquis of Halifax* (2 vols., 1898), vol. I, p. 199; vol. II, p. 139.

formation of anything resembling a reversionary interest. Churchill continued to serve Charles as an officer; in December 1683 he became colonel of the King's Own Royal Dragoons. He also retained his association with James, but no longer advised him on policy matters. But it is clear that he went out of his way to establish the connection with Anne, grabbing the opportunity to travel to Denmark to accompany George on his voyage to England for the marriage in July 1683. Sarah became lady of the bedchamber to Anne. The slight friendship which already existed between them quickly turned into a passionate relationship which came to compensate Anne for the inadequacies of her reliable but extremely dull husband. One of the advantages of the Churchills' position in Anne's household was that they did not become involved in the struggle between the two ministerial and Court factions that began in Charles's last two years and continued until the end of 1686.[9]

Their service to Anne did not involve an association with her uncles Rochester and Clarendon, neither of whom did she ever seem to have liked or even respected, who headed one faction. Churchill would not have fitted comfortably into this Hyde faction since one of its instruments in influencing James was his current acknowledged mistress, Catherine Sedley, who hated Churchill. A clever woman, she had been rejected by him when his parents advised him to marry her for the sake of her dowry. Consequently Churchill's free-standing place in Anne's household meant that he did not go down when the Hyde faction foundered at the end of 1686. On the other hand the increasingly dominant Catholic faction with which Sunderland associated himself – Richard Butler who became earl of Tyrconnel (and whose wife was Sarah's equally capable and assertive sister), the Catholic peers Peterborough,

[9] Frances Harris, *A Passion for Government: The Life of Sarah Duchess of Marlborough* (Oxford, 1991), pp. 34–6. Churchill, *Marlborough*, vol. I, pp. 183, 188.

Huntingdon and Dover, father Petre and Sir Richard Bellings and Robert Brent (the surviving secret operators) – did not target Churchill as a potential rival that had to be removed. James continued to employ Churchill because of his proven military ability, as he did Godolphin and Dartmouth in financial and naval administration respectively, but as Anglicans they were not admitted henceforward to positions which would enable them to influence royal policies.

During the first days of the new reign James gave Churchill a final important confidential task, because of the contacts which he possessed in the French Court. Under cover of a formal mission to announce James's accession Churchill was instructed to ask Louis for a promise that payment of financial subsidies would be renewed, to make the king independent of Parliament if the Commons tried to place restrictions on him as the condition of voting him a revenue. Confirmation of his colonelcy of dragoons, appointment as a lord of the bedchamber and the grant of an English baronage indicated James's recognition of past services. But negotiations for French subsidies were switched to London where Churchill took no part. He received surprisingly modest rewards for his crucial role in suppressing Monmouth's rebellion. And as James turned increasingly to Sunderland and a Catholic group of advisers Churchill lost all political influence, and found himself restricted to the routine performance of his military duties.[10]

Churchill was from the first the most actively involved. News of Monmouth's landing at Lyme Regis (11 June) was brought post haste to London by the mayor who arrived at the house of Sir Winston (one of Lyme's MPs) early in the morning of the 13th. John Churchill took the opportunity to conduct the mayor and his news to James personally. The king

[10] C. J. Fox, *A History of the Early Part of the Reign of James II* (1808), appendix, p. xxiv.

immediately responded by ordering him to collect his dragoons and proceed with the utmost speed to Dorset. Churchill was made brigadier, and named as commander of all regular troops in the area of the rebellion, an unnecessarily restricted remit. Churchill left with the dragoons the same day, reached Bridport on the 17th and quickly instituted aggressive patrolling which harassed Monmouth's improvised force, hampered his recruiting and limited his intelligence gathering. The first regular infantry joined Churchill on the 21st, but he could not seek an immediate engagement because the incompetent lords lieutenant of Dorset, Devon and Somerset and their militia officers were not prepared to give him prompt cooperation, and he had no authority over them.[11]

This gave Monmouth an opportunity to advance to Bristol, which could have resulted in a prolonged civil war developing, but he hesitated. Two separate royal forces were now tracking him. The other was commanded by Sir Theophilus Oglethorpe (father of the founder of Georgia), another rising military officer and rival, who had the advantage of being a Catholic. He too had an able wife at Court, the former Eleanor Wall who had served the duchess of Portsmouth (Charles II's only politically active mistress) and had links with the French embassy. However both Churchill and Oglethorpe were passed over when James appointed as commander-in-chief the earl of Feversham. He was a very long-standing associate (since 1665) and had a kind of military reputation derived from his being Turenne's nephew. He was to show himself totally incompetent, although this did not deter James from re-appointing him in 1688. He lost contact with Monmouth's army. He failed to communicate even to Churchill the campaign plans which James had just authorised. Consequently as Churchill complained in a letter which

---

[11] Robert Clifton, *The Last Popular Rebellion* (1984), pp. 163–4, 165–6. Peter Earle, *Monmouth's Rebels* (1977), pp. 86–9.

reveals that despite all his services to James he felt some insecurity in the new reign, this secrecy inhibited him from giving his opinions freely for fear that his career would be ruined if they ran counter to the king's plans. Finally in the decisive encounter at Sedgemoor (6 July) Feversham's lack of judgement nearly lost the battle. While it was still dark and his forces had not entirely recovered from the initial confusion caused by a night attack, Feversham ordered a realignment of his infantry. Churchill had organised the defence without waiting for Feversham who put in a belated appearance and lacked any appreciation of the situation when he issued his order. This Churchill countermanded on his own authority, realising that it would cause confusion. The army stood its ground, a fire-fight developed with Monmouth's ill-equipped infantry and his cavalry panicked. The battle quickly degenerated into a massacre.[12]

Churchill's achievement in saving his general from the results of his own poor judgement could not be publicised; consequently Feversham got the credit. Churchill was promoted to major-general, but both he and his friends, notably colonel Kirke, felt disappointment at their meagre rewards. They also felt aggrieved at having to remain behind to police the counties where the rebellion had occurred, to protect unpopular and repressive local officials and specifically Jeffreys during his infamous Western Circuit trials. But such was the hatred felt against Jeffreys, who was to become the universal scapegoat in 1688, and the bad reputation acquired by Kirke, that Churchill's part in the repression was not in the future to resurface to be used against him. For the Tory and Jacobite writers who attempted to blacken his reputation after 1710 the victims of 1685 had been rebels,

---

[12] S. W. Singer, *The Correspondence of Henry Hyde, Earl of Clarendon* (2 vols., 1828), vol. II, p. 141. Dalrymple, *Memoirs*, vol. II, appendix part 1, pp. 108–9. Earle, *Monmouth's Rebels*, pp. 91–3, 130–3.

justly punished for treason, and the fathers of their current Whig enemies.

In 1686 Churchill was still sufficiently in James's confidence to accompany him on his provincial progresses. In August at the summer camp at Hounslow Heath he had his first opportunity to drill and manoeuvre units as large as divisions in the annual exercises instituted that year. This gave him valuable experience: the force deployed against Monmouth had been much smaller – about 3,500 men – and apart from the brief Munster campaign of 1690 when he commanded an army of about 6,000 these exercises were the only opportunity he had of controlling an actual army before he assumed the command of the allied forces in the Low Countries in 1702.

From early 1687, when James's policies began to change, many prudent and careerist royal servants and officers began to try to keep wherever possible a distance between themselves and James, and from his ministers and private advisers. Churchill, like Godolphin and most of the bishops, did not make an issue out of unpalatable royal moves – the first Declaration of Indulgence, the dissolution of Parliament, the remodelling of the lieutenancy, the commission of the peace and the corporations – even though they disapproved. Churchill's concerns again came to centre on Anne. Clumsy and intermittent attempts by James and his queen to convert her to Catholicism caused great alarm, but they were counter-productive and strengthened her devotion to the Church. In supporting her stand John and Sarah acted entirely in good faith: both were consistently and genuinely committed in their personal practice, as well as politically, to the Protestant religion. But neither ever equalled Anne's passionate attachment to the Church of England as an institution, or developed an intimate relation with its clergy. This difference was to prove Sarah's Achilles' heel two decades later, but in 1687–8 it did not create problems since the Churchills worked closely and privately with bishop Compton in defending Anne's faith, and it was he who attracted hostility and resentment from James and the camarilla. Churchill did not attempt to conceal his attachment to the Protestant religion from James, but this remained a private matter.

Churchill was in neither James's favour nor his disfavour. He was retained as general because of his proven abilities but, looking ahead, James's reliance on him was likely to be of relatively short continuation. His replacement was already receiving his strenuous military education in the Imperial army fighting the Turks. Having been subordinated to Feversham in 1685 Churchill faced the probability that within a few years his nephew, the duke of Berwick, James's eldest son by Arabella, who had already displayed considerable military talent, would be placed over him as army commander-in-chief.[13]

By encouraging Anne in her resistance to pressure for a conversion from her father and step-mother Churchill was bound to find himself moving closer to Mary, and so to William, both of whom shared his concern. He appeared on the list of English notables whom Dijkvelt, William's special envoy, approached during his first political reconnaissance mission that began in February 1687. Churchill's must have been the most reassuring and informative of all the messages Dijkvelt took back with him. Not only did Churchill pledge himself to do everything he could to protect Anne from forcible conversion, but he assured William that all his undoubted obligations to James would not override his prior loyalty to the Protestant religion. This message marked the start of a correspondence with William, and his agents and

---

[13] The standard life of Berwick is still C.T. Wilson, *James II and the Duke of Berwick* (1876). Also his *Mémoires*, ed. J.J. Hooke (Paris, 1778).

diplomats. By August 1688, as he told Henry Sidney, William's most trusted clandestine representative, he knew exactly what he had to do.[14]

Churchill proved to be easily the most important and influential person in the underground network of army officers who pledged their aid in bringing about a change of royal policy and the elimination of evil ministers. This change he termed a 'change of government', a phrase which did not by any means imply James's deposition. He was uniquely placed to link the various conspiratorial military groups. Anne's household served as the centre during the preparatory phase, before the crisis developed. When it erupted with William's invasion Sarah was able to fulfil his pledge to protect the princess by organising her flight to safety, in order to preempt any attempt by James to seize her and send her to France as a virtual prisoner. Churchill had the advantage of renewing his extensive personal and professional connections within the army during the summer camps that assembled under his command in 1687 and 1688. The regiments which he then inspected and exercised were the units that mattered since they would form any field army sent to oppose an invasion, and they were elite units. The static units on garrison duties were less important, and their fate during the Revolution was to be overwhelmed by improvised forces raised by the neighbouring aristocracy and gentry. Churchill also had long-standing connections with most of the leading military activists who met at the so-called 'Treason Club' at the Rose Tavern in Russell Street: they were a combination of officers and ex-officers, many of the latter being former Whigs and friends of Monmouth. Among them were many Tangerines, several of whom had campaigned with him in 1685.

---

[14] Churchill, *Marlborough*, vol. I, p. 272, with facsimile. Dalrymple, *Memoirs*, vol. II, appendix part 1, pp. 190–1.

We have no specific knowledge of the arguments that were used to induce so many officers to join in the military conspiracy, but the political situation as it was developing in the summer of 1688 provided many good reasons. First, army officers now constituted the sole category of royal servants whom James had not yet brought under systematic pressure to pledge themselves to collaborate with him in securing the repeal of the Test acts and the penal laws. A trial run had been attempted in one regiment but had not been pressed in a determined manner. However there were strong rumours current that a general purge would be carried out during the winter of 1688–9. Officers feared for their livelihood, having recently observed the ruthless and general dismissals of Protestant officers from the Irish army, many of them friends and relations. They also felt threatened by the corrupt partnership of father Petre and the secretary at war, Dover, who were blatantly trafficking in army appointments and promotions, and were poised ready to take advantage of vacancies created by mass dismissals.[15]

As commanding general Churchill was obviously the officer to whom anxious or disaffected subordinates would look for a lead. His subordinates must have grasped the fact that he was in the most exposed position of all and could soon face dismissal. In the second Declaration of Indulgence, issued on 27 April, James stated explicitly that a Parliament would be called by November at the latest to repeal the penal laws and the tests. In that Parliament as a peer Churchill would either have to assist the royal managers or by opposing their efforts make dismissal certain. And by the autumn the threat to his position from Berwick was coming closer; James gave him the appointment of governor of Portsmouth, after London the key citadel of royal authority as the port through

[15] John Childs, *The Army, James II and the Glorious Revolution* (Manchester, 1980), pp. 138–64, 167.

which aid from France could pass. Young but now experienced and blooded in Hungary, Berwick could be seen as
waiting in the wings to take command.[16]

The second consideration that made army officers recep-
tive to approaches on William's behalf was that most of them
were younger sons, or members of cadet branches, of leading
families in the former political nation. Most had close
relations who had already been displaced from offices, and
especially from the commission of the peace in the counties.
The corps of army officers was not an entity separate from the
political nation, with characteristics of its own, but there was
a prospect that this is what it would become, especially as a
result of the influx of Scottish and Irish officers and men,
most of them selected for service in England because they
were Catholics. Consequently religious and professional
insecurity became linked in a lethal combination making for
disaffection. A maladroit move by Dumbarton, a fervent
loyalist and the leading Scottish officer in the English army,
confirmed their fears. During the summer camp of 1688 he
convened a meeting of Catholic officers and asked them to
make and return lists of all Catholics. Finally in the last weeks
before William's invasion a small number of French
volunteers arrived to serve James; although Louis had not left
himself free to send military or naval units to assist James, the
appearance of individuals gave apparent confirmation to
Dutch propaganda about a secret treaty between the two
Catholic sovereigns.[17]

The conspirators' plans to organise defections to William
were furthered by the court-martial of officers of the
Portsmouth garrison for refusing to accept Irish soldiers into

[16] Through administrative inexperience Berwick made serious mistakes as governor
of Portsmouth: A. Coleby, 'Military–civilian relations on the Solent 1651–1689',
Historical Journal, 29 (1986), 955–6, 959–60.
[17] James Macpherson, *Original Papers Containing the Secret History of Great Britain* (2 vols.,
1775), vol. I, pp. 288–9.

their units, a practice that could be extended at will to all other units. Churchill was named as one of the board to sit in judgement and could not invite his own dismissal by opposing or obstructing a guilty verdict and sentence of cashiering. Jacobite polemicists were to claim later that he adopted a severely punitive attitude, urging the penalty of death, but this would not have been applicable to the charges which were being tried.

James made Feversham commander-in-chief, despite his earlier incompetence in suppressing Monmouth's rebellion and the low reputation he had in the army. Similarly although he must have drawn some unfavourable conclusions from Churchill's encouragement of Anne's resistance to religious conversion he promoted him to lieutenant-general on 7 November, when he already knew that William's invasion force was sailing down the Channel. Presumably he hoped to retain Churchill's complete loyalty by satisfying his career ambitions, and give him the power to take decisions if Feversham fumbled the command.

The conspiracy among the officers was instrumental in preventing James from containing, let alone defeating, William's invasion. It represented the culmination of months of skilful canvassing and persuasion of which only vague indications had appeared, too insubstantial for James to take action. There could not be a sharper contrast with what had happened in 1685 when Monmouth hoped, on the basis of past associations and friendships, that James's officers – including Churchill to whom he sent a letter which was passed on unopened to James – would go over to him. However when the defections actually occurred they do not seem to have followed any discernible pattern. Officers took their opportunities when they could, and apparently without consideration of the effect they could have on those who had not yet been able to get away. Churchill could have been fatally compromised, as he had to remain in attendance on James personally, as the king travelled to the army rendezvous at Salisbury. Nor were the defections executed in the way best calculated to ensure the disintegration of James's army. A concerted defection would have had a shattering effect, whereas in the case of several units many of the soldiers either refused to follow their officers or returned subsequently to James's service.

Nevertheless the stream of defections, which began as early as 15 November (by Cornbury), undermined both the morale of the army and James's capacity to take decisive action. When he got to Salisbury on the 19th, to find the army's morale already weakened, his one, fixed idea was to find a simple, clear-cut solution by bringing William to battle. Consequently he did not order the withdrawal of the most advanced units, from which the first defections had been made, because that would involve opening a greater distance between them and William's advance forces. Nor would he act when Feversham and other officers urged him to arrest Churchill and some of his closest associates as the alleged organisers of defections who would betray him. If he did so it was certain that all other officers involved with Churchill would stage a mass defection. Hopelessly at a loss in the extraordinarily abnormal atmosphere of a military headquarters where all the officers were intriguing and backstabbing each other openly, James uncharacteristically became indecisive. Even so Churchill took risks by remaining in the royal entourage until the evening of the 23rd, when he defected after an inconclusive council of war. The only surprise is that he dared to leave it so late, and for no very obvious purpose.[18]

Denigratory Jacobite propaganda after the Revolution

---

[18] Childs, *The Army, James II and the Glorious Revolution*, pp. 184–8, 190–1.

made use of fabricated stories, for which there is no independent evidence, further to blacken his reputation. One allegation was that Churchill had planned to assassinate James. Another that he had had a scheme to seize James and hand him over to William – who would certainly not have welcomed obtaining James as a captive. Another story intended to create mischief was that Schomberg, the veteran Huguenot ex-marshal of France now serving William, greeted his arrival with the insult that he was the first senior general to desert his colours. This was simply not true – Condé and Turenne had defected to Spain during the Frondes – and relations between Churchill and Schomberg were cordial until the end of the following January, when the latter criticised William's delegation of what he thought were excessive powers over the reorganisation of the English army to Churchill.

Sarah Churchill played almost as important a part in the Revolution as her husband. Prince George defected immediately after Churchill, compromising Anne who thereupon became a pawn in what was now turning from a military into a political struggle. James was desperately anxious that his infant son should not fall into William's hands, for fear that he might suffer physically and might not be encouraged to live, or alternatively might suffer spiritual death by being brought up as an Anglican. James therefore decided, as soon as his position began to crumble, to send him to safety in France. Similarly he could prevent William coming to any agreement with Anne only by removing her from Sarah's influence, possibly by shipping her too to France. He ordered Sarah's arrest. It therefore became a matter of urgency to remove both Anne and Sarah to a place of safety beyond James's reach. In cooperation with bishop Compton, who had been persecuted by James since 1686, Sarah arranged a secret flight from London which turned into a triumphant progress with the gentry rallying to escort her to join the peers and their followers who assembled at Nottingham.[19]

John Churchill's pre-planned decision to defect from James and join William was the most important one he took in the whole course of his life. It was also arguably the military defections which he organised that did the most to ensure William's success. He had no illusions about the ways in which his action would be depicted and interpreted by those who continued to adhere to James, and by all who envied him. Moreover since one of his main motives was to found a family or dynasty that would play a leading role in national life after his own death, he was also vitally concerned to justify himself to future generations. Therefore Churchill sent James a carefully composed letter with the objective not of appeasing the king or gratifying William but of vindicating his decision in the eyes of his contemporaries and of posterity.[20]

This letter deserves (but has seldom received) careful analysis. At its start he meets head-on the inevitable charge that his action was self-interested. He acknowledged the 'great advantage' he had enjoyed under James: this he combined with the argument that as he could never expect such advantage 'in any other change of government' his action had been disinterested, not actuated by ambition and opportunism. The crux of his self-justificatory argument was that his own personal obligations to James, and by impli-cation the civil and military duty of obedience, were overridden by the 'inviolable dictates of my conscience' and a concern for the integrity of 'my religion'. This assertion would be received in diametrically opposite ways by the two

[19] Harris, *Passion for Government*, pp. 49–51. J. S. Clarke, *The Life of James II* (2 vols., 1816), vol. II, pp. 169, 224. D. H. Hosford, 'Bishop Compton and the revolution of 1688', *Journal of Ecclesiastical History*, 23 (1972), 209–18.
[20] Churchill, *Marlborough*, vol. I, pp. 299–300.

halves into which Europe was divided. For Catholics, and particularly James and the majority of Jacobite activists, Churchill's disregard of his double duty as a subject and an army officer to give absolute and unconditional obedience to his divinely appointed sovereign was an inevitable consequence of his being an obstinate Protestant, attached to heretical errors including the claim to individual judgement. Fellow Protestants throughout Europe, with few exceptions outside England, recognised the similarity between his meritorious action and the action of literally thousands of Huguenot officers and soldiers who had emigrated since the Revocation of the Edict of Nantes in 1685 and were to fight against their persecutor Louis XIV in the Dutch, Prussian, Hanoverian, Danish and English armies.

Unlike the Jacobites who claimed after 1688 that they fought for their rightful king and his allies against an usurper and his allies, the Huguenots fought for their religion. So did Churchill. For the rest of his life he consistently expressed his determination to defend the Protestant religion, which he saw as insecure unless, or until, the power of Louis was drastically reduced. This was no pose adopted to impress the public or pander to religious prejudice. His private correspondence is full of expressions that reveal his fear that if Louis retained the power to intervene in the affairs of other countries the Protestant religion would continue to be in real danger, and this concern – often expressed in vehement terms – is the strongest argument for regarding his connections with agents for the exiled Stuarts as nothing more than personal insurance policies.

Churchill expressed himself obliquely in his letter on the central issue of the constitution. He followed William's model (in his *Declaration*) of putting the responsibility for attempts to destroy the constitution on the royal ministers, not on James himself. He made a bold, some at the time might have said impudent, contrast between ministerial conduct as that of 'inconsiderate and self-interested men' and his own 'dutiful' behaviour to James. By inconsiderate he meant that they had ignored all considerations of the law and constitution in their 'designs', a word that implied a malevolent conspiracy against the undoubted rights of the nation. This provided a reply to those who would make (well-founded) charges that Churchill and the defecting officers had constituted a military conspiracy: what they had done had been necessary as counter-action to the subversive activities of the ministers to break the laws and destroy the constitution and the Protestant religion.

By contrast Churchill cited his own 'dutiful' behaviour in the worst of times, that is during the Exclusion Crisis when the Whigs had pressed unconstitutional policies. That is he had defended the constitution then, when it had been threatened by demagogues and populists, and was now doing so again in the face of the threat from a totally different quarter, the official and clandestine advisers who had misled the king. He went on to show why, having continued to give James service right up to the present, it was imperative that he should dissociate himself in the most dramatic fashion imaginable from this service at this particular moment. His argument was that William's invasion had created an entirely new and extremely dangerous situation. Most ominously James and his most loyal servants had been vehemently in favour of bringing about a decisive battle with William, on which the fate of the kingdom, the constitution and the Protestant religion would depend. If James won, then the designs of the evil ministers would be realised. A royal victory would give him absolute power as a conqueror: he would have defeated not only William but also the causes which the latter had featured in his *Declaration*, and great emphasis had been laid on the Protestant religion as the principal one. In addition James would be able to act, if he so pleased, against the liberties of the bishops, the peers and the gentry, all of whom were conspicuously failing to give him any assistance in trying to defeat the invaders. Their refusals meant that the designs of the evil ministers could only succeed if the army continued to serve and obey James blindly. In his letter Churchill declared that he could not do so, could not in effect assist James to conquer his own subjects and their rights. If a battle came, and of course his purpose in defecting was to make it far less likely that James could fight one, his place must be on the side of those fighting for, not against, the religion and rights of the nation.

In reality Churchill was pre-engaged by his promises to Henry Sidney to join William once he had established himself in force. But this promise did not pre-engage Churchill to work for any specific constitutional solution to the crisis. He actually ended his letter by promising James that he would endeavour to preserve his royal person and 'lawful rights', implying that this is what he would try to do when he had joined William. There is no evidence that he made any attempt to do so, and like many other servants of James he probably thought himself absolved from this undertaking when James left the country.

Churchill's letter is unique in one important respect. Every other statement in favour of William's action or denouncing the conduct of James's ministers saw as the solution to the crisis the calling of a 'free' Parliament to legislate for the protection and perpetuation of constitutional liberties and the Protestant religion. Churchill did not, and he was not to be active in the Convention of 1689. Surprisingly too, in the light of his later career, Churchill (in this like all but one of those who adhered to William) did not lay any emphasis on what was for William the main issue, the blow to French influence and power which the humbling and curbing of

James and the destruction of his ministers' designs must involve. Curiously only Anne's consort George made this point in the letter which he sent to James to justify his defection to William: one may of course suspect that this letter was at least drafted in consultation with the Churchills.[21]

Churchill prudently maintained a low public profile during the sessions of the Convention Parliament of 1689–90. He did not play a prominent part in any of the legislative processes that led to the enactment of the Bill of Rights. To have spoken or voted for the placing of William and Mary on the throne would have contradicted his promise to James in the justificatory letter that he sent him on his defection in November, that he would endeavour to preserve his lawful rights. On the other hand to have opposed the settlement would have alienated William. Churchill's behaviour after his defection to join William shows that he was determined to exploit the opportunities which now opened up. Even before William got to London, or James fled the country, Churchill committed himself to active collaboration, taking on the most urgent and difficult of all practical tasks. He and Grafton were given the job of reforming and restoring order and discipline in what was left of James's army, after Feversham had obeyed royal orders to disband it (without disarming the soldiers), orders that had the malevolent intention of creating the maximum confusion; and the situation had been aggravated by William's instructions that all units must immediately move away from London and its vicinity.[22]

This mission entailed a great deal of detailed work, but no officer was better qualified through knowledge of the officer

---

[21] Ibid., vol. I, p. 300.
[22] Childs, *The Army, James II and the Glorious Revolution*, pp. 195–8.

corps to undertake it. The powers which Churchill exercised in confirming or purging officers and men gave him the opportunity to build a new patronage network, and many of his beneficiaries were to remain associates for over two decades. However the eagerness with which Churchill grasped his opportunities generated criticism. Officers of the Anglo-Scottish regiments in Dutch service, who had come over with William, saw Churchill as the leader of a rival military interest. His self-confidence and transparent appetite for power and influence alarmed William, who knew that between them the Churchills entirely dominated Anne and her husband. He had no intention of submitting to any Englishman's influence, and Churchill appeared to be the first to thrust himself forward. As early as 30 December 1688 William told Halifax that Churchill was 'very assuming', but that he would not be governed by him. Furthermore looking ahead William knew that, whatever settlement was reached, Mary was going to have to be left in charge of the government while he campaigned overseas, and it was also probable that she would outlive him. She might be as susceptible to the influence of the Churchills as her sister. William's relation-ship with Mary was still based on the dominance which he had established in the first days of their marriage, and at the small Orangist Court at the Hague Mary had never met anyone (except Monmouth briefly) with the charming personality and ambition of John Churchill. William's stated determination not to be his wife's subordinate – her gentleman usher, as he put it – was founded on the belief that an inexperienced Mary would be in danger of being exploited by English politicians and courtiers. This is why he played off Whigs and Tories, Halifax and Danby, against each other and why he restricted Churchill's opportunities.[23]

[23] Foxcroft, Halifax, vol. II, p. 202.

Nevertheless William incurred one major obligation to the Churchills. They used their influence to persuade Anne to accept the significant variation in the line of succession made by the Bill of Rights. She did not oppose William sharing the throne with Mary and continuing as sole sovereign if, as was thought unlikely, Mary predeceased him. Anne was agreeing to being displaced in the line of succession; in constitutional law she ought to succeed her elder sister, and the proposal made nonsense of all the concepts of divine right formerly articulated by the Tories. Anne's uncles, Clarendon and Rochester, were strongly opposed to the proposal so that her acceptance was not a foregone conclusion, but was very much to the credit of the Churchills. William recognised their services at the time of the coronation, when Churchill was given the title of earl of Marlborough.[24]

William also confirmed Marlborough as lieutenant-general. The appointment he received for the campaign of 1689 was predetermined by the task he had already been given of reorganising the English army. Many officers and men deserted, often to join James in Ireland, or had to be purged as politically unreliable, but a force of 8,000 was assembled and sent to Flanders; it was logical that Marlborough should command them. The Anglo-Scottish regiments, the Dutch and Huguenot units and new English regiments raised during the summer were to be sent to reconquer Ireland, first under Schomberg and then in 1690 under William himself. Marlborough greatly distinguished himself in the Flanders campaign of 1689. In character his English contingent closely resembled the units he had commanded in the French service in 1673–5: the men were brave but raw, poorly trained and equipped but aggressive. Marlborough made them into an effective fighting force. Under the overall

[24] Singer, *Correspondence of Clarendon*, vol. II, pp. 255, 257, 260–1. W. King (ed.), *Memoirs of Sarah, Duchess of Marlborough* (1930), pp. 15–16.

command of prince Waldeck they (and he) were very largely
responsible for inflicting a sharp defeat on the main French
army at Walcourt (25 August).[25]

This achievement and Waldeck's generous recognition of
it, which was echoed by William, counter-balanced the
negative impression made by Anne's quarrel with William
and Mary over her receiving a grant of £50,000 annually from
Parliament (rather than from the king and queen, at their
pleasure). It became common knowledge that Sarah was
encouraging Anne in her stand, and it was she who incurred
most of the blame for the general deterioration of relations
between the two royal sisters. But this did not prevent
William giving Marlborough further key positions for the
campaign of 1690. While the king was campaigning in
Ireland the country was to be governed by Mary, assisted by a
Council of Nine. Marlborough was one of them and he also
became commander of all troops and militia in England. This
turned out to be a key post when on 30 June the French
defeated the Anglo-Dutch fleet off Beachy Head. French
control of the Channel exposed England to invasion along the
south coast. With few resources at his disposal – some 6,000
regulars – Marlborough made energetic preparations to
organise an effective defence. Assembly points were arranged
to which the militia rallied with enthusiasm and in thousands
but their military value, as he knew from his experience in
1685, was extremely problematical.[26]

The French proceeded to fritter away their opportunity.
Their army was fully committed in Flanders, on the Rhine, in
the Alps and in the Pyrenees, and they had a contingent in
Ireland. Consequently no invasion army had been prepared

[25] John Childs, The Nine Years War and the British Army (Manchester, 1991), pp. 100,
121–3.
[26] Lord president Carmarthen (the former Danby) sought to consolidate his position
as chief minister by disparaging Marlborough; Browning, Danby, vol. I, pp. 479–
81; vol. II, pp. 175, 178, 181. Harris, Passion for Government, pp. 54–8.

and they had no plan ready to exploit their naval superiority: they did not even send ships into the Irish Sea to destroy William's transports and detain his army in Ireland after the victory at the Boyne. Their inaction was in very sharp contrast with the imaginative strategic project which Marlborough conceived and executed with outstanding success. Once the French fleet had retired to Brest Marlborough concluded from its lack of enterprise that it would not reappear to cover an invasion. He therefore advanced to the Council the bold plan of an invasion of the Munster ports, to take the remaining Jacobite forces in Ireland in the rear. Six of the nine councillors opposed his plan because it would drain England of troops at a time when they assumed that invasion by the French was still possible. Despite this majority Mary sent on the plan to William, who approved it (14 August).[27]

Although the Council remained pessimistic, and bad weather retarded the sailing of his transports, Marlborough pressed ahead with his project with great urgency. He landed with some 4,000 troops near Cork on 22 September, linking up with cavalry from William's army who crossed Jacobite-held territory under Würtemberg, who gave Marlborough his first major exercise in handling awkward allied generals. His tact secured Würtemberg's full cooperation and his energetic drive ensured a quick success. Cork fell after five days. The more formidable defences of Kinsale were overcome by 15 October. As a result communications between France and the Jacobite armies were restricted to the far less accessible ports of Limerick and Galway, and French aid did not get through to save them during the final campaign of 1691.[28]

There is a suggestive possibility that this successful

---

[27] Browning, *Danby*, vol. II, pp. 167, 188–9.
[28] J. G. Simms, *War and Politics in Ireland 1649–1730* (1986), pp. 117–27. Churchill, *Marlborough*, vol. I, pp. 326–34.

Munster campaign had a considerable effect on the outcome of World War Two exactly two and a half centuries later. Winston Churchill's account of it was published in the first volume of his biography of Marlborough, which was published in 1933. Seven years later he followed his ancestor's example in the middle of an even more acute crisis. In August 1940 at the height of the Battle of Britain, when a German invasion in overpowering strength was judged to be imminent, he made a similar decision to despatch several of the few available, fully trained army formations, with half the tanks in the army, to a theatre of war where they could be used offensively. Their arrival enabled Wavell to hold the Middle East, rout the invading Italian forces and conquer their colonies. There is no direct or explicit evidence of a link, but in general it is clear that the intensive study of all Marlborough's campaigns, and his relations with the allies, gave Winston Churchill an unrivalled education in grand strategy and the conduct of war by a heterogeneous alliance.[29]

Marlborough drew important conclusions from his experiences during 1690. Profoundly unimpressed by the way that the Council of Nine members had directed affairs, he told Halifax that executive decisions ought to be concentrated in a Cabinet Council of only five members. Such a concentration was necessary to produce quicker and firmer decisions: this judgement anticipated the triumvirate of Marlborough, Godolphin and Harley which was to direct the Spanish Succession War during its first years. His articulation of such an idea also demonstrated Marlborough's ambition and growing self-confidence.[30]

In critical situations such as that of 1690 (and 1940)

---

[29] Winston Churchill, *The Second World War* (4 vols., 1949), vol. II, pp. 375, 378–9. Martin Gilbert, *Finest Hour* (1983), pp. 755–6.

[30] Foxcroft, *Halifax*, vol. II, p. 129.

politicians and soldiers must utilise their capacity to deploy
latent powers and abilities to the utmost if they are to ensure
survival. What they need above all is a belief in themselves,
and the ability to make others accept this belief. Marlborough
had the former, but not yet the latter quality. Marlborough
acted in 1690 in the same way as the elder Pitt during the
crisis of the Seven Years War, that he and he alone knew how
England was to be saved. But unfortunately a crisis of equal
intensity to that of 1690 did not recur until 1702 and 1704.
From William's viewpoint he was no more than a competent
but overambitious general: it was the king who was entitled
to be regarded as the saviour of England, having delivered it
from tyranny in 1688 (not to speak of having saved the Dutch
Republic from mortal danger in 1672). But even though there
was currently room only for one great man, no other English
soldier impressed William with his strategic insight and
military skills. A bitter dispute was to send Marlborough into
the wilderness the next year, and the two men never
developed any kind of personal rapport, but these initial
impressions were eventually to lead William to give Marlborough his greatest opportunity. When his own health and
powers began to decline, after 1699, it was to Marlborough
that he turned to ensure the continuation of his own life-long
mission to subdue the power of France.

During 1691, when Marlborough accompanied William on
an almost entirely featureless and fruitless campaign in
Flanders, very similar to his own in 1703, hostility to him and
Sarah steadily built up at Court. William consistently relied
on and therefore favoured English and Scottish officers who
had been in the Dutch service. He saw Marlborough's
championing of those whose pre-1688 service had been in
France or under Charles and James as potentially divisive.
However it was criticism of long-serving senior Dutch and

German officers that William found most unacceptable. Marlborough also incurred the lethal hostility of Portland, William's trusted servant and friend since boyhood. No two men could have been more dissimilar in personality. Portland had none of Marlborough's natural charm and good manners, his ability to please and persuade. Stubborn, taciturn but determined to hold on to his powers and influence he had to act on William's behalf as his chief intermediary and front man in a polished, cynical Court where he was hated and openly derided. Marlborough sneered at him as 'a wooden fellow'. This kind of sniping was damaging because William off-loaded on him the thankless work of rejecting petitions and disappointing aspirants for office and favours, making Portland the most hated man in England. Seeing Marlborough as a threat Portland counter-attacked, exploiting both his disparagement of Dutch officers and the increasing friction between Mary and Anne, to discredit the Churchills. Sarah got the blame for Anne's defiant behaviour. In January 1692 Mary ordered Anne to dismiss her, but she refused. Anne demonstrated that her loyalty to her friend came before loyalty, or even respect, to the king and queen.[31]

This personal dispute, nasty and petty-minded on both sides, precipitated Marlborough's dismissal from all his military posts, which was accompanied by orders to sell his civil offices and to stay away from Court, in the same month. This abrupt fall from a position of apparently increasing power and influence created a sensation, which was stimulated by the fact that William gave no reason for his action.[32]

---

[31] William Coxe, *Memoirs of John, Duke of Marlborough* (3 vols., 1818–19), vol. I, pp. 33–4. *Private Correspondence of Sarah, Duchess of Marlborough* (2 vols., 1838), vol. I, pp. 173–4. David Green, *Queen Anne* (1970), pp. 59–60.

[32] Harris, *Passion for Government*, pp. 62–6. Foxcroft, *Halifax*, vol. II, pp. 151, 152–5.

Subsequently the rift between Marlborough and the Court steadily widened. Anne provoked Mary by refusing to part with Sarah, to the point of leaving her official residence when the court chamberlain barred Sarah from living there. Undoubtedly Anne was allowing Sarah to manipulate her; Mary fell into the trap of personalising the issues because she was living under great stress. William left for the Hague to prepare for the campaign on the continent despite mounting evidence of French preparations for an invasion of England. Mary and the Council became alert to the danger of internal subversion by the Jacobites, or even a concerted rising. Informers came forward with well-timed but fabricated allegations that implicated Marlborough in an alleged plot (May); even at first sight the evidence was unimpressive but at a time of acute apprehension Mary and the Council took no chances. Marlborough was one of those arrested and sent to the Tower. Some historians have concluded that this action reflected William's fear of Marlborough, but it was actually Mary who ordered his arrest. When he learnt of it William reacted with caution, suspending judgement on whether, as he wrote, it was well done or not until he knew all the circumstances. On examination the falsity of the charges became evident to the Council. Marlborough was released on 15 June.[33]

It is significant that while this experience made the Marlboroughs' relations with Mary irreparable, the first tentative (if unsuccessful) attempt at a reconciliation of Marlborough with William came as soon as three months after Mary's death on 28 December 1694. But before this Marlborough made trouble for the administration. During the parliamentary session of 1692–3 he aligned himself with the factious section of the Tories, protesting against the

[33] N. Japikse, *Correspondentie van Willem III en van Hans Willem Bentinck*, RGP kleine serie 23 (6 vols., the Hague, 1927), vol. I, p. 171. Harris, *Passion for Government*, pp. 64–6.

rejection of a Country-sponsored bill to disable placemen from the Commons and encouraging obstruction of the land tax. Even more provocatively he continued with his attacks on the employment of foreign troops, a line that made it impossible for William to consider restoring his commissions during the rest of the war. Marlborough's factious behaviour encouraged Jacobite agents and sympathetic MPs to work out a plan for Marlborough to move in the Lords for the dismissal of all foreign officers and troops, while declarations of support would be organised among army and navy officers. James claimed to the French that this would make William powerless, but there is no evidence that his agent had actually established the kind of clandestine network that had been behind the organised defections of 1688.[34]

There was always more talk and speculation than substance in the reports of Jacobite agents and the claims made to impress the French by the ministers at Saint-Germain. There is no doubt that Marlborough like a great many other prominent persons talked to avowed Jacobite agents and maintained an intermittent correspondence with Saint-Germain, giving general assurances of loyalty and service. The generally accepted historical view is that these connections were in the nature of insurance policies, entered into just in case the wheel of fortune turned yet again (as in 1649, 1653, 1660, 1681 and 1688) to bring about wholesale change, a revolution in public affairs.

This conventional judgement certainly applies to Marlborough in the years after 1698, and particularly during his command of the allied army in the Spanish Succession War. He never gave any serious consideration to Jacobite offers

---

[34] Foxcroft, *Halifax*, vol. II, p. 161. Macpherson, *Original Papers*, vol. I, pp. 440, 456–9.

during that war. In 1714 he was committed to taking command of the forces being prepared to resist the Tory administration if it attempted to restore James III when Anne died. Marlborough in his dealings with both Jacobites and the French employed the same modes of negotiation which French diplomats of this period had perfected. He 'chicaned'. That means he subtly used ambiguous language and carefully constructed empty phrases, promises containing implied but unstated conditions and reservations. He allowed his correspondents to assume agreement when he had not explicitly committed himself. He had contrasting success. Jacobite agents were invariably deceived, but the professional chicaners in the French diplomatic system understood what he was doing and reacted sceptically.

However there were at least two instances in which Marlborough's actions cannot be described as non-committal or insurance policies. In December 1691, before his dismissal, he persuaded Anne to write a penitential letter to James, although the agent to whom it was entrusted could not deliver it until the next spring, when James was at La Hogue expecting to accompany a French invasion. Its publication during this brief but extremely dangerous crisis, which ended when the French fleet was heavily defeated at Barfleur–La Hogue, would have created great confusion and an irreparable breach with William III.[35]

The second instance is the 'Camaret Bay letter'. A Jacobite major-general, Sackville, sent James the transcript of a letter from Churchill to him, with a covering memorandum which was dated 3 May 1694, presumably Old Style since the letters originated in England. In the transcription of Churchill's

---

[35] Churchill, *Marlborough*, vol. I, p. 385. Green, *Queen Anne*, p. 59.

letter, translated into French, he confirmed earlier reports that a combined fleet and small army were preparing to attack Brest, and gave details of the force, the name of the military commander, Tollemache, and the date at which it would sail. If the transcribed document which survives is a faithful record of an authentic original, and this has been strenuously questioned by Winston Churchill and other apologists, this letter did not give the French their first warning of the intended attack. Louis had already instructed Vauban to go to strengthen the Brest defences, and delays in England caused by the shortage of ordnance for the bomb-ketches gave him all the time he needed, and also made the time-table allegedly communicated by Churchill obsolete.

At the very least it was totally improper for Marlborough to give additional credibility to the reports of the attack, even if security about the employment of the fleet was lax, indeed almost non-existent. Marlborough's detractors have gone much further, alleging that he wished to ensure that the attack ended in disaster, with the aim of either discrediting Tollemache as a rival for high command or, as was to happen, eliminating him altogether by getting him killed. Tollemache certainly was a professional rival: he had replaced Marlborough as lieutenant-general and gained credit in the army among English officers by taking up their grievances against foreign officers, but in a more skilful and less provocative way than Marlborough.

All conclusions and judgements must be speculative. The letter may be authentic, but the original has not survived. However the attempts to rubbish it, notably by Arthur Parnell and Winston Churchill, are unconvincing. But if the evidence is valid it does not follow that Marlborough had prime reponsibility for the disastrous attempted landing in Camaret Bay (8 June). The alarm had been given, the French were ready. Tollemache pressed the attack despite this, and the availability of only five of the stipulated sixteen bomb-ketches.[36]

Whatever the truth about Camaret Bay it is significant that in the last major Jacobite attempt of William's reign no part was assigned to Marlborough. By the end of 1695 James and his ministers became aware that despite assurances to the contrary Louis was now ready to negotiate a peace that would not include his restoration. The Jacobites therefore made a last attempt to impress Louis with the strength of their support in England, with the objective of persuading him to authorise a last attempt at invasion. Louis had always demanded as a condition an undertaking by James that his partisans would stage a rising or seize a port at which the French could disembark. In none of the succession of plans for armed insurrection was any part delegated to Marlborough or the other prominent men who appear on Jacobite lists as ready to welcome James, nor was he expected to use his army connections: the men given these tasks were zealous Jacobites of much less influence, such as Sir John Fenwick and Sir John Friend. Even more revealing of the low valuation placed on Marlborough and doubts about his zeal was the failure of Berwick, his nephew, to contact him during the secret visit he made at the end of 1695 to see whether a rising could be staged effectively.

Berwick's negative report led to the substitution of a plan to assassinate William. When this was discovered Fenwick tried to save himself by incriminating Marlborough and others whom he knew were in contact with Saint-Germain, but he had no evidence other than the letters they had sent to James, and William already knew of these in general terms, and had

[36] Churchill's partisan account, *Marlborough*, vol. I, pp. 420–50, includes a facsimile of the letter at p. 436. John Childs, *The British Army of William III* (Manchester, 1987), pp. 215–37.

discounted them. Naturally Marlborough consistently supported the attainder bill which liquidated Fenwick, but the latter's allegations failed to interrupt a slow rapprochement between William and Marlborough. This had begun at the end of March 1695 with the first meeting since the latter's dismissal. It became firm in June 1698 when William appointed Marlborough to be governor to Anne's only surviving son, the nine-year-old duke of Gloucester. This establishment of a separate household for the duke was an act of state: the appointment of Marlborough to its key office was virtually a formal recognition of his headship of the reversionary interest.[37]

Marlborough obtained this appointment because for William he represented the best hope of ensuring the continuation of his foreign policies and war strategy after his own death. If, for example, Anne's uncle Rochester gained such influence he would certainly try to institute an isolationist policy. This would have particularly disastrous consequences since if any lead was to be given to the former allies it would have to be by England – William would have no heir, either personal or political, in the Dutch Republic capable of influencing the policies of other states.

Marlborough was restored as a privy councillor, and in July his return to favour was signalled by his being named a lord justice to govern in William's absence in the Low Countries. In an increasingly critical political crisis William desperately needed Marlborough's help to resist intense parliamentary pressure, backed up by an inflammatory pamphleteering campaign, to force the disbandment of most of the army and of all foreign troops in English pay. In the past Marlborough had consistently disparaged foreign troops and officers, but he was now ready to help William in his attempt

---

[37] Coxe, *Memoirs*, vol. I, p. 48. G. P. R. James, *Letters Illustrative of the Reign of William III* (3 vols., 1841), vol. I, pp. 49, 64, 97n, 138–9.

to retain his Dutch Guards because many of his own English military associates faced disbandment as well, and because he believed that the army as a whole was being reduced below the safety line. He also shared a personal resentment for the virulent attacks made by Country Whig journalists on the alleged characteristics of military men – greed which led them into corrupt practices, brutality to inferiors and subservience to superiors, including a willingness to serve rulers and ministers with absolutist ambitions and disorderly private lives.

The crisis over army disbanding restored Marlborough to political influence as well as personal favour. The Junta minister Somers, who thought himself in William's confidence, was astounded when he discovered that the king was having private discussions with Marlborough about tactics, which included even a brief but unsuccessful move to revive, in the form of a pressure group, the network of officers that had as the Rose Tavern Club organised the defections from James's army in 1688. The connection between William and Marlborough was facilitated by the absence (in the Paris embassy) from Court of the latter's old enemy Portland, and the growing influence of William's new favourite Albemarle. Marlborough also helped himself by improving relations between William and Anne; he was instrumental in reaching a compromise over George's debts.[38]

As William's health and stamina declined he accepted as inevitable the fact that Marlborough was the only man fully equipped to continue his work. For that reason he did not allow Marlborough's participation in the parliamentary action against Irish land grants to do more than cause a temporary cooling of relations. A sequence of critical developments drew the two men closer together. On 30 July

---

[38] James, *Letters Illustrative*, vol. II, pp. 258, 262–3. William Coxe, *Private and Original Correspondence of Charles Talbot, Duke of Shrewsbury* (1821), p. 573.

1700 the duke of Gloucester died, leaving the question of who would succeed Anne a matter for urgent parliamentary action. On 1 November Carlos II died in Madrid. Just over two weeks later Louis announced his acceptance of the will made by this last Habsburg king, which bequeathed the whole Spanish Empire to Louis's second grandson, Philip of Anjou. By doing so Louis reneged on the second Partition Treaty which William had negotiated with him. Although most English politicians reacted with equanimity, since the treaty had been fiercely criticised by commercial interests, William and Marlborough knew that Philip's accession would give Louis indirect control over Spain and its possessions and trade, and that such an enormous accession of power and wealth would enable him to 'give the law' to Europe. Throughout the coming war Marlborough believed that England's aim in fighting and negotiating should be to deprive Philip of all, or all but a few, of the Spanish territories.[39]

Although both William and Marlborough believed that English and Dutch participation in a new war was both inevitable and essential they knew that the run-down in army strength would make the southern territories of the Dutch Republic extremely vulnerable. For this reason alone they were ready to enter into negotiations in order to postpone the outbreak of war until 1702. They had also to reconstruct the alliance against France.

It was an act of faith for William to designate Marlborough as the continuator of his policies. The two men, one now ailing, the other still belatedly in his prime, had both been born in 1650, with Marlborough actually five months older. But he was immensely less experienced. William had fought fourteen continental campaigns in all of which he had been

[39] Japikse, *Correspondentie*, vol. I, p. 350.

commander-in-chief. Marlborough had served in only five and had never commanded a large army or formulated the strategy for a continental campaign. His only independent command, in southern Ireland in 1690, had been of a force of under 6,000 men. Yet William clearly saw a promise of greatness in him.

However as developments were to show Marlborough's long exclusion from public and military affairs, while in Anne's service, had some advantages. He had the mental freshness and physical stamina of a much younger man. His Dutch contemporaries – Overkirk, Ginkel, Slangenburg – had vastly more military experience, but it was experience of a somewhat disheartening and mentally deadening kind, acquired as subordinates of William in a series of bloody campaigns of attrition that had achieved no more than a precarious containment of the French army. They did not believe, as Marlborough did, in the practical possibility of total victory; they had not developed the tactical and strategic ingenuity to work out the methods by which it could be achieved. Like their French counterparts they were tied to conventions and rules of war that Marlborough and Eugène (and, to do him justice, Peterborough in Spain) were to shatter.

Chapter 2

French hegemony destroyed

When on 1 July 1701 Marlborough left England with William his role was to act as the king's deputy. The dual appointments which he held also reflected a situation in which war against France was highly likely, but not yet inevitable. As ambassador extraordinary he received instructions to negotiate with French and Spanish diplomats at the Hague for a settlement on what by later standards were very generous terms – a French evacuation of the Spanish Netherlands and satisfaction to the Emperor for his claims. His instructions did not spell these out because it was for Marlborough to negotiate them in working out the terms of the Grand Alliance. Secondly, as commander-in-chief of the English and Scottish forces assembling in the Dutch Republic Marlborough was to assume the active role of general which William's failing health made it impossible for him to sustain. However William would still have been in the background, and had he lived longer would certainly have intervened, a serious complication which Marlborough was spared. William's choice of Marlborough, despite their mutual dislike and past antagonisms, was dictated by the king's life-long commitment to subordinate all personal considerations to the mission of containing and reducing the excessive and aggressive power of France. William knew that

the recent parliamentary and journalistic onslaughts against
the employment of foreign soldiers made it impossible to
nominate a Dutch general, such as the experienced Athlone
(Ginkel) or the royal favourite Albemarle to whom he had
recently given the Garter, still withheld from Marlborough.
But the latter had far less military experience than his one
British competitor, the duke of Ormonde, who had served as
general in Flanders under William and had Dutch connections through his mother, a member of an illegitimate branch
of the Orange family. Ormonde wanted the command and
was aggrieved at not obtaining it, and was eventually to
satisfy his ambition by superseding Marlborough in 1712.
However he lacked the diplomatic skills which were to play
as important a part in Marlborough's career as his military
genius. But the crucial point in Marlborough's favour was his
possession of Anne's confidence. William knew that he had
not long to live, but through Marlborough's influence on
Anne he could hope for the continuation of his own policies,
and indeed in all his references to the allied objectives during
the war Marlborough used the same phrases as William; to
prevent Louis 'giving the law' to Europe, to preserve the
'liberties' of Europe and to establish a 'lasting peace', that is
one which France could not break when it was in its interests
to do so.[1]

The situation of the allies in 1701 was far more adverse
than at any time during the Nine Years War. Then William
had managed to preserve the Spanish Netherlands in difficult
defensive campaigns. But he and the Dutch suffered a severe
psychological shock when in February 1701 the French
occupied the barrier fortresses which the Dutch occupied
under the terms of the Rijswijk Treaty, releasing their
garrisons only when the States General recognised Philip V.

[1] Snyder, vol. I, pp. 41, 268. All the many citations from these volumes refer to
correspondence originating with, or addressed to, Marlborough.

This brought French troops right up to the frontiers of the Dutch Republic and made it possible for them to repeat their blitzkrieg strategy of 1672 if Louis declared war. It is this desperately unfavourable position that accounts for the defensive mentality of all Dutch generals during the first years of the war, an attitude that William fully shared in 1701–2. They insisted on maintaining large garrisons in largely obsolescent fortresses, and they were determined to avoid becoming involved in major set-piece battles. In 1674–8 and 1691–7 William had repeatedly engaged the main French army, but he had won none of the battles and had suffered heavy casualties, and subsequent losses of precious territory, in a number of defeats. These had been in the Spanish Netherlands, but after their occupation the price of defeat would be unacceptably higher, the loss of Dutch cities and popular panic producing an irresistible demand for peace.

In 1702–3 Marlborough lacked the prestige and authority to override the defensive attitudes of the Dutch, but he could not accept them indefinitely. The premise underlying all his strategic thinking was that French military predominance must be destroyed, or at least reduced, and only through winning set-piece battles against their main armies could this be achieved. Dutch attitudes also posed two more immediate dangers. Limited campaigns, in which offensive operations carrying an element of risk were avoided, could produce only piecemeal gains, but would nevertheless be financially expensive. The resulting stalemate would strengthen the appeal of the arguments advanced by the Tory 'blue water' school who wished to concentrate on naval and colonial operations, restricting the English role in the Low Countries to that of auxiliaries. Secondly, during the rather desultory negotiations of 1701 with the French he became aware of Dutch susceptibility to approaches for a separate agreement, on terms that would be advantageous to France. This would leave both England and the Emperor isolated. This left a lasting impression. Unlike most Tories and many Whigs at home Marlborough constantly emphasised the interdependence of England, the Dutch Republic and the Emperor and, despite his frequent exasperation (and occasional fury) at their conduct, always strove to maintain good relations with the allies.

The initial agreement which Marlborough negotiated on the army strengths which the allies were to maintain in 1702 reveals the extent of English dependence on her allies: while the Emperor was to put in the field 82,000 men and the Dutch 100,000, the English contribution was only 40,000. The English war-effort also depended on the provision of troops by the minor allies – the newly created king of Prussia and elector of Hanover, Denmark, Hesse-Cassel and other German princes. From the beginning in 1701 these negotiations, and subsequent doubts about the willingness or ability of these princes to fulfil their obligations, caused Marlborough constant anxiety; as early as September 1701 he described himself as 'tormented' by the negotiations with Prussia, a word he used to indicate extreme stress. His task was greatly complicated by the outbreak of what developed into the Great Northern War of 1701–21. This prevented northern sovereigns and princes from concentrating their attention on the war against France and posed the possibility that their contingents might have to be withdrawn at short notice to defend their homelands. In the years down to 1709 Marlborough also faced the nightmare possibility that the French might persuade Karl XII of Sweden to attack the Emperor in central Europe, altering the whole balance of the war, just as Gustavus Adolphus had done, with French support and subsidies, in 1629–31. Consequently Marlborough always had to pay particular attention to Sweden: in

1701 he carefully submitted all the treaties which he concluded to the ministry at home for approval, except the one with Sweden which he signed himself; he knew that any delay could tempt the Swedes into accepting the offer of an alliance which the French were pressing on them.[2]

Marlborough enjoyed considerable freedom of action under William's almost nominal supervision, but the recent attempted impeachments of the Junta ministers warned him that his real accountability could be to Parliament. Consequently he was dismayed when William in the autumn of 1701 turned again to the Whigs, as the party more likely to support the war-effort, and dissolved Parliament in order to take advantage of a rising tide of anti-French sentiment that would strengthen their representation in the Commons. Marlborough never at any time wanted to become involved in the envenomed disputes between Whigs and Tories, but to have to work with an administration increasingly Whig in composition, backed by a Whig-dominated Parliament, would put him in a false position, as it did in 1708–10. Had it come to a forced choice he would stick with his associates, who in 1701–2 were Tories, notably Godolphin and Rochester, and risk dismissal by William. It is difficult to see how Marlborough could have continued long in command if William had not died on 8 March 1702. It was doubtful whether he could, or alternatively would be allowed to, work with partisan Whig ministers. Moreover William fully shared the defensive preoccupations of his Dutch generals, making it even more difficult to take the offensive, and would have been appealed to by all who became dissatisfied by Marlborough's conduct.

Anne's accession secured Marlborough's position. Her favour was demonstrated immediately by the gift of the

---

[2] Ibid., vol. I, pp. 36–7.

Garter, the lucrative office of master-general of the Ordnance and appointment as captain-general. Godolphin's installation as lord treasurer provided double security. However the question of who was to take command in the Low Countries became temporarily complicated by Anne's wish that it should be by her consort, George. Because of his dependence on her favour Marlborough had to support this unrealistic claim, and no doubt he could have supplied George with the brains he lacked, and actually directed operations – as able German generals did in 1914–18 while nominally serving under princes. For this reason the Dutch opposed George's appointment, and it would never have been accepted by rival aspirants, the king of Prussia and the elector of Hanover. In the compromise adopted when Anne abandoned George's claim no generalissimo was appointed: it was agreed that Marlborough should command the Dutch and allied contingents, but only when they were operating in conjunction with the English, as they were throughout 1702–3.[3]

This solution was not a tribute to Marlborough's personal capabilities, but a recognition by the Dutch that with French armies on their vulnerable frontiers it was essential to commit the English to concentrate on their defence, and by the minor allies of the fact that England was their paymaster. Serious doubts persisted. Marlborough was seen as a royal favourite, and Dutch experience – of Leicester in the 1580s and Buckingham in 1625–6 – had been of disastrous incompetence. In terms of military experience Marlborough was a lightweight compared to a generation of Dutch generals – Overkirk, Opdam, Slangenburg, Athlone. He had fought in only one Flanders campaign (1689) and commanded only one smallish army, in the Munster expedition of 1690. This is why the Dutch imposed and rigidly enforced

[3] Ibid., vol. I, p. 52 and note. Winston S. Churchill, *Marlborough: His Life and Times* (4 vols., 1933–8), vol. II, pp. 57–63.

close controls over him. All major decisions had to be approved by the field deputies representing the States General and they, after consulting their generals, consistently erred on the side of caution. Their minds were set within the military conventions of the age; the use of defensive lines, siege operations, careful advances with well-secured lines of communication (and retreat). They were to be profoundly dubious about the innovative strategy which Marlborough wished to follow – bold advances by means of forced marches with the army carrying its own supplies and, above all, the deliberate seeking of battle with the enemy's main army.

Marlborough's open objectives in his first campaign were to clear the enemy from the territories bordering on the Dutch Republic, and particularly from their positions on both sides of the Maas, from which they could advance to and even cross the lower Rhine. Privately he hoped to do more, to open the way for an advance into the heart of the Spanish Netherlands.

Initially the Dutch forces were concentrated to cover their frontier fortresses, limiting their offensive operations to a siege of the isolated fortress of Kaiserwerth, east of the Rhine. Louis waited for the allies to declare war (on 4/15 May) and saw Italy, where hostilities against the Emperor had begun in 1701, as the main theatre of war. However the veteran Boufflers kept Dutch fears alive by taking up a forward position between the Maas and the Rhine, from which he made a surprise attack (10 June) that narrowly failed to encircle and destroy Athlone's army. The Dutch retreated in disorder, saving themselves only by retiring within the Nijmegen defences. This near disaster frightened them and made them refuse to consider the excessively bold offensive proposals which Marlborough put to them when he arrived

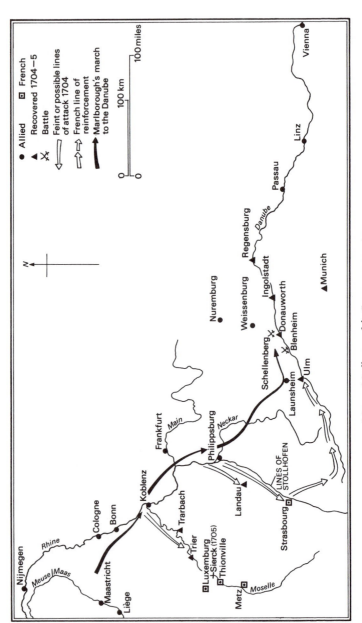

Map 2 Marlborough's German campaigns

Legend:
- ● Allied
- ▣ French
- ▣ Recovered 1704–5
- ▲ Battle
- ⤬
- ⇨ Feint or possible lines of attack 1704
- ⇨ French line of reinforcement
- ➤ Marlborough's march to the Danube

Scale: 0 — 100 km / 0 — 100 miles

N

Locations: Nijmegen, Liège, Maastricht, Cologne, Bonn, Koblenz, Trarbach, Trier, Luxemburg, Sierck (1705), Thionville, Metz, Frankfurt, Landau, Philippsburg, Strasbourg, LINES OF STOLLHOFEN, Launsheim, Ulm, Nuremburg, Weissenburg, Schellenberg, Blenheim, Donauworth, Ingolstadt, Regensburg, Munich, Passau, Linz, Vienna

Rivers: Rhine, Meuse/Maas, Moselle, Main, Neckar, Danube

to take command on 2 July. He wanted to force the French to retire from their threatening positions by launching an offensive sixty miles into enemy territory in Brabant, which would involve breaking enemy defensive lines, in order to attack Antwerp, a major fortress, strongly garrisoned. It is not surprising that the Dutch generals dismissed this plan as fantastic, and that it coloured their response to all subsequent proposals from a commander who was new to them.[4]

Marlborough had to modify his second plan so as to meet Dutch defensive mindedness. He had to depart from his principle that success, especially in offensive operations, demands the concentration of forces by agreeing to detach substantial forces to reinforce the static defence of Nijmegen while the rest of the army crossed the Maas. As he expected, this move threatened Boufflers's lines of communication and forced him to withdraw to the west of the Maas. Indeed by rapid forced marching, a characteristic that was to mark all his later campaigns, Marlborough manoeuvred Boufflers into an unfavourable position of having to march across the front of the allied army. Marlborough had earlier obtained the theoretical consent of the field deputies to attack if circumstances appeared to be favourable, but now that such a situation had been brought about they vetoed a general assault. From their perspective Marlborough's manoeuvring had forced the enemy to retire, lifting the threat to their frontier fortresses: why put this gain at risk by provoking a set-piece battle? At the back of their minds there must have been the thought that no French army equivalent in strength to Boufflers's had suffered defeat in the Low Countries since the 1650s. Unfortunately Marlborough confirmed their suspicions of his rashness when on the next day (3 August) he again requested their approval to attack, although by then

---

[4] Snyder, vol. I, pp. 70, 72, 79–80, 85. *Historical Manuscripts Commission, Portland*, vol. IV, pp. 40–2.

the enemy had entrenched themselves strongly. But after again out-manoeuvring Boufflers Marlborough did finally get the deputies to approve an attack on 23 August at Hechteren on a seriously disorganised enemy. However the plan of attack depended on an early and swift advance by the allied right wing, but its commander the elderly Dutch general Opdam failed to move forward as ordered and this wrecked all chance of a general engagement. This fiasco sank Marlborough in despondency, but although cheated of a major opportunity to defeat the enemy's main army he had created the opportunity for significant successes in the last weeks of the campaign. He covered the sieges of Venlo, Stevensweert and Roermond, clearing the enemy from the Maas, and followed by taking Liège which cut easy access to the remaining French garrisons on the middle Rhine.[5]

These successes distinguished Marlborough as the out-standing allied general in the Low Countries. Ironically this could have precipitated the end of his career. As the campaign finished he was returning to Holland by boat, down the Maas, when his party was ambushed and captured by a raiding force based on the isolated fortress of Geldern. Fortunately a clerk travelling with Marlborough slipped him a pass issued by the French for his brother George. Although it was time-expired the officer commanding the enemy force ignored the discrepancies and clearly did a deal: he was an Irish exile who had deserted the Dutch service to which he was now soon to return, with a pardon and promotion. This was a fortunate escape. Marlborough's position as Anne's adviser made him a great prize. His successes in the field had also personally affronted Louis. Initially Louis had highly optimistic expectations of the 1702 campaign. He therefore sent his favourite grandson, the duke of Burgundy, to take

[5] Snyder, vol. I, pp. 89–94, 102, 110, 115, 121, 126. T'Hoff, pp. 17, 19, 27–9. Murray, vol. I, p. 12.

nominal command. This meant that not only Burgundy's prestige but the glory of the House of Bourbon demanded military victories, and the rout of Athlone before Nijmegen seemed to provide the first. From Versailles Louis ordered Burgundy to continue with offensive action, without taking into account problems of supply. But when it was Marlborough who went on to the offensive Louis warned his grandson that it would be an affront to his own and the young duke's glory to allow the allies to conduct successful sieges in the presence of a French army impotent to interfere. When this actually happened Louis withdrew Burgundy to Versailles, and had Marlborough been retained as a prisoner it is most unlikely that Louis would have been prepared to exchange him even for Villeroy, the marshal captured by Eugène in Italy.[6]

By his successes in 1702 in taking fortresses to give the Dutch secure frontiers and himself bases for future offensive action, Marlborough did more than affront Louis and establish his own reputation as a general. He also validated the strategy of concentrating first on the war in the Low Countries. In 1702 the now predominantly Tory administration also invested heavily in the alternative strategy. They sent a large naval and military expedition to take Cadiz, and this also gave Ormonde, its general, and Marlborough's only real rival, the chance to make his reputation. But Ormonde proved to be lamentably ineffective and the expedition failed. In contrast Marlborough's successes showed that there was a realistic prospect of dislodging the French from at least part of the Spanish Netherlands. They convinced a majority of the ministers to augment his forces there for the next year.

---

[6] Snyder, vol. I, pp. 140, 141. Murray, vol. I, pp. 54–5. Churchill, *Marlborough*, vol. I, pp. 605–9. F. E. de Vault and J. J. G. Pelet, *Mémoires militaires relatifs à la succession d'Espagne sous Louis XIV* (11 vols., Paris, 1835–62), vol. II, pp. 7, 48–9, 54–6, 83–4, 91–2, 94–5, 98–9, 100–1, 105.

This commitment reassured the Dutch, who were seriously alarmed by the naval and colonial strategy advocated by Rochester and other insular Tories. His arguments reflected blatant national self-interest by claiming that colonial conquests would be made to produce an expansion of trade and the enrichment of England. Such a selfish concentration on national advantage would lead to imitative action by the other allies and disrupt the common cause. Acting to defend the Habsburg claimant's interests, but also with Imperial approval, Wratislaw protested against tentative proposals for a joint Anglo-Dutch expedition to the Caribbean because it envisaged the retention of colonial conquests and the destruction of the Spanish trading monopoly. The so-called blue water strategy also, if illogically, assumed that Spain and its colonies would voluntarily rally to the Habsburg claimant Karl, but there had been absolutely no response when Ormonde's expedition appeared off the coast of southern Spain.[7]

In planning the campaign of 1703 Marlborough had to overcome persistent Dutch fears, despite the successes of the previous year, that the French intended to make an offensive to overwhelm their defences. However he was able to turn these fears to advantage by negotiating an augmentation, an agreement to levy more men and provide more money for the army. When the initial French force dispositions indicated that they intended to stand on the defensive, he also persuaded the Dutch to agree to two plans of campaign that were strategically risky. In the first Marlborough accompanied the veteran of siege warfare, Coehorn, in an attack on Bonn so as to secure the middle Rhine. Some five days march away another army, under Overkirk, covered the main

[7] David Francis, The First Peninsular War 1702–1713 (1975), pp. 19, 40–52, 55–6.

French army on the Maas, but was greatly inferior in numbers. The impatience which Marlborough showed at delays in beginning, and then in pressing, the siege reveal his awareness of the risks he was running with such widely separated forces. The rigidity of the French command structures prevented their generals exploiting the situation. Louis was trying to run the war from Versailles. Like Hitler in 1941–5 he gave the generals detailed instructions from which they could not depart without his permission – which took at least four days to obtain. Nevertheless Marlborough was in a hurry to concentrate his forces again, and made the concession that the Bonn garrison should march out to rejoin their main army rather than surrender as prisoners of war.

Marlborough also rejected pleas from the allied commanders on the Rhine, prince Lewis and the elector Palatine, that the bulk of the forces freed by the fall of Bonn should be committed to an advance up the Moselle so as to divert French forces which were putting their own under pressure. Such a diversionary attack would need careful preparation and logistical support if it was to produce any permanent gains and nothing was ready. In any case Marlborough had already planned an ambitious offensive at the other, northern, end of the front – but he was in future years to return to the idea of an invasion of France via the Moselle. For the offensive of 1703 he had conceived what he called his 'great design', a coordinated attack to capture Ostend and Antwerp. The former would give England an independent supply base, the latter control over the main river lines opening a way into Flanders and Brabant.[8]

So high were the expectations which Marlborough had of this offensive that for the first time in his private correspondence with his wife and with Godolphin he held out the

[8] Snyder, vol. I, pp. 174, 180, 192, 206–12. T'Hoff, pp. 68, 73, 74–9. Churchill, *Marlborough*, vol. II, pp. 192, 197, 209–19, 220–33.

prospect that its success would break French predominance and lead to a lasting peace. This would be brought about by posing such a direct threat to the French control of the entire Spanish Netherlands that they would be forced to risk the set-piece battle which Marlborough was confident he would win decisively – although he did not spell out this calculation to the Dutch.

Compared with his strategic plans for later campaigns the 'great design' contained both political and military weaknesses. The proposal to take Ostend renewed Dutch suspicions that the purpose was a long-term English occupation as a counter-weight to their own barrier fortresses and as the means of preventing them monopolising the trade of the Spanish Netherlands, a war aim which was already beginning to take covert shape. In addition it seemed that the Dutch would have to do most of the fighting. Militarily the plan entailed splitting the army into four separate forces, and relying on each general keeping to a programme of timed, coordinated movement and attack. If the 'great design' was to succeed each movement had to go according to plan. This consisted of an attack on Ostend by Coehorn, whose conduct of the siege of Bonn had in its slowness reflected his age and poor health.[9] Two Dutch forces, under Spaar and Opdam, were to penetrate the French lines and in a pincer movement attack Antwerp. Finally Marlborough, at the head of the main allied army, would move rapidly north to confront Villeroy who now commanded the main French army.

The underlying principle of the 'great design' was to present the enemy with a series of options, each of them posing difficult choices and potential losses. If the French did not send help to Ostend from Antwerp the port would fall. If help was sent Spaar should be in a position to intercept it, and

[9] Snyder, vol. I, pp. 165, 176–7, 178–9. T'Hoff, pp. 63, 67, 68. Churchill, Marlborough, vol. II, pp. 211–15.

in any case Antwerp's garrison would be weakened. Seeing this Villeroy could despatch reinforcements from his own army, but at the price of making himself vulnerable to the impending threat from Marlborough; if he kept his army intact Spaar and Opdam would take Antwerp. Plans like this for coordinated attacks may look impressive on paper, but interdependent actions depending on adherence to a predetermined plan can quickly collapse if one part goes wrong. In 1703 almost everything that could, went wrong. Coehorn, a general of immense prestige and influence, refused to attack Ostend, but preferred a pillaging expedition into the Pays de Waes from whose booty he stood to gain. But although this would not divert enemy troops from Antwerp Marlborough allowed the rest of the plan to continue. Spaar's advance did not draw off troops either and, separated from Opdam by the Scheldt, he could not give the latter support. Opdam put himself in a position of great peril by advancing prematurely, and then staying in an indefensible advanced position facing numerically superior troops from the Antwerp garrison. He disregarded warnings from Marlborough and advice by his own subordinates to withdraw while he could in good order. Marlborough's march north was hampered by heavy rain and he had to march along exterior lines.

Moving along shorter distances Villeroy arrived in the Antwerp area first, and his vanguard under Boufflers went on ahead, joined with a force from the garrison and made a surprise attack on Opdam, who was out-numbered by four to one. Opdam panicked, abandoning his men and sending despatches to Marlborough and the States General that his whole army was lost. In reality a fighting retreat by the Dutch infantry under the veteran general Slangenburg (who was later to achieve prominence as a bogeyman for Marlborough, who was to blame him for blocking all proposals for offensive action) brought back most of the army in relatively good order, and the States General took immediate and effective emergency action. However this second escape from near disaster at the hands of Boufflers greatly increased the reluctance of Dutch deputies and generals to agree to offensive operations that they judged to be risky. Unwisely in these circumstances, and giving the impression that he would rashly press for action regardless of an adverse situation, Marlborough proposed making a frontal attack on Villeroy, although the French were strongly positioned behind their defensive lines and their morale had been lifted by their recent victory. Privately, he did not expect approval, and after a five-hour council of war the Dutch refused to authorise an attack that would have been costly in casualties and uncertain in outcome.[10]

Subsequently Marlborough recognised the need for a conventional operation that would restore Dutch confidence in themselves (and in himself). He undertook the siege of Huy, a very minor fortress fifteen miles down the Maas from the southern end of the enemy lines. This safe operation took only eleven days, which left two more months of the campaigning season. Marlborough proposed that in this time the army should force a breach in the southern section of the French lines, arguing that these were not as strongly held or as elaborately constructed as the section which covered Antwerp and which the Dutch had refused to attack. He pointed out that this would prevent the enemy sending forces to the middle Rhine where prince Lewis and the German contingents were hard pressed. But it was obvious that he was not interested so much in creating a diversion but in bringing about a general engagement with Villeroy's army. His generals were divided on the proposal. Dutch generals and deputies tried to avoid giving a direct opinion, but

---

[10] Snyder, vol. I, p. 222. Churchill, *Marlborough*, vol. II, pp. 226–30.

concentrated on emphasising the difficulties. The commanders of the allied contingents which were in either Dutch or English pay supported Marlborough's plans: he made considerable play with this, pointing out that it was unusual for officers who commanded what could be called mercenary forces to favour offensive action that could cause heavy casualties and consequently a reduction in the financial subsidies they received.

The resulting impasse led to the matter being referred to the States General in the Hague, who of course knew nothing in detail of the situation in the field. Constitutionally they were right to refuse to make a decision but to send the issue back to their field deputies. But they did not want to be responsible for a decision that might be criticised not only by Marlborough but by the English administration and Parliament, and could lead to weakening of their commitment to the war in the Low Countries. Inevitably after all this havering the field deputies decided against an attack on the lines. These days of disputes and uncertainty, coming on top of the failure of the 'great design', affected Marlborough's health, producing severe headaches, but not his self-confidence. He made a parade out of his discontent at being constantly frustrated, declaring that he saw no point in staying in command of an army that did nothing but consume forage (and taxpayers' money, he might have added). His talk of retiring and refusing to serve in future campaigns was intended to put pressure on Heinsius and the States General to give himself greater freedom to take decisions.[11]

The last part of the campaign saw two minor military successes, which each brought political difficulties. The Prussians took Geldern, which threatened their neighbouring territory of Kleve, only for the Dutch to claim it as theirs

[11] Snyder, vol. I, pp. 225, 226, 233, 234–5, 236–7, 239. T'Hoff, pp. 82–3, 85–6, 88–9, 90–1. Murray, vol. I, pp. 165–6. Churchill, *Marlborough*, vol. II, pp. 241–6.

and try to install an administrator. The Dutch also claimed sovereignty over Limburg when it was captured, although the area had never been theirs, and excluded Imperial officials acting on behalf of the Habsburg claimant. Both these disputes gave Marlborough a foretaste of major troubles to come; the king of Prussia, knowing how important his military contingent was for allied plans used it as a bargaining counter, and when the Spanish Netherlands were recovered the Dutch were to disregard Karl's nominal rights to sovereignty in order to impose their own control over government, finance and commerce.

The inconclusiveness of the 1703 campaign ominously strengthened a growing sentiment in England, among Whigs as well as Tories, that it was useless to concentrate more resources on the war in the Low Countries. The alliance with Portugal revived plans for a major expedition to the Mediterranean which would certainly divert resources from the Low Countries and, if successful initially, could become the theatre of war in which the main English offensive would be mounted.[12] In the discussions which followed the winding-up of the campaign it was essential for Marlborough to create a situation for 1704 in which it would be possible for him to strike at the enemy. He wrung out of the Dutch a recognition that he must be allowed greater independence to make and implement decisions. The dispositions for the placing of troops in winter quarters which were agreed made it possible to go on to the offensive in the spring. This was to be launched up the Moselle valley, by an army predominantly composed of English and English-paid forces, while the Dutch remained on the defensive further north. By pressing a vigorous offensive Marlborough would force the French to concentrate against him so that no

[12] Snyder, vol. I, pp. 182, 224. T'Hoff, pp. 71–2. Churchill, Marlborough, vol. II, p. 253.

major attack could be made on the Dutch, and by providing ships it would always be possible to transfer troops down the Moselle and Rhine to reinforce them if an emergency should arise. The Moselle offensive would take the war to the enemy and constitute the first major invasion of French territory for over half a century.

This might be the last opportunity for offensive action. Marlborough was becoming intensely depressed by accumulating evidence of divisions and even demoralisation among the Dutch. The States General was divided by factions which Heinsius found it increasingly difficult to control. The cost of the war, especially the hiring of foreign contingents, was overstraining governmental finances. The war in the Baltic and the depredations of French privateers were depressing the economy. War-weariness and defeatism, such as had forced William out of the war in 1678, and hampered him in 1695–7, were apparent in all provinces and sections of society.[13]

Marlborough's initial decision to concentrate in 1704 on an offensive campaign on the Moselle reflected the disappointments of the previous year, and particularly the waste of the autumn months in virtual inaction. The combination of extensive lines of defence, behind which the French could move quickly on interior routes, and Dutch caution made it unlikely that Marlborough would be able to revive in some new version his ill-fated 'great design'. An offensive in the southern part of the Spanish Netherlands, such as he had been denied the previous autumn, would probably mean that a whole campaigning season would be consumed by a siege of Namur, which would mean repeating the pattern of William's strategy of attrition. By contrast an offensive up the

[13] Snyder, vol. I, pp. 197, 216, 233, 257, 261–2, 264–7.

Moselle, aimed first at the fortress of Thionville and then widening into an invasion of Lorraine, would create a threat to which the French were certain to respond. Active campaigning would result with opportunities for Marlborough to force a major battle. The plan also had the advantage of reassuring the Dutch about their security; if an emergency developed in the Low Countries Marlborough would be able to send back troops to assist them in a matter of days. A Moselle campaign would also reduce enemy pressure against the allied forces on the upper Rhine.[14]

This plan attempted to take into account the interests and problems of the allies. Although Marlborough never tried actually to direct the allied war strategy he consistently attempted to keep himself informed about military and political developments in every sphere. Unlike almost all other allied generals, except Eugène, he consciously tried to see and formulate his own strategic plans and decisions in the context of the war as a whole. He obviously had to give English interests prime consideration, but he genuinely believed, and consistently acted on the belief, that the 'common cause' necessitated mutual confidence and supportive action among the allies. When during his stay in London, during the winter of 1703–4, Wratislaw the Imperial ambassador convinced him that an extremely dangerous crisis was developing in southern Germany Marlborough's response was privately to prepare, if any further deterioration occurred, to scrap all his plans for a campaign on the Moselle. He knew that if he marched his army to the Danube instead this would require formidable logistical organisation, and he would become entirely dependent on the cooperation from the allies which Wratislaw promised him would be forthcoming. However he must have seen from the first that here

[14] Ibid., vol. I, pp. 277–9. T'Hoff, pp. 101, 105–6.

76

was an unrivalled opportunity for decisive and offensive action since the problems and dangers which he faced were nothing like as serious as those which the enemy would incur if Louis was really determined to stand by his new ally, Maximilian the elector of Bavaria.[15]

Maximilian had suddenly, even treacherously, changed sides during the first year of the war. He had previously supported the Emperor and was actually negotiating to provide the allies with substantial military contingents when, in September 1702, he concluded a mutual support treaty with France and seized the Imperial free city of Ulm. This alliance opened up entirely new opportunities for Louis in Germany, tilting the balance of strength against the Emperor and the allied princes, but a policy of supporting Bavaria also represented a major commitment whose extent and disadvantages gradually became apparent. Bavaria had few natural boundaries and was surrounded by hostile territories. It could be used to undermine the entire allied position in southern Germany, but equally it might be totally overrun unless Louis provided substantial military support. When in answer to Maximilian's appeals Louis sent an army commanded by Villars to fight its way through the rugged terrain of the Black Forest to join the elector's army, a serious threat to the allies began to emerge. But the form which this threat would take had not yet been determined.

Characteristically the ebullient and aggressive Villars immediately formulated on his arrival a simplistic offensive plan. After systematically devastating neighbouring territories in order to intimidate their rulers into remaining on the defensive, the entire Franco-Bavarian army would advance down the Danube, living off the unravaged Habsburg lands, to attack Vienna, which was weakly defended. However no

---

[15] Snyder, vol. I, pp. 147, 163, 267. T'Hoff, p. 30.

logistical preparations could be made, unless the operation was postponed, so that it must be doubtful whether Vienna, assuming that it could be stormed without a regular siege, could be held for a sufficient length of time to compel the Emperor to come to terms. In other words, although he refrained from using them, Villars was proposing what could only amount to a raid.[16]

This 1703 plan by Villars represents the hypothetical danger which most historians have described as the reason why Marlborough decided to march the following year to the Danube. Their view is that Marlborough intervened on the Danube to save or, as most English panegyrists after Blenheim put it, to 'rescue' the Emperor and prevent Vienna being occupied. French forces on the Danube are seen as being primarily aimed at Austria, with the objective of forcing the Emperor to make peace on French terms, which would involve abandoning Habsburg claims to the Spanish succession. The elements of the situation in southern Germany in 1703–4, one that was constantly changing, were far more complex and at the time more difficult to discern and appreciate. Both sets of combatants had to confront serious problems whose full extent only gradually emerged. The Emperor and the allied princes could not eliminate the Franco-Bavarian threat without assistance from Marlborough, and unless this was accomplished they could make no effective contribution to the war elsewhere. On the other hand once Louis had decided to send an army into Bavaria he found himself forced to despatch successively two sets of reinforcements for fear that either Maximilian would be forced to renege on the French alliance or that the Franco-Bavarian armies would be destroyed. And he took these decisions despite mounting evidence that his forces there

[16] Vault and Pelet, vol. III, pp. 593, 601–2. C. C. Sturgill, *Marshal Villars and the War of the Spanish Succession* (Lexington, KY, 1965), pp. 40–1.

found themselves in an increasingly precarious military and logistical position, indeed one that was ultimately untenable even had the decisive battle of Blenheim not been fought on 13 August 1704.

The plans advanced by Villars in May 1703 for an offensive into Austria came to nothing. For diplomatic reasons Louis ordered him to act under Maximilian's command, and the latter was primarily intent on making territorial acquisitions not on implementing a grand strategic plan. Maximilian also feared that his own unprotected territories would be devastated if the joint army was entirely committed to an invasion of Austria. In 1703 he concentrated first on an (unsuccessful) invasion of the Tirol and then in the autumn on the capture of the free cities of Augsburg and Regensburg. Villars had to defend the integrity of Bavarian territory, which he did by a victory at Hochstadt (20 September). By that time relations between the two had become impossible, but Louis in sending as replacement the soldier-diplomat Marsin made the mistake of thinking that the causes of friction were personal. He took no notice of Villars's scepticism about the value of the Bavarian alliance. Despite Hochstadt Villars saw that Bavarian territory was difficult to defend. He suspected that, actuated as he was entirely by self-interest, Maximilian might make a settlement with the Emperor that involved abandoning the French forces sent to aid him. In despatching Marsin as replacement for Villars Louis was making the assumption that the Bavarian alliance was an asset, not a liability, and going far to making a commitment that Maximilian must continue to receive military aid, ultimately to match the additional strength which Marlborough brought to the allied side.[17]

[17] Vault and Pelet, vol. III, pp. 653–4, 664–5, 686–7, 695, 697, 711. Sturgill, *Villars*, pp. 44–51.

At first developments elsewhere seemed to justify the French decision. Another spectacular defection occurred in November 1703, this time in the opposite direction when the duke of Savoy made an alliance with the Emperor. This could give the allies the opportunity to drive the French out of northern Italy: this made the French army in Bavaria all the more valuable in order to prevent Imperial armies being concentrated in Italy, or alternatively if substantial Imperial forces had to be transferred to the Danube the allied position in Italy could collapse and Savoy be overrun. Another less dramatic change, when Portugal signed an alliance with England and the Dutch, also made it essential to prop up Maximilian as an ally.

Initially the Emperor and the allied princes pinned their hopes on negotiations and inducements to persuade the cynical Maximilian to abandon the French alliance. He was offered generous subsidies (which the English and Dutch would have to provide) if he changed sides and supplied regiments to serve with the allied armies. Even more generously he was promised territorial acquisitions, so that he would be well rewarded for a double treachery, first betraying the Emperor and then Louis. Knowing Maximilian's lack of scruples, these negotiations caused the French considerable disquiet. Louis therefore responded to Marsin's appeals to strengthen his influence over the elector: 7,000 replacement troops were sent to bring his army up to strength, who were passed through the Black Forest defiles in May 1704.[18]

Marlborough had anticipated some such move, and by the end of April came to the conclusion that his planned Moselle offensive would have to be postponed. At this point the flexibility of his forward planning proved to be an enormous

---

[18] Vault and Pelet, vol. IV, pp. 400, 417, 446. Snyder, vol. I, pp. 315–16, 325–38.

advantage. He had ordered the assembly of troops and supplies at Koblenz, the confluence of the Rhine with the Moselle. These preparations would serve equally efficiently for a march towards the Danube with the objective of intensifying pressure on Maximilian to accept the terms offered him. If this happened Marlborough could join with the Imperial forces in preventing Marsin's army retreating and annihilate it. If Maximilian at first refused he might be intimidated into acceptance by subjecting Bavaria to devastation, and with the addition of Marlborough's army the allies would be superior to the Franco-Bavarian forces. In short Marlborough's projected plans had the advantage of being adaptable to a variety of situations, and during the months between April and August the general situation was constantly changing.

Marlborough had to overcome one momentarily threatening difficulty. In February the Dutch had agreed to contribute forces to the proposed Moselle offensive, but their ingrained caution led them to have second thoughts: in April they scaled down their contribution and decided to recall some of their troops, although with difficulty Marlborough got them to revoke this move. This incident made it necessary for the design of a march to the Danube to be kept from them: on 29 April Marlborough wrote to Godolphin that he would wait until the army assembled at Koblenz before informing the Dutch for the first time about the march into Bavaria. Strict security was also to be maintained in England; this letter was to be communicated only to the queen and her husband, and in a letter to Sarah Marlborough confined himself to saying that he was going to the Moselle 'and if the service requires into Germany', which could mean the upper Rhine. Disquieted as the Dutch were about what they considered to be the risky Moselle plan, it is certain that the Dutch would have vetoed the use of their contingent (about 12,000 strong) in a campaign in far-away Bavaria.[19]

On 23 May Marlborough learnt about the arrival of reinforcements for Marsin, which made it less likely that Maximilian would either wish, or be able, to abandon the French alliance. At the very least Marlborough's arrival was now urgently needed to keep up pressure on him and to prevent the French from overwhelming the entire allied position in southern Germany. As in previous decades Louis's primary aim was to strengthen his power and influence in German lands that neighboured France; he was interested in the politics and position of central Europe only as a means to achieve that primary end. The French plan of campaign for 1704 did not, as is usually suggested, envisage an invasion of Austria or a knock-out blow against Vienna. French strategy was to use the armies in Bavaria and those positioned on the upper Rhine, from Landau southwards, to batter Swabia and Franconia into total submission. These were circles (kreiss) which provided substantial military contingents and essential supplies. Without their support the Imperial army on the Rhine would not be able to maintain itself. Secure French communications would be established with Bavaria. Contributions would be levied from both circles and they would be forced to disband all their troops, so that they could not be transferred into Imperial service. While Tallard with one army advanced across the Rhine into Swabia, the Franco-Bavarian army would besiege Nordlingen and Weissenburg, to be followed by Nuremburg.[20]

Marlborough's counter-move had the immediate effect of wrecking this French plan of campaign. When the army assembled at Koblenz, instead of moving up the Moselle,

---

[19] Snyder, vol. I, pp. 275, 276–7, 279, 281, 282 and note, 286.
[20] Vault and Pelet, vol. IV, pp. 394–5, 407–9, 446, 448, 461, 871–3. Snyder, vol. I, pp. 300, 303. Murray, vol. I, pp. 274, 279.

crossed the Rhine and began marching south the French assumed at first that his objective was Landau and an invasion of Alsace from the north. Tallard could not now invade Swabia. By 6 June Marlborough's army was nearing Phillips-burg, where a bridge would enable it to re-cross to the west bank of the Rhine. By then Tallard had joined with Villeroy's forces from the Spanish Netherlands which on a parallel route had been shadowing Marlborough's southern march. It was only on the 7th, when he turned east away from the river that the French realised that Bavaria was his real objective. On 10 June Marlborough went ahead for his first meeting with Eugène, who he had insisted should be sent to take a command. By 22 June the army completed its march and joined up with allied forces already in Bavaria.[21]

This celebrated march to the Danube has always and justly been regarded as a masterpiece of military organisation. Its success was so considerable that in a later critical situation Marlborough proposed moving his army from the Low Countries to northern Italy, which would involve the prodigious feat of crossing the Alps. Along the route Marlborough took in 1704 only the Swabian Jura presented great physical difficulties, and most of it ran parallel to the Rhine and Neckar through friendly territories. But supplies had had to be organised at short notice, bridges prepared and discipline preserved. The patient attention to detail in ensuring that bread and forage, camps and hospitals, even boots and clothing were ready when needed, and paid for, meant that the condition of the army did not deteriorate. It was ready for action as soon as it joined up with prince Lewis's army at Launsheim, twenty miles north of Ulm and the Danube, on 22–3 June. In addition, Marlborough had made arrangements for future supplies to be provided from

---

[21] Snyder, vol. I, pp. 300, 303, 312–13, 314–15. Churchill, *Marlborough*, vol. II, pp. 314–64. Vault and Pelet, vol. IV, pp. 454, 461–3, 466–7, 487, 489.

Franconia, from bases which his arrival made secure since Marsin and Maximilian had quickly to abandon all thought of attacking in that direction.[22]

The efficiency with which Marlborough organised his march south was not matched by his French opponents in their admittedly much more difficult transit of reinforcements through the Black Forest. The troops who were to arrive in Bavaria less than a month before Blenheim were in poor physical condition and there were no local magazines and depots to remedy their deficiencies in equipment. Nor could the reinforcements which Louis sent in be fed for more than a few weeks, and by beginning systematically to devastate the rural areas Marlborough deprived them of a substantial part of the ripening harvest. Marsin became seriously concerned at the logistical crisis that could not be avoided since it was impossible to send supplies of any kind in quantity by routes through the Black Forest. Tallard's arrival with substantial reinforcements in July greatly worsened the supply position, and in sending them Louis seems to have entirely lost sight of logistical practicalities. Moreover these troops were sent despite explicit warnings that most of the French forces would have to be pulled back in the autumn to winter in Alsace. On the other hand without these reinforcements Marsin's and Maximilian's forces faced annihilation once Marlborough's arrival upset all the calculations on which the French strategy had been based. Louis bears the responsibility for placing an army of very substantial strength in a position that became increasingly untenable for both military and logistical reasons. The only rationale for this inept set of decisions can be found in a contempt for his opponents, a belief that they were not

---

[22] On the importance and problems of logistics in this period, see G. Perjes, *Army Provisioning, Logistics and Strategy in the Second Half of the Seventeenth Century* (Budapest, 1970).

sufficiently determined or astute to exploit a favourable situation.[23]

This was possibly true of only one of the three allied generals. Eugène by his recent successes and enterprise in Italy had further enhanced an outstanding reputation as an aggressive military leader. He still overshadowed Marlborough whose failures in 1703 partly effaced his achievements the previous year and who had never yet commanded an army in a major battle. But the two men immediately established a rapport, including an understanding of each other's intentions and a mutual confidence, that is a tribute to their good sense and tact, their lack of arrogance and selfishness. The same could not unfortunately be said of the third general, prince Lewis, the margrave of Baden (and therefore a real, hereditary sovereign prince of the Empire). Lewis was a veteran in terms of experience, but cautious and slow-moving with a preference for sieges and the use of defensive lines. He was also in poor health and ageing. From the first he was suspicious of the adventurous, aggressive plans of his colleagues and he became openly jealous of their successes. His negative characteristics did not prove as damaging in 1704 as in the following year, but it is significant that Marlborough and Eugène were not displeased at his absence at Blenheim. However there is no direct evidence to show that they deliberately contrived this absence (at the siege of Ingolstadt), at the price of being deprived of his army.[24]

Marlborough's advance into Bavaria put the French army in great peril. Marsin now had additional reason to fear that Maximilian would use the negotiations which he knew were continuing to come to terms with the Emperor. He doubted whether Maximilian would insist as part of a settlement that

[23] Vault and Pelet, vol. IV, pp. 469, 475, 491, 493, 495–6, 510.
[24] Snyder, vol. I, pp. 345–6.

Marsin's army should be allowed to retire undisturbed to the Rhine, and he had no illusions that his forces would be able to fight their way out of Bavaria and through the Black Forest. Maximilian's awareness of his increasing vulnerability found expression first in his early prediction that Marlborough's advance was directed against Bavaria, at a time when Louis and his generals thought the target was the upper Rhine, and then in the appeals for reinforcements with which he bombarded both Marsin and Louis. The latter realised that if he failed to respond this would be used and cited to justify Maximilian in abandoning France, but he also received warnings from Marsin that supplies and arms were lacking in Bavaria, and that the French army might have to abandon the idea of exacting contributions from neighbouring territories. Marsin advised that the exhaustion of supplies in Bavaria would probably cause the withdrawal in the autumn of Marlborough's as well as his own army. In deciding to despatch Tallard with a further substantial army Louis was reinforcing not so much failure as weakness. He did not see that he was placing very large forces in a vulnerable strategic position which would ensure that any defeat would be likely to turn into catastrophe. His error was the product of a complacent assurance of military superiority; the possibility of defeat in a major and decisive battle does not seem to have entered his thinking.[25]

In the first agreed allied operational plan Marlborough and prince Lewis were to concentrate in Bavaria, with the objective of compelling Maximilian to accept the Emperor's terms and desert France, while Eugène commanded substantial forces covering Tallard's army on the Rhine. From the start Marlborough applied ferocious pressure. Early on 2 July he and prince Lewis learnt that a Franco-Bavarian army was

---

[25] Vault and Pelet, vol. IV, p. 481, 491, 495–6, 510.

hurriedly fortifying the Schellenberg, a ridge that dominated the riverside city of Donauworth. Realising that this defence position was hourly becoming more formidable they decided to attack that same day, although this meant a fifteen-mile march which took the enemy by surprise but also taxed the stamina of his soldiers. There followed a bloody action, not generally ranked as one of Marlborough's major victories but important because it was his first, and because his direction of the assault displayed many of the characteristic calculations and tactics that marked his later triumphs. First he was careful to ascertain the state of the enemy defences and the topography of the ground on which they were set. Then he moved his forces with great rapidity, his men out-marching prince Lewis's units and arriving well over an hour before them. Marlborough had as his objective not just the taking of a defended position, a city and a bridge over the Danube, but the total destruction of the defending force. To achieve this he was prepared to accept heavy initial casualties. There is a strong resemblance between his battle plan at the Schellenberg and those he used at Blenheim, Oudenarde and Malplaquet: attacks were to be pressed home which he did not expect to break the enemy defences, but they would force those commanding them to weaken other sectors in order to prop them up. Then the coup de grâce would come against weakened defences away from the first sectors to be attacked. In the end result overall casualties would hopefully not be excessive; Marlborough was never prodigal in sacrificing the lives of his men, and they knew it.

Marlborough always acted on the principle that well-timed attacks by massed forces were the only certain way of achieving decisive victory. At this first test of his generalship in command of substantial forces he had the advantage of an overwhelming superiority in numbers; it would seem inevitable that an army of 40,000 must defeat even a strongly entrenched one of 14,000. But it was not an easy task for tired men to advance uphill, without cover, to attack trenches containing a good deal of artillery, especially as losses in regimental officers marching in front of their men were very heavy. The first wave of attack lost over half its effectives. A second assault was also repulsed, but only after hand to hand fighting in which the defenders lost heavily. They had to switch men from their left flank and this consequently became vulnerable when prince Lewis, arriving over an hour after Marlborough, launched an attack over easier ground. His units overran the weakened defence and then proceeded to roll up the enemy line from the flank, while continuing pressure from Marlborough made it impossible for the defenders to realign their forces. Their formations began to disintegrate and masses of men fleeing downhill were ridden down and slaughtered by the allied cavalry. The Franco-Bavarian army lost over half its strength in the battle and more in its disordered attempts to retreat.[26]

This display of purposeful ferocity should have acted as a warning to the French not to underestimate Marlborough, but for them the heavy allied losses suffered in his repeated attacks masked his achievement. French generals saw him as a blundering butcher of his men (some English units lost 40% of their men) and attributed the victory to prince Lewis.[27] However Marlborough left Maximilian in no doubt of his aggressive intentions. He ordered a systematic devastation of the Bavarian countryside, although privately he expressed his distaste for this French-pioneered method of frightfulness. It proved very effective. It forced the elector to disperse valuable troops in garrisons designed to protect his own estates, not those of his subjects. It also brought him to the

---

[26] Murray, vol. I, pp. 332–41, 344. Snyder, vol. I, p. 327. Churchill, *Marlborough*, vol. II, pp. 374–91.   [27] Vault and Pelet, vol. IV, p. 908.

verge of accepting the Emperor's terms and abandoning the French, which had been the primary reason for Marlborough's original decision to march to the Danube. Maximilian gave Marsin warning that unless he heard by 15 July that, as promised, Tallard's fresh army had arrived he would have to accept a settlement with the Emperor. The despatch with news that he had just arrived came through on 14 July. Consequently on that day Wratislaw, who had expected the elector to arrive in person to conclude the treaty, met only the latter's secretary who announced that the negotiations were now broken off.[28]

Although the arrival of substantial reinforcements with Tallard obviously improved the military position of the Franco-Bavarian armies it actually exacerbated their logistical difficulties. For this reason, and uncertain of allied strength, their generals did not work out a new strategy; they seem to have expected the allied armies to retire before them and evacuate Bavarian territory, but Tallard moved very slowly and only joined with Marsin and the elector on 6 August. Prince Lewis on the allied side behaved in an equally cautious fashion, seeing the rest of the campaign as a series of sieges. Eugène saw a concentration of his army with Marlborough's as the prerequisite for early offensive action. He had followed Tallard from the Rhine but with an inferior force. Too weak to fight alone against Tallard and Marsin Eugène outmanoeuvred his opponents, not only linking up with Marlborough but also drawing the French north of the Danube. This meant that Lewis could continue to besiege Ingolstadt and needed no close covering force while he did so. A series of difficult and potentially hazardous manoeuvres would have been necessary, and would have taken time – perhaps a few weeks – to undertake, if Marlborough and

---

[28] Ibid., vol. IV, pp. 520, 524, 525, 527, 551, 904–7. Murray, vol. I, pp. 295, 307, 315, 328, 348, 352, 357–8, 455–6. Snyder, vol. I, pp. 332–3, 335, 337, 342.

Eugène had thought it necessary to wait until Lewis and his army gave them numerical superiority before seeking a general battle (and there was a high risk that Lewis would not agree).[29]

Marlborough and Eugène needed an early engagement; to have to go into winter quarters in Bavaria and surrounding territories would leave both the Low Countries and northern Italy vulnerable in the spring of 1705, even though Louis left an army in Bavaria. Both the allied generals were set on reaching a decision, but their French counterparts did not realise this, and do not seem to have expected to have to fight a battle. Tallard had only just arrived; Marsin was not an aggressive leader. They anticipated that Eugène and Marlborough would withdraw before the cautious French advance, and then divide, with Marlborough protecting his Franconian supply bases and Eugène covering the Danube route into the Habsburg territories. Consequently although the two combined armies were in contact on 12 August they expected to be able to do no more the following day than press the allied rearguard. They were therefore taken by surprise by the general allied advance to seek a battle, which began before dawn on 13 August.[30]

This fact, that the French had not anticipated the allied move and were consequently slow to get into formation, determined the early pattern of the battle. They were not able to prevent the allies deploying according to their battle plan; an army on the alert could have disrupted, or at least impeded, their initial movements. This would have been particularly the case with Eugène's units moving to their position on the

---

[29] Vault and Pelet, vol. IV, pp. 528–9, 548, 563, 904–7. Snyder, vol. I, pp. 344–6, 347–8. Murray, vol. I, pp. 366, 381, 386n.
[30] Vault and Pelet, vol. IV, pp. 555, 563. Snyder, vol. I, p. 344. *Historical Manuscripts Commission, 14th Report*, appendix 9, pp. 200–1. Churchill, *Marlborough*, vol. II, pp. 431–4, 437.

allied right, which entailed an oblique march across the enemy front. But the allied movements, which took up most of the morning, were undisturbed. Action occurred only on the allied left where Marlborough's men moved in strength to within cannon range of Blenheim village, and incurred casualties. On their side the French and Bavarian dispositions were largely determined by where their units had camped the night before, with a large proportion of the infantry on their right, near the road, Blenheim village and the river Danube, and with the allies advancing it was not thought prudent to try to switch large numbers of slow-moving infantry. Another major disadvantage was the lack of a battle plan. This meant that the three generals, Tallard, Marsin and Maximilian had to respond to allied moves as they were made, and they also failed to detect the allied plan of massing overpowering strength in the centre. Each of the generals had to make and execute independently decisions which were forced on them by a rapidly developing but confusing situation in the afternoon. Tallard had to leave his sector of the front, on the French right, in order to confer with Marsin and was therefore absent when the English troops began a strong attack on Blenheim village. Facing an apparent crisis his subordinates, who had not been left instructions, committed strong reserve forces to assist the defence of the village; this proved to be one of a number of grave errors. The village could have held out without this reinforcement, and these reserve battalions were not available when the real crisis developed in the centre. Again when this main allied attack on the centre was gaining momentum Tallard could not coordinate effective counter-attacks because he was not physically in a position to see what was happening or to communicate orders to units which came under increasing pressure.

When the allied attack went in against the enemy centre

Marsin and Maximilian were out of reach on the enemy left, Tallard equally out of touch on their right. By contrast Marlborough had the freedom to place himself where he was most needed. He could leave Eugène to conduct the fighting on the right, and trust Cutts to execute orders – which Marlborough was in a position to vary when he thought it necessary – in his repeated attacks on Blenheim. At a later stage Marlborough did not turn up by accident when a momentarily dangerous situation developed on his right, in the only sector where men under his command faced Marsin's rather than Tallard's forces. Counter-attacks by the strong infantry garrison sortieing from the village of Oberglau, quickly supplemented by cavalry attacks, threatened to disrupt the allied formations which were massing for the decisive breakthrough. Marlborough saw what was happening, made counter-moves and sent for and received aid from troops under Eugène's command.[31]

The allied battle plan that led to a decisive victory provides a text-book example of how to create a local superiority that will carry all before it, despite the fact that at Blenheim the Franco-Bavarian army was superior in numbers. It is also a model of how to make maximum use of those elements in which one has an edge over the enemy. The allies had a considerable inferiority (25%) in infantry, but a very useful superiority (33%) in cavalry. The plan depended for its success on the allied infantry attacking enemy positions held by numerically superior forces, which meant that they had little or no chance of achieving their apparent objectives. On the allied right Eugène kept up for most of the day attacks by eighteen battalions on the twenty-eight of Marsin and the elector. In the centre the enemy garrison of Oberglau, with

[31] The most vivid accounts by participants are accessible in David Chandler (ed.), *Military Memoirs: Robert Parker and Comte de Merode-Westerloo* (1968), pp. 37–50, 166–84.

fourteen battalions, was stronger than the allied assault force of ten. In the most important move of all Cutts with twenty battalions attacked a force initially of about the same strength, but one that was very strongly entrenched behind palisades in Blenheim village. Crucially these attacks were repeated even though previous ones had been repulsed with heavy casualties and although the village garrison had been heavily (but unwisely) reinforced. These were the tactics Marlborough had used with effect at the Schellenberg, to make attacks that were primarily intended to draw in troops from other sectors so that in these, that is in this case in the centre, the allies could achieve massive superiority and use their cavalry. The enemy generals did more than Marlborough could have expected to contribute to the success of his plan. They made two crucial errors of judgement. First, while Tallard was avoidably absent, a staff officer succumbed to the temptation of committing the general reserve of eleven infantry battalions, which had been left too far to the French right (that is off-centre). It stood where it had camped, temptingly near to Blenheim village, and so it was easy to move when Cutts made his second set of attacks. But by maintaining this pressure Marlborough persuaded Tallard to keep the reinforcements there. Subsequently, when he saw that his centre was collapsing, Tallard tried to move them out, but the confusion caused by the excessively large number of soldiers crammed into a small, congested area, and exacerbated by the smoke caused by houses on fire, made it impossible to do so. As a result, but at the price of far heavier casualties than those suffered by the French, the numerically weaker battalions of Cutts were pinning down twenty-seven of the enemy including most of his elite infantry regiments.[32]

---

[32] Vault and Pelet, vol. IV, p. 588. Churchill, *Marlborough*, vol. II, pp. 444–6.

Secondly, Tallard in person made the decision to allow Marlborough to move large forces across the Nebel stream in the centre, without immediately subjecting them to attacks before they could establish themselves. The reason was apparently to avoid getting his troops bogged down in the marshy land on the west side of the Nebel, but this did not prove an obstacle to the allied advance. This failure was followed by a disaster which reflected the obsolescence of French military thinking and practice on both the employment of cavalry and on ways that infantry, cavalry and artillery should be disposed in order to give each other mutual support. The French infantry and cavalry were not effectively integrated in a combined defensive system, whereas Marlborough interlaced the two arms in his decisive advance in the centre. Once the French cavalry had been driven back in rout their infantry had to stand their ground without support. They were simply annihilated by a combination of the allied infantry with the artillery which was brought right forward as quickly as possible by the redoubtable colonel Blood. But the inferiority of French military doctrine showed up most clearly in the comparative uses made of cavalry.

The French practice was still largely stuck in past tradition. Their cavalry still relied on the fire-power of pistols and carbines, although their range, accuracy and penetrative power were very limited, in tactics evolved a century before by Maurice of Nassau. Using precise drill movements successive waves of horsemen advanced, fired and then withdrew. Charges would then follow. The French should have been warned about the limited effectiveness of their cavalry tactics by their repeated failures to rout William in the major battles of the Nine Years War when, worsted by superior French numbers, he had nevertheless been able to bring off his forces in good order by fighting retreats which the French cavalry had not been able to do more than harry. By contrast Marlborough did not use cavalry until he thought that they could achieve decisive results. Then he committed them to massed charges at the trot developing great and hopefully irresistible momentum. At Blenheim Marlborough's use of cavalry proved decisive at two stages. First, in order to snuff out a momentarily dangerous attack on the flank of his centre, Marlborough got Eugène to order his Austrian cavalry to charge and restore the situation. Then in the centre it became possible to launch the English into a massed charge that pressed back the French cavalry with such force that the latter disintegrated into a horde of fugitives many of whom were stampeded over the low cliffs into the Danube, where they drowned. This was the most dramatic incident of the battle, made much of by English panegyrists who often compared the doomed French horsemen with the drowned hosts of Pharaoh in the Red Sea.[33]

However the sequel reflected a weakness in English cavalry practice that was never to be fully rectified: once committed to an all-out charge developing dynamic momentum it was almost impossible to bring the horsemen back into formation so that they could be used for further charges. Consequently after shattering the enemy centre Marlborough could not use his cavalry again to attack from the flank the forces of Marsin and Maximilian which now began to retreat from the enemy left. They were able to withdraw in relatively good order. But he could use the infantry again. They cut off all retreat for the large forces crowded into Blenheim village, into which the battalions led by Cutts had been able to penetrate only at a few points. Disgracefully abandoned by their commander who tried to cross the Danube (as Saint-Simon suggested,

---

[33] Churchill, *Marlborough*, vol. II, pp. 446–56. Robert D. Horn, *Marlborough: A Survey Panegyrics, Satires and Biographical Writings* (Folkestone, 1975), pp. 45–6, 52–3, 62–3, 70–6, 79–80, 82–6.

doubtless to live as a hermit) but was drowned, some 10,000 largely elite troops had to surrender ignominiously. It was this wholesale surrender, unprecedented in recent French military history, that made the deepest contemporary impression, dispelling the myth of French military invincibility.[34]

Marlborough's tactical skill offset the enemy's superiority in numbers. He exploited Tallard's faulty concentrations of his main strength, misleading his staff into sending unnecessary reinforcements into Blenheim village, so squandering reserves who were not available when the French centre came under attack. Assuming that allied units which were allowed to cross the Nebel could be driven back with great loss they allowed Marlborough to build up a decisively strong concentration of all arms, including artillery. But the allied battle plan involved high risks: in particular Eugène had to fight all day against superior numbers, and did so by keeping them under pressure by repeated attacks, and the same tactic was used in front of Blenheim village. As a result allied casualties up to the point when the decisive attack began in the centre were undoubtedly much heavier than the French – Winston Churchill says double, but how could he know? But this was the necessary price for setting up a situation in which a total victory could be achieved.

Tallard's section of the enemy army was virtually annihilated. Marsin and the elector led their forces off the field in good order, but their armies subsequently disintegrated, losing large numbers through desertion. Marsin's surviving men pulled back to the Rhine.[35] Of course all figures of casualties were approximations. The allies had about 13,000, that is 25% of the personnel engaged. Enemy losses

---

[34] Churchill, *Marlborough*, vol. II, pp. 477–80, at his most rhetorical. Murray, vol. I, p. 435, 439. Chandler (ed.), *Military Memoirs*, pp. 176–84.

[35] Murray, vol. I, pp. 413–14, 417, 420, 464, 465–6.

were much higher and included some 11,000 prisoners, a humiliating number almost unmatched during this period. In addition all their wounded fell into allied hands, either on the field or later when Ulm was taken. The allies gained 3,000 recruits from among the prisoners. Marlborough expected French losses in officers to be lasting in their effects; they would make it more difficult to reform lost regiments, and morale throughout the French officer corps would be damaged. Surprisingly Maximilian rejected the still very generous terms which were renewed to detach him from France, although the whole of his Bavarian territories were quickly conquered: he retired to the Rhine with a mere remnant of his army.[36]

Writing to Godolphin in November, Marlborough evaluated the victory at Blenheim as bringing the end of the war in sight. Putting great emphasis on the need to follow it up with the greatest possible vigour, he predicted that another successful campaign would force Louis to agree to terms that would ensure a satisfactory peace – that is one that would last for the remainder of Anne's reign. As a cautious politician, absorbed by affairs at home, Godolphin disagreed. Counselling caution he thought that Marlborough had done as much as could ever be expected in a single campaign. He also wanted to exploit Blenheim in terms of domestic politics by having the all-conquering general back in London and Westminster as soon as possible to help the hard-pressed administration overcome its difficulties.[37]

An exhausted army would probably have agreed with Godolphin and ended the campaign when the French retired to the Rhine. But in the late autumn Marlborough led his

[36] Ibid., vol. I, pp. 417, 439, 455–6, 474n, 476, 488. Snyder, vol. I, p. 363. T'Hoff, pp. 125–6, 137, 138, 140.   [37] Snyder, vol. I, pp. 366, 368, 369–70.

army into a further and successful campaign, west of the Rhine. He intended to establish bases for a major and hopefully decisive offensive at the earliest possible moment the next year. This was to take the form of an offensive up the Moselle valley, the project which he had intended to undertake in 1704 had not the deteriorating situation in Germany forced him to march to the Danube. Unless advances were made west of the Rhine it would be necessary to put his army into winter quarters to the east of the river, in the territories of allied princes who would therefore find it difficult to provide their quota of men and supplies for the campaign. In addition the territories which Marlborough was confident he could conquer at a very late date for open warfare (the last week in October) would absorb the energies of the allies for an incalculable length of time the following spring, if they were now left undisturbed.

In September joint operations by Marlborough and Eugène established a superiority in the field to enable Lewis to besiege Landau, the key fortress controlling north–south routes to the west of the Rhine. They were ineffectively opposed by an army under Villeroy which was numerically their equal. However he seems to have lost confidence in the ability and determination of his army to withstand a full-scale allied assault, even though very few of his men had been at Blenheim. Rather than fight a battle he precipitately abandoned two strong river lines of defence.[38] This sign of French demoralisation made it feasible for Marlborough to take what would earlier have been regarded as unacceptable risks. While Eugène covered the siege of Landau, which was very slowly and incompetently pursued by Lewis, with a relatively small force Marlborough crossed the difficult and barren Hunsruck mountains, going across the contours of the

[38] Ibid., vol. I, pp. 382–3, 386–7, 389–90. T'Hoff, pp. 129, 133–4, 143–6. Murray, vol. I, p. 464.

country. He knew that a strong French force was on its way to install a garrison in Trier. Consequently he drove his men into forced marches that enabled them to reach Trier before the French. Then they reconstructed its defences, while the enemy prudently kept their distance. This seizure of Trier isolated the fortress of Trarbach, further down the Moselle. It could be taken at leisure and the valley became available for allied troops to winter in, while supply depots could be built up to ensure the earliest possible start to the offensive planned for 1705.[39]

But although the capture of Trier virtually completed operations for 1704 Marlborough could not yet return to England, where a serious political crisis was developing over a new Occasional Conformity bill. He had to cap his arduous months of campaigning with a long winter journey to Berlin and Hanover. The purpose of this mission, unlike those undertaken in later years to prevent the alliance disintegrating, was military rather than diplomatic. If pressure on France was to be intensified in 1705 Marlborough had to ensure that allied princes provided the stipulated number of troops. In addition, taking his characteristically wide perspective he was also concerned that the allied position in Italy should be strengthened and Savoy saved from conquest and capitulation. Although as he wrote his heart ached at the prospect of an 800 mile journey he knew that additional troops for Italy could be provided only by the king of Prussia.[40]

On the return journey Marlborough travelled out of his way to conduct a public relations exercise in Amsterdam. Past experience made him suspicious of the Regent oligarchs who operated its municipal government and possessed great influence in the States General. They insisted on maintaining

---

[39] For the autumn campaign in detail, Churchill, *Marlborough*, vol. II, pp. 489–505.
[40] Snyder, vol. I, pp. 397–405. Murray, vol. I, pp. 532, 542, 543, 546, 550–1.

financial and commercial links with France and Spain. In previous wars they had exerted pressure on William to accept terms of peace offered by Louis, although these had the effect of separating the Dutch Republic from its allies. Once Blenheim altered the balance of military strength Louis renewed his approaches for a negotiated peace, but Marlborough saw that again his primary aim was to split the allies. It was in order to block these French tactics that he visited Amsterdam, and he reported afterwards that he had persuaded the Regents of the need to intensify pressure on France, so as to ensure an entirely satisfactory and durable peace.[41]

In the discussions in Amsterdam and the Hague Marlborough obtained Dutch acceptance of his plans for an offensive campaign in 1705 up the Moselle into Lorraine. Eugène had also agreed to them, but would be commanding in Italy. However there was a fatal flaw from the start in the preparations for an offensive. Although prince Lewis's dilatory conduct of the siege of Landau should have warned Marlborough that plans depending on a prompt start by the Imperial forces were at risk unless the allied generals and princes were tied down he had not consulted them about either the size of their contingents or their quotas of logistical support. Marlborough's other mistake was personal. He returned to London very late, on 14 December. This resulted in a delayed return to the continent: he arrived at the Hague only on 14 April, and this was far too late to ensure the early start on which the whole success of an invasion of France depended.

The total failure of all Marlborough's ambitious plans in 1705 was largely, but not entirely, caused by his lack of effective

---

[41] Snyder, vol. I, pp. 401, 405, 407.

authority over the allied forces and generals on whose cooperation they absolutely depended. It proved an entirely blank year, sandwiched between two years of great success. In 1704 the victory at Blenheim was primarily due to the understanding established between Marlborough and Eugène, but in 1705 the latter was in Italy. In 1706 the Dutch by conceding what amounted to sole command of the allied army enabled Marlborough to defeat the French at Ramillies and to conquer a large part of the Spanish Netherlands. The States General, their field deputies and the Dutch generals were then abashed by their behaviour during the previous year. Personal jealousies of Marlborough's success and prestige, continuing professional distrust of his constant advocacy of aggressive tactics and strategy, provoked them to wreck the second stage of the 1705 campaign in the Low Countries. But this behaviour only reflected, at the operational level, the limited character of Dutch war aims. Although theoretically committed to satisfying the claims of the House of Austria to the Spanish succession, the Dutch were primarily concerned to secure an effective barrier. They favoured a strategy of piecemeal advances, like that of 1702. Each successful siege would mean an improved barrier, whereas a major battle fought and lost could mean a reversion to the position of 1701, with no barrier of fortresses between them and French power. Nevertheless the conduct of some Dutch generals in July and August 1705 was by any standards entirely indefensible and amounted almost to direct sabotage of Marlborough's campaign.[42]

By contrast the failure of the first phase of the campaign of 1705, the planned invasion of France via the Moselle valley, was only partly attributable to allied shortcomings, in this

[42] Before the campaign opened Marlborough sent Heinsius a 'coded' warning, stressing that success in 1704 had been due to acceptance of a subordinate position by Imperial generals: T'Hoff, p. 166.

case to Lewis and the other German princes. In his eagerness
to take the offensive Marlborough showed himself to be
overoptimistic about a project that proved to be impracticable. His confidence was based on the belief that he had
sufficiently prepared for it by taking Trier the previous
October so that large magazines of arms and supplies could
be established during the winter, and by obtaining from
Lewis his agreement to participate in a coordinated offensive.
Lewis would attack Saarlouis, in order to secure Marlborough's rear while he advanced up the Moselle to invest
Thionville. Lewis would join him in the siege, and while
covering it Marlborough hoped to create the opportunity for
a set-piece battle with Villars, commander of the defending
army in the field. His defeat would be a second shattering
blow to French strength and morale, and would necessitate
the transfer of substantial enemy forces, leaving the Spanish
Netherlands vulnerable. The fall of Thionville could be
followed by a siege of Metz, the key eastern fortress in French
defences. This part of the plan, in the view of Winston
Churchill and many historians, would then open a way into
the heart of France, and they saw the Moselle as the start of the
'surest road to Paris'.[43]

This view is questionable and distorts Marlborough's
intentions. In pre-railway days there was no direct invasion
route that an army could follow from the Moselle: it would
have to march across very difficult and extremely barren
country, through the Argonne and then across the Meuse, in
order to reach the barren plains of the Champagne pouil-
leuse. Such a march would be a logistical nightmare.
Marlborough's eyes were set on a different kind of decisive
outcome, the defection to the allies of the duke of Lorraine, a
sovereign prince. While keeping his links with France the

---

[43] *Ibid.*, pp. 174–5, 185. Snyder, vol. I, pp. 415, 420, 432. Murray, vol. II, pp. 20–1,
33–4, 50–2. Churchill, *Marlborough*, vol. II, pp. 524–6.

duke was secretly negotiating with the allies and waiting to see who would emerge victorious. His defection, like those of the elector of Bavaria and the duke of Savoy, would alter the strategic situation overnight. The French would find Alsace untenable, and would have to withdraw from the whole length of the Rhine. France would be deprived of its main defences along its entire eastern borders.[44]

These high expectations were to be disappointed. When Marlborough arrived at Trier very late indeed, on 26 May, he found that all the essential conditions for success were absent. The magazines for food were not full: the commissary left unsupervised in charge had been embezzling and fled to the enemy. The Rhenish princes had not provided the horses needed to draw the artillery and there were insufficient carts. The Palatine and Prussian contingents had not arrived and indications were that it would be several weeks before they did. Most seriously the Emperor had had to draft reinforcements for Eugène in Italy, leaving Lewis with an army too weak to carry out the planned attack on Saarlouis. Marlborough had to agree to drop that attack. But he could not wait for Lewis to join him at Trier with a relatively small force, and as he advanced up the Moselle Villars withdrew before him to a strong prepared defensive position at Sierck.[45]

The usually impetuous and aggressive Villars inadvertently followed the correct tactics to foil Marlborough. He remained at Sierck in the erroneous belief that the allied army was far stronger than his own. Deadlock ensued. With a weaker army Marlborough could not risk a frontal assault on a superior army in a naturally formidable and well-entrenched position. With insufficient draught horses and few carts he was tied to the Moselle and could not venture on

[44] Snyder, vol. I, p. 424.
[45] Ibid., vol. I, pp. 433, 435–7, 445, 464–5. T'Hoff, pp. 173, 174–5. Murray, vol. II, pp. 55, 57, 63.

manoeuvres to outflank the Sierck defences. His existing supplies enabled him to maintain an advanced position for only a limited time, and even if an assault had carried the French defences – inevitably at the cost of heavy casualties – his army would be too weak to undertake a siege of Thionville until the Palatine and Prussian troops arrived. Moreover the army would not be able to live off the country since Villars had scoured it for supplies to maintain his own army. In other words Marlborough found himself in an impossible situation of his own making, and had no option but to withdraw. Surprisingly in view of his experience of the natural advantages which the topography of the valley gave to the defence he thought of returning to the Moselle in the late summer, if the supply problems had been rectified, and he also thought of using it in future years, but he never had the opportunity.[46]

Marlborough's withdrawal was expedited by urgent calls from Overkirk, who had been left commanding the Dutch army on the Meuse, where Villeroy advanced re-taking Huy and the city (but not the citadel) of Liège. Marlborough left an adequate garrison in Trier, but although it was not directly threatened with an enemy attack its commander soon abandoned the city, which ended the idea of a renewed Moselle offensive in the autumn. As Marlborough approached Liège the French abandoned the siege of the citadel, withdrawing behind their defensive lines to the west. Despite their losses the previous year the French had a slight superiority in numbers, which made Marlborough's Dutch colleagues reluctant to agree to a move to breach the lines. Marlborough's plan of attack depended on deceiving Villeroy, who had over fifty miles to cover, about the point at

---

[46] Churchill, *Marlborough*, vol. II, pp. 535–44, Snyder, vol. I, p. 497. Murray, vol. II, pp. 69, 76, 81, 87, 102, 104, 106–8, 116–17. Sturgill, *Villars*, pp. 63–5. *Historical Manuscripts Commission, Portland*, vol. IV, pp. 186–7.

which the breach would be attempted. He sent the Dutch to make a feint opposite a sector where the defences were not particularly formidable, while he moved his English units under cover of night to one of the more strongly fortified sectors which was not so heavily manned by defenders. The Dutch show of force attracted Villeroy with his main force while the English broke through several miles away. Once the breach was made Marlborough rapidly deployed cavalry beyond the lines who in a brisk engagement routed a counter-attack by enemy cavalry, capturing two generals. He personally led the charge and narrowly escaped death in the mêlée which ensued. This led to his being rewarded by spontaneous and prolonged applause from his men, an unusual military tribute during the pre-Romantic period. But having achieved this breach and minor victory at Elixem (18 July), the rest of the operation went sour.[47]

First the enemy infantry manning adjacent sectors of the lines withdrew almost intact and in good order. Secondly there was a flaw in the plan: Villeroy was bound to arrive at the scene of the breach first, before the Dutch, because he could march by a shorter route behind his lines, and the Dutch were too exhausted to move fast – they had had to make a night march to reach the point at which they had appeared in front of the lines. Marlborough did not have the numbers to advance to fight an encounter battle or to make an immediate attack on Leuven. He therefore confined his actions to rounding up some 2,000 stragglers. And by the time the main Dutch units arrived the French army was establishing itself in a strong position behind the river Dyle to cover Leuven and Brussels.

This position had to be attacked if the offensive was to maintain any kind of momentum. The allied army had

---

[47] Snyder, vol. I, pp. 449, 458. T'Hoff, pp. 177–82, 186–7, 188–90. Murray, vol. II, pp. 133–4. Churchill, *Marlborough*, vol. II, pp. 545–6, 551–67.

consumed most of its supplies and would become dependent on convoys from as far away as Liège, which would require escorts. Prolonged heavy rain made movement difficult. But when Marlborough put forward proposals for an attack, on 23 and 27 July, the Dutch generals in the council of war argued strongly against one; on the first occasion saying it would be an unacceptable risk to attack the main French army in a fully prepared position, and on the second because of difficult terrain. He could not openly show his exasperation when the Dutch generals justified their negative response by arguing that a repulse would 'spoil the whole campaign'. From Marlborough's perspective nothing would ever be achieved if all decisions had first to be approved by councils of war in which all possible risks were magnified. Nevertheless by diplomatic persuasion he did obtain consent for an offensive across the Dyle on 30 July: the Dutch crossed in strength and established themselves on the left flank. But as usually happens in war things did not go according to plan, and the Dutch generals were unwilling to vary the plan which they had agreed to in the prior council of war. The advance of the English troops was delayed, and as their crossing point over the river was nearer to the enemy's approaching forces any bridgehead they established would be difficult to hold. Marlborough therefore wished to vary his plan by ordering the Dutch to leave the positions in which they were entrenching themselves and advance on the far side of the Dyle to give support to the English.

The Dutch insisted on holding a new council of war to discuss the proposed variation in the original plan, which would undoubtedly mean hard and possibly desperate fighting under none too favourable circumstances. The arguments in the council went on as the situation unfolded only to end in the Dutch insisting that the whole operation should be called off. In fact Marlborough had not waited for the deliberations to conclude but had already ordered the Dutch to withdraw, and this was probably the right decision. The delay to the English advance imperilled the whole operation. As he had shown at Sierck earlier in the year Marlborough would not press an offensive under unfavourable conditions.[48] However he was determined to gain more (if still not full) freedom of decision and action. Otherwise, as he wrote to Heinsius on 2 August, nothing could ever be achieved. If he had to convene councils of war on every occasion it was inevitable that on occasions security would be breached and the enemy forewarned. The format of councils encouraged disagreements. A change was needed if he was to be able to act offensively and bring the war to a 'good end'. Marlborough sent a Dutch general who was favourable to his views, Hompesch, to persuade the States General to modify the limitations imposed on him, but the results were largely cosmetic. Hompesch obtained a resolution telling the field deputies that they were not to convene a council of war unless they thought it absolutely necessary. But they were to do so if proposals were being made that seemed likely to produce a general engagement of the main armies. Furthermore Marlborough had still to consult Overkirk, the senior Dutch general, and the deputies before making major decisions, and as civilians the latter would obviously have to take advice from the other generals about the line they should adopt.[49]

When tested in the operations on the Yssche, in the last phase of the 1705 campaign, the modification failed to prevent an even greater fiasco that, but for Marlborough's restraint and

---

[48] Snyder, vol. I, pp. 458, 461–2, 463. Murray, vol. II, pp. 172–7, 178–81. T'Hoff, pp. 196–8. Historical Manuscripts Commission, 14th Report, appendix 9, p. 203. Historical Manuscripts Commission, Portland, vol. IV, pp. 212, 252, 254–5.

[49] Snyder, vol. I, pp. 465, 471. T'Hoff, pp. 199, 201. Murray, vol. II, pp. 197–8.

tact, would have completely poisoned Anglo-Dutch relations. Renewing the offensive operations on 15 August he
took with him sufficient stores for two weeks so that he
would not be tied by having to protect lines of communication. He was also accompanied by his artillery train to enable
him to fight a battle or begin a siege. By moving boldly to a
position south of Brussels he gave himself several options and
kept Villeroy guessing about his intentions. He could move
north to attack Brussels and Leuven; south to begin a siege of
Namur; or, to the south-west, Mons; while to the east lay the
main French army, which was his actual target. Moreover by
posing this multiple threat to several fortresses Marlborough
prevented Villeroy transferring men from their garrisons to
reinforce his field army, and by this means the allies had for
the first time in the war a superiority in numbers.

By skilful manoeuvring Marlborough misled Villeroy
about his movements and on 18 August achieved a tactical
surprise, confronting the enemy in open country where they
had no choice but to stand and fight. Overkirk agreed that the
French were in an extremely disadvantageous position and
accepted Marlborough's plan of attack. But although the
allied infantry were ready to launch an immediate attack
against the French who were frantically improvising
defences, not all the artillery was yet in position. This was
because, unbelievably, part of the train had been held up in a
narrow defile by the personal baggage waggons of the Dutch
general Slangenburg who insisted on priority for them.
During the delay the field deputies insisted on consulting the
Dutch generals before authorising an attack. To Marlborough's astonishment they unanimously advised rejection,
with Slangenburg particularly vociferous in his opposition. A
totally absurd – but dangerous – situation ensued with the
heated debate continuing for two hours, while the French
organised their defences. Marlborough could obtain no more

than permission to make a reconnaissance of these defences, but this revealed only that the situation was steadily becoming less favourable. Significantly all English officers present fully shared Marlborough's fury, which for once he did not entirely mask. He refused to receive the report on the reconnaissance and abruptly ordered a withdrawal without seeing the Dutch generals.[50]

The withdrawal left the army to complete two minor tasks. Part of the French lines were demolished (but they could easily be rebuilt). The small fort of Léau was taken. Slangenburg put himself in the wrong again by refusing to undertake this latter operation unless he was given a large force, twice the strength of the one which quickly forced its surrender. So sickened was Marlborough by the Yssche fiasco that in effect he abandoned the campaign, although two months of campaigning weather remained. With a distinctly ironical comment he promised to undertake with the army any scheme put forward by the Dutch generals and approved by the deputies. He knew that there was only a slight chance of their doing so, because if they did they would be committed in advance to carrying it out.[51]

Although it only became apparent the next year the Yssche fiasco had one immensely important, if indirect, consequence. Villeroy naturally did not publicise the way in which he had been out-manoeuvred and French (and at home Tory) observers dismissed arguments that only Dutch obstructionism had robbed Marlborough of a great victory as empty boasting and a cover for incompetence. Those who wished to think in that way were confirmed in their belief that he had been lucky at Blenheim, and that his indifferent performance

[50] Snyder, vol. I, pp. 472–3, 474, 477, 479. Murray, vol. II, pp. 220, 226. T'Hoff, pp. 203–4, 205. Historical Manuscripts Commission, 14th Report, appendix 9, pp. 205–6. Historical Manuscripts Commission, Portland, vol. IV, pp. 230, 254–5. Churchill's account is very highly coloured: Marlborough, vol. II, pp. 578–92.
[51] Churchill, Marlborough, vol. II, pp. 596–7. T'Hoff, pp. 206, 211–12.

in 1705 as well as in 1703 showed that he was not to be feared. The readiness of Louis to authorise Villeroy to meet Marlborough in a general engagement early in the campaign of 1706 was a product of the French judgement condemning his generalship on the Moselle and in Brabant in 1705.

The Yssche fiasco could have had disastrous political repercussions had Marlborough not gone out of his way to exercise a restraining influence. He protested privately to Heinsius that he could not exercise effective command under existing restrictions.[52] But it was to his ministerial colleagues at home that he freely expressed his full resentment. They were incensed, and they also faced an outburst of popular anti-Dutch indignation, but he realised that their understandably harsh reaction in deciding to send one of their number to make a formal protest in person to the States General would be counter-productive. Instead he persuaded the Cabinet Council to substitute a warning that would make the Dutch lift their restrictions on his freedom of action. The States General was told that the English would not be able and willing to continue to bear a large share of the costs of the war in the Low Countries unless they committed themselves to a vigorous prosecution of the next campaign. They could only do this by placing their trust in Marlborough, a clear indication that they must abolish their restrictions on his ability to take and implement decisions.[53]

Marlborough never lost sight of the necessity of maintaining good relations with the Dutch, although he was also particularly critical of their continuing trade with the enemy and financial links which enabled Louis to meet the costs of the war. But in August 1705 he was aware of the revival of

[52] T'Hoff, pp. 203–5; the letter was routed via Slinglandt, a colleague of Heinsius, to keep it secret.
[53] Snyder, vol. I, pp. 482–3 and note. Murray, vol. II, pp. 224, 276.

Dutch sentiment in favour of an early peace; in his judgement any terms offered by Louis would be unsatisfactory and fail to produce a durable peace unless another major blow could be inflicted on the French army. The first French approach in the previous spring was no more than mischief-making: Louis would not specify conditions but suggested that the English and Dutch should do so, hoping that they would find agreement difficult and also antagonise the Emperor. In August extremely specious terms were specified. As in 1678 and 1696–7 emphasis was placed on French commercial concessions to the Dutch (but these could be revoked at will – for the third time). The establishment of the Spanish Netherlands as a republic which would be saddled with paying for the Dutch garrisons in the barrier fortresses was a formula calculated to cause continual friction. The French proposed that Naples and Sicily should go to the Habsburgs as compensation for their claims, but not Milan which they valued more highly. But Naples and Sicily were more important for the English and Dutch because of their trade. Similarly Louis implicitly promised to recognise Anne as queen, but not the Protestant succession, which would remain as a further bargaining counter.[54]

In arguing for the end of restrictions on his power as general Marlborough explained to Heinsius that without freedom of action he would be unable to achieve the decisive victory in battle which was essential if a satisfactory peace was to be won. In spelling out what such a peace should contain he made it plain that the English administration would insist that the Spanish monarchy should go to the Habsburg claimant, Karl. This constituted the first explicit mention to Heinsius of what was to become the declared war aim of England, and an unattainable one, 'no peace without Spain'.

[54] T'Hoff, pp. 160, 164–5, 189, 202–3, 205, 209n, 214. Snyder, vol. I, pp. 424, 452–3, 477–9, 481, 492–3, 505, 557. Murray, vol. II, pp. 361–2.

The Dutch had to give ground to English pressure, the beginning of a process that was to continue for the rest of the war. Slangenburg, who had put himself technically in the wrong by impeding the artillery, was disgraced. Buys, the pensionary of Amsterdam, explained a workable compromise over his powers as general. The constitution imposed on the field deputies the duty of supervising and consulting with the generals. They could not be dispensed with, but as in William's day only those likely to prove acceptable to the captain-general would be selected.[55]

The campaign in the Low Countries at least ended in stalemate, but when Marlborough looked at the war as a whole the prospect was depressing. Lewis remained almost inactive on the Rhine, despite having a superiority in numbers. A large Imperial army was tied down in trying to suppress a rebellion in Hungary. Relations between Prussia and the Dutch deteriorated to the point where the king was threatening to withdraw his contingents from the Rhine and Italy. In northern Italy the campaign had gone badly, leaving Savoy in a precarious state. The capture of Barcelona represented a major success but also a new commitment for the allies which would demand substantial additional resources. And from England Godolphin urged Marlborough to return early to assist preparations for the next parliamentary session and to help avert a rift with the separate Parliament of Scotland.[56]

Marlborough preferred to devote himself to preparations on the continent for the next campaign rather than involve himself in the preparatory detail of home politics. Ever since July he had seen it as essential to visit Vienna. Originally his purpose was to persuade the Emperor to dismiss Lewis and

[55] Snyder, vol. I, p. 496. Murray, vol. II, p. 249.   [56] Snyder, vol. I, pp. 491–2.

replace him with Eugène, so that another offensive could be launched up the Moselle in 1706. But a spurt of activity by Lewis in late August made his removal politically impossible and his retention ruled out a Moselle offensive the next year. Nevertheless Marlborough still travelled to Vienna, meeting Lewis and the elector Palatine en route, although all the business which he had to transact was concerned with wider issues of the war as a whole and not his own plans for 1706. His foremost concern was to ensure the reinforcement of the allies in Italy. In Vienna he completed arrangements for the first major loan raised on the London money market to go to a great power ally, as distinct from subsidies. He had to ensure that the money was spent exclusively on the war in Italy. During his visit to Berlin he persuaded the king to retain his contingent in the Italian theatre of war. Secondly Marlborough tried to arbitrate in disputes involving allies, but with little success: between the Emperor and both Prussia and the Hungarian rebels, and also between Prussia and the Dutch.[57]

---

[57] Ibid., vol. I, pp. 464–5, 497, 502, 507, 509. T'Hoff, pp. 214, 218, 221. Murray, vol. II, pp. 273–4, 294–5, 303, 321–2, 323–5.

Chapter 3

More victories but an endless war?

In military terms the campaign of 1706 was to prove the most successful of all in Marlborough's career, but in the weeks before it began he was consistently pessimistic about the prospects of the allies. He had expended a great deal of time during the winter in trying to persuade them to make a major and early military effort to put the maximum forces into the field, and he had attempted to allay their mutual suspicions and jealousies. But when he reached the Hague on 14 April it seemed that his work had had at best only limited effects. He feared that allied weaknesses could produce a succession of disasters since they faced a confident enemy who was fielding larger forces than ever before in a conscious attempt to reestablish an ascendancy in all theatres of war. Marlborough found his apprehensions about Dutch attitudes sadly confirmed. The concentration of French strength in the Low Countries continued to intimidate their political and military leaders, making them ultra-cautious, yet it was increasingly obvious that the public was becoming war-weary and would question the vast expenditure which yet another inconclusive campaign would necessitate. The danger of the States General being induced into accepting French offers of a separate peace (as in 1678) was now very real. Another expensive and indecisive campaign, together with any indications of the

Dutch defecting, would also greatly strengthen Tory 'blue water' arguments in favour of switching English resources away from the Low Countries to concentrate instead on naval and colonial campaigns.[1]

A serious situation was developing in northern Italy, as Marlborough had anticipated. He had tried during his winter tour to ensure that substantial reinforcements were sent there at the earliest possible moment, but when the campaign opened the French seemed to be close to achieving a decisive victory. The Dutch were helplessly aware of the predicament of their allies, the Emperor and Savoy; Marlborough with his eyes as always on the overall war situation was ready to provide a solution. He formulated an ambitious and daring plan to intervene in northern Italy with an army composed exclusively of English and English-paid troops; he knew that the Dutch would not agree to their troops disappearing beyond the Alps under foreign command. This audacious move would be undertaken by a smaller army than that which he had marched to the Danube in 1704, but it would have to march over much longer distances and infinitely more difficult terrain. It would at first take the same route up the Rhine and then across to the Danube, but it would then have to move down the river and then cross the Alps.

In Marlborough's judgement the critical situation in northern Italy necessitated such a move. Eugène with the main Imperial army was being held in eastern Lombardy, while a second French army had overrun most of Savoy and was now laying siege to its capital, Turin. Its capture would face the duke with the choice of either following the elector of Bavaria's example, abandoning all his territories to become the dependant of his chief ally, or of accepting whatever peace terms Louis would concede. The conquest of

[1] Snyder, vol. I, pp. 521, 523, 527.

Savoy would probably be followed by a further French offensive to drive Eugène to evacuate all positions south of the Alps, and it would ensure that no Imperial forces could be sent to reinforce prince Lewis on the Rhine. It would rule out for the forseeable future any question of Eugène being sent with an army to join Marlborough to fight the decisive campaign in the Low Countries on which the latter pinned his hopes of forcing France to agree to a satisfactory, that is durable, peace. Finally, to complete a woeful prospect, if the French won decisively in northern Italy, Philip's control over Naples and Sicily would become unassailable, and the Emperor would be unable to send any help to his brother Karl in Spain, leaving England and the Dutch with the entire burden of the war there.

This plan for a march of nearly a thousand miles to retrieve a critical situation in Italy provides perhaps the best single example of Marlborough's ability to conceive a bold and innovative strategy which would necessitate overcoming formidable difficulties. The obvious comparison is with Napoleon's spectacular passage of the Alps to overwhelm the Austrians in 1796, but in that case the main problems were operational: Napoleon had to fight his way through the passes and then debouch to attack an enemy in prepared positions. Once his army broke initial enemy resistance it lived off unravaged country. Marlborough's problems both on the long march and in northern Italy would be logistical. No advance preparations had been made; this meant that the army would have to depend on supplies procured from Habsburg authorities (which had not been the case in 1704). The coolly hostile neutrality of Venice would prevent the Mediterranean fleet escorting seaborne supplies for a campaign in Lombardy. By contrast French forces in 1705–6 as later in Napoleon's time were accustomed to Italian campaigning, but English armies had absolutely no experience of it, and were not to operate in Lombardy until after the Caporetto disaster of 1917. Three destructive campaigns had reduced much of the countryside to a state of destitution so that a new army would find it impossible to live off contributions or plunder. The logistical problems were so formidable that without Marlborough's confidence in his quarter-master Cadogan's ability (which had been tested and proven in the Blenheim campaign) the plan could never have been seriously proposed. Nevertheless if the duke of Savoy was to be preserved as an ally and – unlike most English and Dutch politicians and generals – Marlborough consistently upheld his interests and valued highly his contribution to the war, great risks might have to be taken.[2]

In the event Marlborough had to leave Eugène and the duke to save themselves by their unaided exertions, because a deterioration of the allied position in Germany made impossible an unimpeded march up the Rhine and then across to the Danube. The arguments which he had advanced during his winter tour of German Courts had failed to produce results. The Imperial Court showed no intention of settling the rebellion in Hungary, which tied up large military forces, by the kind of compromise the English ministry advocated. Prince Lewis had promised to supply Marlborough with his campaign plans so that coordinated action could be prepared. He delayed doing so, and when they arrived it was in impracticable form: he suggested an attack on Strasbourg that he must have known he would not have the resources to mount. The backwardness of Lewis's preparations meant that no operations on the Saar or Moselle would be possible in 1706, and they resulted in his suffering a major setback. At the end of April a surprise attack by Villars drove the German forces back across the Rhine. There he

---

[2] Ibid., vol. I, pp. 523, 528, 530; Godolphin's reaction was sceptical, pp. 526, 530. T'Hoff, pp. 227, 228.

could be expected to remain on the defensive for most of the rest of the summer with an inadequate army because the German princes had failed to provide him with full strength contingents. He would also be unable to guarantee an unimpeded passage for Marlborough's proposed march across southern Germany.[3]

The king of Prussia continued to create acute problems. At Berlin the previous December Marlborough had persuaded him to sign a new treaty for the supply of troops for both the Low Countries and Italy. The king held these contingents back as a means of exerting pressure on the Emperor and the Dutch, with both of whom he had long-running disputes. Their absence left Marlborough with a significantly smaller army than the French. But even more serious were the indications that the king was now giving consideration to the approaches being made to him by France for a separate peace on very favourable terms.[4]

In the Low Countries Marlborough faced the same problem as in 1705; he had to manoeuvre the enemy into a vulnerable position so that, despite the French superiority in numbers, the Dutch deputies and generals could be persuaded that an all-out attack would be successful. Marlborough expected his opponent, Villeroy again, to stand on the defensive using new lines, and the fortified camps that had proved so effective the previous year on the Moselle, to hold off the allies without becoming involved in a major set-piece engagement. He had the advantage of field deputies who were likely to be more amenable, but the overall Dutch attitude was still one of caution, dominated by the concern

---

[3] Snyder, vol. I, pp. 532, 537. Murray, vol. II, pp. 431, 436, 487–8, 498, 500–2n, 505; vol. III, pp. 18–19, 22, 27–8.

[4] Murray, vol. II, pp. 391–2, 441, 471–4, 475, 477–8n, 478–9, 480–1, 492–3, 510 and note. T'Hoff, p. 233. Snyder, vol. I, p. 571.

that loss of a single major battle could precipitate the collapse of their main defences, and force a submission to French peace terms. A crucial difference existed between the defence systems of the two sides in the Low Countries, one that Winston Churchill constantly ignored in his denigration of the Dutch. The French possessed defences in great depth, lines of strong fortresses modernised by Vauban, most of them containing purpose-built magazines to supply not only the garrisons but also armies operating in the field. By comparison the Dutch had only one thin line of modern fortresses, and the great rivers could easily be out-flanked (as in 1672 and as it was thought of doing again in 1702) by wide moves across the Rhine to invade the Dutch Republic from the east. Consequently defeat in a major battle could result in what remained of the Dutch army being pinned back in a desperate defence of the homeland.

Marlborough certainly did not expect Villeroy to go on to the offensive right at the start of the campaign as he did, without even waiting for reinforcements from the Rhine. Louis had authorised Villeroy to follow an active strategy to defend the Spanish Netherlands: he was not instructed to concentrate on avoiding battle. His instructions reflect a general recovery of confidence on the part of the French and an underestimate of Marlborough's abilities derived from his failures the previous year. They were made possible by the remarkable achievements of the French war minister, Chamillart, in replacing losses suffered in previous years, in mobilising and supplying armies of unprecedented size. Villeroy was well aware of the delays to the Prussian and other German princely contingents and thought that Marlborough would not be ready to attack immediately.[5]

Events moved with unparalleled swiftness, especially for

[5] Vault and Pelete, vol. VI, pp. 16, 19, 32. Snyder, vol. I, pp. 535, 543. Murray, vol. II, p. 468.

the opening phase of a campaign. Villeroy moved forward from his lines on 19 May. Marlborough completed the assembly of all the forces available as yet on the 22nd. The decisive battle of Ramillies was fought on the next day. This exceptionally early date for a major battle meant that the whole summer could be used to exploit the victory and that the French had to move troops in numbers from other theatres in order to replace their losses.

As at Blenheim Marlborough's success followed from his creation of overpowering local superiority on a part of the battlefront where he saw that a sustained and massive attack was made possible by the open terrain. Secondly he took advantage of faulty dispositions by Villeroy, although it is not possible to say whether he was aware of them from the start or became aware at some later stage. Villeroy placed the mass of the French infantry, with strong cavalry support, in what was physically a strong defensive position on their left, around the hamlet of Autre-Eglise and behind a stream, the Little Gheet. On the other, right, wing over four miles away he placed his main cavalry force behind a relatively small infantry force defending the village of Taviers. The remainder of the French infantry were stationed in the centre, behind Ramillies village, too far distant from either flank to move in time to stem an allied attack.

The considerable length of the French front, together with the undulating ground which meant that there were several extensive areas of dead ground which Marlborough skilfully used, made it impossible for a general on either side to survey the whole battlefield. This gave a crucial advantage to the general who had worked out a clear battle plan and took the initiative, over one who merely stood to await the enemy and then responded to his moves as they became evident. Marlborough as usual gave his subordinates clear and unambiguous orders, and knew that they would be obeyed.

He made Villeroy react from the start, but as the French general could not personally observe all allied moves time was lost by him in setting counter-moves in motion. As at Blenheim Marlborough began by launching an attack in very considerable strength on the sector which was most formidably defended. This attack on the French left – like the assaults on Blenheim village – was not expected to succeed in the sense of dislodging and driving back the numerous defending units, although the local commander (Orkney) was not aware of this aspect of the battle plan. Marlborough's objective was to pin down the enemy's forces and draw in reserves to that sector, particularly from the centre. On the other flank the Dutch, by attacking and taking Taviers on the French right, also drew forces away from their centre. Villeroy's faulty dispositions complicated his task of organising a counter-attack, forcing him into an improvisation that seriously weakened his cavalry. The main French infantry reserves behind Ramillies were too far away for him to use them, so that Villeroy had to order his dragoon regiments to dismount in order to attack as infantry. Of course dragoons were accustomed to such a role, but their attack was repulsed and as they were trying to reform as remounted cavalry they were effectively charged by Marlborough's Danish cavalry and thrown into confusion.

These allied attacks on each of the flanks prepared the way for the main attack, by the massed cavalry moving forward irresistibly in the centre, just as they had done at Blenheim. Marlborough brought most of his squadrons round from the allied right, where they had put in a highly visible appearance to show the French where they were, and to create the impression that they were waiting for the allied infantry to make a breakthrough in that sector. The switch to the centre was concealed by the use of dead ground and, again as at Blenheim, the main cavalry advance was combined with one by infantry: they attacked Ramillies village in order to prevent the cavalry being charged on their flank.

The allied cavalry did not break through without a protracted struggle. During the prolonged mêlée units lost their formations, and Marlborough became personally and dangerously involved while characteristically leading from the front. His behaviour in this battle recalled that of William in his desperate and usually less than victorious engagements of the 1670s and 1690s. Marlborough was unhorsed; his equerry Bringfield was decapitated while helping him to remount and he narrowly escaped capture. Even at the time many criticised such taking of risks, but it was by this kind of display of courage that both William and Marlborough endeared themselves to their armies, enhanced the morale of their troops and made an impact on their enemies. Louis XIV did not share the dangers and hardships of those who earned him his 'glory'; the respect which their former comrade John Churchill exacted from French officers and men was, as with Rommel in the Western Desert in 1941–2, a considerable allied asset inculcating a sense of inferiority among them.

Marlborough halted Orkney's attacks towards Autre-Eglise before the attack went in in the centre. Orkney at once protested, and claimed later that his men were about to drive their more numerous opponents from their positions. But the cavalry which could have converted this unplanned local success into a rout of the enemy's whole left wing were needed to form part of the cavalry mass in the centre, on whose attack Marlborough depended for decisive victory. Consequently he had good reasons for halting Orkney's infantry, who could have driven their opponents back but probably not broken up their formations and routed them. More questionably in the situation Orkney had created, but as part of the original battle plan, Marlborough also ordered him to send some of his infantry to reinforce the centre; the success of the allied cavalry made this move unnecessary, whereas renewed attacks on the French left, coinciding with the collapse of their centre, could have produced the encirclement of substantial enemy forces.

The final stage of the battle saw a substantial part of the allied cavalry, reformed after they had broken up the enemy's main cavalry – the elite units known as the *maison du roi* – wheeling across what had been the rear of the French line. This forced a precipitate retreat. French losses were heavy, probably as many as 10,000 killed and wounded and another 5,000 prisoners. In addition there were several thousand desertions as Villeroy's army broke up in great confusion with fragmented units retreating in different directions.[6] He had absolutely no chance of forming a defence line along the Dyle, in front of Brussels. Two days after Ramillies the allies took Leuven without resistance. On 27 May, that is four days after the battle, representatives of the city and of the States of Brabant made their formal submission; Marlborough promised that their privileges would be confirmed. This public act of recognition would hopefully persuade other major cities and provinces to submit voluntarily.[7]

By his victory at Ramillies Marlborough saw that he had created an opportunity to gain possession of the whole of the Spanish Netherlands in a single campaign. As after Blenheim he demonstrated his ability to gain the maximum advantages from a success, calculating that normally unacceptable risks could be taken while the enemy was disorganised and shocked by defeat. As early as 25 May he called on the Dutch to move troops from their fortress garrisons to reinforce the field army, since he considered the enemy was now too

---

[6] Winston S. Churchill, *Marlborough: His Life and Times* (4 vols., 1933–8), vol. III, pp. 102–29. David Chandler (ed.), *Military Memoirs: Robert Parker and Comte de Merode-Westerloo* (1968), pp. 58–65.   [7] Murray, vol. II, pp. 529, 534–5.

demoralised to attack, although this was before any signs appeared of such neighbouring enemy garrisons as Antwerp being prepared to defect.[8]

In exploiting the situation created by Ramillies Marlborough combined the application of relentless military pressure with painstaking diplomatic negotiation. The latter sphere of activity is a less familiar story, but one can see in it a clear picture of Marlborough's ideas about the character of the war and its objectives. There was now at last the prospect of achieving a satisfactory peace, with the French being forced to make sufficient concessions to ensure that the individual allies obtained their own particular demands. For example, overlooking the king of Prussia's extremely negative attitude in holding back his troops, he flattered him into sending them to give extra impetus to the campaign by promising that Anne would uphold his interests in what must now be a relatively early peace settlement. This implied supporting his claims against other allies – the Emperor and the Dutch – but their satisfaction would now be more easily arranged in a peace which gave the major allied powers most of what they wanted.[9]

Marlborough devoted a great deal of attention to what proved to be abortive negotations with the exiled elector of Bavaria. Although Maximilian had become entirely dependent on France, and was in process of losing most of the provinces which he ruled as Philip V's governor-general, this was a negotiation for the highest stakes imaginable. The elector commanded the troops garrisoning the four key fortresses which controlled the southern parts of the Spanish Netherlands; Mons, Namur, Charleroi and Luxemburg. Villeroy's defeat and the confusion among the enemy which followed it meant that the French, for a few weeks at least,

[8] T'Hoff, p. 234.   [9] Snyder, vol. II, p. 665. Murray, vol. II, pp. 514, 521.

would not have the physical strength to prevent the elector defecting to the allies. They offered him generous terms. Possession of these four fortresses would give Marlborough immense strategic advantages, far greater than those he actually obtained in 1706. First it would give Brussels and Brabant total security so that troops would not have to be stationed in static defensive garrisons, whereas after 1706 Marlborough when on the offensive had always to look over his shoulder to their defence. Secondly, and positively, each of the four fortresses could serve as bases, with magazines, for offensive action giving Marlborough the option of three alternative invasion routes into the heart of France; up the Moselle from Luxemburg, the Meuse from Namur and towards Valenciennes and Cambrai from Mons and Charleroi, and these last two were not covered by French defences in depth. The availability of these options would have given Marlborough far more freedom of action than he was to possess after 1706. The French defences would be stretched to cover an almost impossibly wide front, giving free scope to his superior skills in mobile campaigns of rapid movement.[10]

Surprisingly, since the French defeat at Ramillies would make it more difficult for Louis to honour his earlier promises, Maximilian hesitated to abandon his patron and consequently he lost all value in Marlborough's eyes once the French recovered sufficiently to take precautionary moves to secure the four fortresses. Once they knew about the secret negotiations Louis and his ministers misjudged Marlborough's motives. Stereotyping him as covetous and grasping they thought that he was concerned to safeguard the principality of Mindelheim which the Emperor had granted him as a reward for Blenheim out of the sequestered

---

[10] Snyder, vol. I, pp. 565–6, 572, 574, 588; vol. II, pp. 589, 617, 633, 642, 646. T'Hoff, pp. 248–9, 251.

territories of Bavaria. They also concluded that because the negotiations had been personal the elector would now be a useful channel in making an approach for a general peace. Marlborough regarded all consideration of peace at this time to be premature. His objective was to use the gains of 1706 to mount a final, decisive offensive the next year. But he realised that he could not prevent the Dutch wanting to explore French proposals and that for the first time in the war these would be relatively attractive to them. The energy with which he exploited enemy weaknesses after Ramillies had two long-term aims. First he showed the Dutch that their desired Barrier could be achieved by conquest more surely than by entering into negotiations which would give the French plentiful opportunities for their usual duplicities and chicanery. Secondly he was intent on creating a springboard for the offensive which he planned for 1707.[11]

Marlborough made spectacular advances during the summer. Ghent, Bruges, Oudenarde and the province of Flanders followed the example of Brussels and Brabant in voluntarily submitting and recognising Karl as their sovereign. At Antwerp, the biggest prize, the Spanish governor and his Spanish and Walloon regiments also declared for Karl, prevented French units seizing the citadel and forced them to capitulate: this saved the allies from having to mount a siege. Only at Dendermonde were the French able to overwhelm an attempt by the townspeople to surrender. This necessitated a siege which was made difficult by the inundations that formed the most effective part of its defences; it fell only on 5 September. By then other important places had been taken. Ostend (6 July) improved the supply position, giving the army a direct link with England for the first time. Kortrijk was occupied without resistance to serve as the main forward

[11] T'Hoff, pp. 253, 255–6, 262–3, 266, 269. Murray, vol. III, pp. 166, 167–8, 214–15.

base. After long delays caused by the difficulty of moving supplies in bulk and the artillery, because the depth of water in several of the rivers was controlled by sluices retained by the enemy, the army could lay siege to well-defended fortresses. Marlborough did not get his way in the choice of targets. He wanted to attack Mons, seeing it as a 'portal' opening up the way into France. Godolphin unhelpfully urged him to attack Dunkirk, although it lay beyond both Ypres and Nieuport and was protected by polders which could be flooded even more effectively than those around Dendermonde; the reason for this advice was political, the mercantile community were suffering heavy losses to privateers based on Dunkirk.[12]

Marlborough had to accept the Dutch choice of targets for siege warfare: this was because siege operations were a Dutch speciality, with their engineers directing the work under the supervision of the deputies. But despite their expertise he believed that they were often lethargic and overcautious; in 1706 he intervened to ensure that a maximum bombardment was maintained, overriding the deputies who wished to economise in the expenditure of powder and shot. Two important successes were achieved. Menen fell on 22 August, to act as an allied check on the Ypres garrison. By taking Ath on 4 October a threat to Brussels was removed. But after that the army went into winter quarters. A period of heavy rain made it impracticable to switch men and the heavy guns across country to attempt the siege of Mons, which Marlborough wanted to occupy as an alternative base for his planned invasion of France in the spring.[13]

During these sieges Marlborough gave cover with the field

---

[12] Snyder, vol. I, pp. 552, 556, 558, 565, 573, 589, 657–9. Murray, vol. III, pp. 117–18, 121.

[13] Snyder, vol. II, pp. 648–9, 652–3, 667, 679, 690, 692, 696. T'Hoff, p. 272. Murray, vol. III, pp. 15, 164.

army. He did not expect the French to attempt actively to try
to interfere. By transferring troops from the Rhine Louis
actually managed by the end of July to rebuild his field army
to a nominal strength greater than Marlborough's. He also
transferred Vendôme from Italy to command it, but although
the new general talked in confident terms of meeting and
beating Marlborough in battle, the latter rightly discounted
his boasts as a morale-boosting device particularly suited to
the French temperament. He described the real mood of the
French soldiers as 'cowed'. He did not expect Vendôme to
dare to attack, despite his superiority in numbers. Another
unhelpful intervention by Godolphin explains this superiority. He had persuaded his ministerial colleagues that after
Ramillies it was safe to detach six regiments of infantry to
embark in transports for a 'descent' on France from the sea.
This was a strategical concept which he inherited from
William who had experimented with it in 1692, unsuccess-
fully. The arguments in favour were that a descent, or even
the threat of one, would bring pressure to bear on France
from an unexpected quarter and force a diversion of troops to
defend long lines of coast. Winston Churchill in his
biography consistently overstates both the practicality of this
strategy and its attractiveness to Marlborough. At the time the
language which the latter used revealed a cool attitude: he
hoped the descent would cause *embarrassment* to the enemy and
bring us a 'happy success', that is limited and less than
decisive results. The project ended in a fiasco, like most
similar ones. The transports were delayed; the weather
turned adverse; no soldiers even got near the French coast.
Worst of all Marlborough never recovered the six regiments
detached for this expedition; subsequently, they went to
Spain as reinforcements.[14]

---

[14] Snyder, vol. II, pp. 613, 622. Murray, vol. III, pp. 6, 36.

In terms of politics the victory at Ramillies and its brilliant exploitation created some new problems. The voluntary adherence of representative bodies, cities and most of the nobility to the cause of the Habsburg claimant, Karl, created some illusions. If this happened in the Spanish Netherlands, once the occupying forces of France had been expelled, why not also throughout Spain, where already Catalonia and most of Valencia had also declared for him? It is from the position of strength achieved in 1706 that Marlborough committed himself to the formula of no peace without Spain, that the allies should continue the war to ensure that the Spanish Empire should go 'entirely' to Karl, and this despite his failure to establish himself in Madrid during the summer. Galway had marched there with an allied army based in Portugal, but Karl's delays in joining him there and the nearness of a superior French army poised to retake the city resulted in very few Castilians rallying to him. However developments in Italy during 1706 encouraged the growth of allied ambitions with a stunning reversal of fortunes. Vendôme won an early victory at Calcinato (19 April), and the French invested the Savoyard capital, Turin, from 15 May. But Eugène outflanked their forces by marching south of the Po, relieved Turin and inflicted a shattering defeat which forced the main French army to retreat across the Alps. A second army based on Milan, and garrisons in Lombardy cities, were left perilously isolated.[15]

It is a truism that when what appears to be a decisive victory has been achieved coalitions of allied states tend to start falling apart as each of the partners begins to concentrate on pursuing its own interests. In his correspondence with allied statesmen Marlborough consistently and sincerely

[15] David Francis, *The First Peninsular War 1702–1713* (1975), pp. 222, 224–41. N. Henderson, *Prince Eugen of Savoy* (1964), pp. 115–35. T'Hoff, pp. 259, 262–3.

emphasised the necessity of maintaining 'the common cause', arguing the necessity of continuing to exert the maximum pressure on France. The Imperial Court blatantly ignored his advice. When the French had to weaken their forces on the Rhine to replace their losses in Flanders the Emperor took no notice of Marlborough's pleas that Lewis's army should take the offensive. On the contrary the temporary disappearance of a French threat led to the Emperor transferring troops from the Rhine to Hungary. This decision had serious consequences. It destroyed all possibility of a compromise settlement, as urged from London, and the Hungarians continued throughout 1707 to tie down large Habsburg forces. The opportunity of strengthening the allied armies on the Rhine was forfeited, allowing the French to stage a major recovery in 1707. This rebuff sickened Marlborough in the second part of the 1706 campaign; he wrote reproachfully to an Imperial minister on 24 July: 'when such an opportunity has been cold-bloodedly thrown away, I see no hope for the future'.[16]

Habsburg policies in Italy became even more ruthlessly self-centred. Their successes in 1706 were followed by a convention with the French in March 1707 that allowed them to withdraw their isolated garrisons from Lombardy: this gave the Habsburgs the main cities without sieges, but freed French units for service in other theatres, particularly Spain. However instead of sending matching reinforcements to Spain, the Emperor planned an expedition to take Naples. He not only wanted British naval cooperation but also expected the British and the Dutch to provide (and pay for) the additional troops needed to retrieve the allied position in Spain.[17]

Marlborough saw the long-term dangers from Habsburg

[16] T'Hoff, pp. 249, 260, 261. Murray, vol. III, pp. 23, 55, 69, 87, 92, 114, 143.
[17] Murray, vol. III, pp. 371, 375. T'Hoff, pp. 307, 309.

preoccupation with its own interests, but although he offered advice he could not intervene. His most urgent problems were the result of emerging Dutch policies towards the newly conquered provinces of Brabant and Flanders. These were also to be exacerbated by the Emperor's intervention. Marlborough had been careful to consult the Dutch deputies who accompanied his victorious army before he gave formal undertakings, on behalf of the British Crown, the States General and their sovereign Karl, to confirm the rights and privileges of the provinces and cities that voluntarily submitted. He thought that the deputies agreed also that no policy decisions should be made or enforced in relation to the governing bodies of the provinces – the Council of State and Chamber of Finance, judicial courts and the municipal administrations – without the approval of both English and Dutch representatives, but the Dutch deputies began to act at once, being on the spot, whereas a delay ensued before Stepney, the English representative, took up his duties. Knowing already how strained Dutch finances had become Marlborough cannot have been surprised at the determination of the deputies to raise a maximum amount in money and services from the conquered provinces in order to support their army. The consequences of their exactions troubled him. Within a month of its submission Marlborough had evidence of the strength of pro-French elements in Brussels, and by the end of August he expressed fears that Dutch fiscal demands were already leading most of the population to want the return of the French.[18]

In more general terms the question of the future administration of the recently conquered cities began to threaten Anglo-Dutch relations. The treaty of 1701 promised the Dutch a sufficient Barrier but did not define the way in which

---

[18] T'Hoff, p. 257. Murray, vol. III, p. 93.

it would be administered, nor had it received detailed attention since, and Karl and the Emperor had not given it their agreement. The English ministers had interests of their own to protect: they did not want the ports of Ostend and Nieuport (the latter still in French hands) to become part of the Barrier, for fear that the Dutch would use control over administration of customs rates to hamper or even effectively exclude English imports into the Spanish Netherlands as a whole. Marlborough believed that he had been deceived about the administration. On 26 June he wrote to the deputies at Brussels approving, with a minor amendment, their nomination of the Council of State, without being aware that the authorisation already given to them by the States General in a resolution of 19 June omitted any need to consult or get the approval of a representative of the queen. The text of the actual resolution had been left in Dutch when it had been transmitted to Marlborough, and he did not ask immediately for a translation so that it was not until 9 July that he informed himself of its content. The frigid tone of the letter which he wrote the next day to pensionary Heinsius can be seen as marking a deterioration in their relationship which was never to be fully rectified. But by then Marlborough had much more personal causes of grievance against the Dutch, and they had been given long-lasting grounds for suspicion of his ambitions.[19]

Before he left for Spain Karl, who according to his allies was rightfully king and therefore sovereign over the Spanish Netherlands, had deposited with his brother the Emperor signed blank commissions for offices in territories which might be recovered from the enemy. The Emperor now used one to name Marlborough to the great office of

[19] Snyder, vol. II, pp. 616–17. Murray, vol. II, pp. 633, 686–7. R. Geikie and I. A. Montgomery, *The Dutch Barrier* (Cambridge, 1930), pp. 25–30.

governor-general of the Spanish Netherlands.[20] His motive was only too obvious. The Dutch had already demonstrated in the relatively unimportant territories already recovered their intention to control and exploit local administration for the duration of the war, and do their utmost to predetermine the eventual shape of their Barrier. They had prevented Goes, the Imperial envoy, asserting any control over administration; the English government had acquiesced. But by appointing Marlborough the Emperor could obtain effective authority: only he, with the backing of the ministers in London, could uphold Habsburg rights and interests during the remainder of the war and in the peace settlement which was expected within a year or two.

The offer was not explicit about tenure. It seems that the Emperor intended only a short-term appointment, either until Habsburg authority had been consolidated, or for the duration of the war. Marlborough failed to appreciate this and undoubtedly thought of it as a long-term, if not life, appointment and when the offer was renewed in 1708 Karl knew that anything less than a life tenure would not attract him. Nothing could have been more attractive than this office to Marlborough. He could rise no further in terms of honours and offices under the English Crown – apart from converting the tenure of his post as captain-general into one for life. He had revealed to the Emperor his ambition for European honours, status and monetary rewards by the eagerness with which he had canvassed about the details of the principality of Mindelheim, granted to him in recognition of Blenheim. Lack of a male heir would prevent the Churchills becoming hereditary princes of the Empire, but the Governorship of the Spanish Netherlands gave its holder quasi-regal status and virtually autonomous power: it had customarily been held by

[20] Snyder, vol. II, pp. 591–613. T'Hoff, pp. 239, 241–7.

brothers of the king of Spain and Imperial archdukes, and recently by the elector of Bavaria. It was also worth at least £60,000 a year, and disposed of wide patronage. Marlborough could expect to receive the order of the Golden Fleece, the most prestigious in Europe.

Naturally Marlborough wanted to accept. He had to refer the offer to Anne, but the queen made no difficulty in authorising acceptance. However neither she nor Marlborough and his colleagues took account, in their initial reactions, to the great and indeed insuperable objections. Acceptance would shake the unity of the allies. The Emperor intended the offer to detach Marlborough, and through him England, from the Dutch Republic so as to prevent the States General establishing a predominance in the Spanish Netherlands that would leave Karl with only an empty title. This was a particularly dangerous divisive political strategy. Any sign that their allies intended to go back on their undertaking to establish a full Barrier would provoke the Dutch into accepting French offers of negotiations for a separate peace – as in 1678. After Ramillies they no longer had reasons to be desperately afraid of France, and Louis could now be expected to hold out the prospect of generous terms.

Marlborough does not seem to have anticipated the difficulties he would encounter in executing the duties of the office. His humble, non-noble origins would have formed a barrier to his acceptance by the nobility and his unshakable Protestantism would provoke intense suspicion in one of the most dévôt regions of Europe. It would be used against him by the strong clerical party within the Imperial Court at Vienna and by Karl's anglophobe German ministers in Barcelona. Above all, once the war had been brought to a successful end the Emperor would no longer depend on English support; Marlborough's importance as an influence on Anne, his ministerial colleagues and Parliament would diminish.

Furthermore, this influence would certainly be eroded by his absence in Brussels from the Court, Council and Lords.

In practical terms the Governorship involved its holder in so much complex and time-consuming detail that it is difficult to see how its duties could be combined with continued command of the allied army. Questions of providing money, carts, horses and boats for transport, labourers for sieges, would have engaged him in constant contentions with the exigent Dutch deputies, and faced him with a series of conflicts of loyalty between the needs of the army and the interests of the provinces. At a higher level political issues would have inevitably provoked running battles with the Dutch, with Marlborough having to combine the advancement of Karl's rights with the protection of English interests and effective prosecution of the war.

Unfortunately for future Anglo-Dutch relations Marlborough did not conceal his wish to accept or his mortification when under pressure he had to decline (12 July).[21] His reluctance encouraged Karl to renew the offer on two occasions. He made a direct offer in December from Barcelona, and another in August 1708. On both occasions he ignored the earlier Dutch outcry. In 1708 the offer was renewed precisely because Karl and the Imperial ministers knew that Marlborough blamed Dutch maladministration and fiscal extortion for the defection to the French of the cities of Ghent and Bruges, which had precipitated a serious crisis, retrieved by Marlborough by the battle of Oudenarde. This time the offer was explicitly for life, and the suggestion that it should take effect only after peace had been concluded revealed Karl's objective. As future Governor Marlborough would be bound to work with him in trying to restrict the

---

[21] Murray, vol. II, pp. 670, 688–9, 701. In all these notifications of his decision to decline Marlborough stressed that it was the need to preserve allied unity that actuated him.

rights and powers which the Dutch would acquire along with the Barrier. He was also aware by then of the alarm in British mercantile and industrial circles at Dutch attempts to exclude or discriminate against imports from England by the alleged manipulation of customs duties. This would ensure that Marlborough would have his home government's backing in working to uphold Karl's interests, and this gave him an advantage over any alternative candidate, including the most obvious, Eugène. By 1708 there were two new reasons for hoping that Marlborough might now be greatly tempted to reconsider his earlier refusal. His relations with Anne were deteriorating, and the Godolphin administration found itself increasingly in difficulties in Parliament, so that the Governorship would offer him an assured position of the greatest eminence and influence that would continue into a post-war world in which he had ceased to be the queen's indispensable servant. Secondly if Anne predeceased him, Marlborough would as Governor be in a strong position to ensure that the Protestant succession went into effect. In the immediate future this would reduce the pressure on the British administration to concede maximum Dutch demands on the Barrier, because of their eagerness to obtain in return a Dutch guarantee of the succession.

In 1708, remembering the earlier outcry, Marlborough kept the renewed offer secret for some time. He must have known that he had to refuse it, but an abrupt rejection might provoke Karl to appoint a Governor with whom Marlborough, as well as the Dutch, would find it difficult to collaborate. His hesitation made Karl persist. He replied to the letter in which Marlborough eventually declined the offer expressing the hope that he would reconsider his decision once peace had been concluded.[22]

---

[22] Snyder, vol. III, pp. 1086–7, 1088, 1092, 1302, 1303, 1305. The correspondence continued into the second half of 1709.

Marlborough's rejection of the offer made in 1706 damaged his standing with the Emperor, cooling his previously excellent relations with Wratislaw, the most sympathetic Imperial minister. This was particularly unfortunate when a new crisis developed in the last months of 1706 between the Emperor and Karl XII, the king of Sweden. After successful campaigns in Poland the latter had overrun and established himself in Saxony. From there he began to exert pressure on the Emperor to withdraw encroachments made on Protestant rights in Silesia, which had been agreed in 1648 in the Treaty of Westphalia, and of which Sweden was a guarantor. A combination of inept diplomacy and pressure from the clerical party in the Imperial Court led to negotiations becoming bogged down. A real danger emerged that the impulsive and aggressively Protestant Karl would launch an attack on Habsburg territories which they were in no position to repel: an ominous repetition of the intervention of 1629 by Gustavus Adolphus seemed likely. That had destroyed Imperial predominance; a Swedish irruption in 1707 would disrupt and perhaps destroy the alliance. Although the Swedes had resisted French attempts to involve them in the war, either as combatants or as mediator, general hostilities with Imperial forces would certainly lead to a full alliance with France. Denmark, Prussia and other north German states would have to recall their contingents, critically depleting Marlborough's strength. The Emperor would not be able to provide any forces for the Rhine and the Low Countries. The extension of hostilities would seriously affect the Dutch economy, heavily dependent as it was on Baltic commerce.

Marlborough could not achieve any military success in 1707, but by his personal diplomacy he saved the alliance from the catastrophe of a war between Sweden and the Emperor.

Marlborough's mission to Karl XII delayed the start of the campaign for over a month, but his plans for an offensive would in any case have been put off by the late arrival of several allied military contingents which were needed to give him a margin of superiority over the French.[23]

Marlborough's mission to Karl XII confirmed his de facto position as the effective leader of the alliance against France. No other allied statesman, diplomat or general could have undertaken it with any prospect of success. It put Marlborough on equal terms with the sovereign whose victories and conquests gave him domination over northern and eastern Europe. Marlborough did not have plenipotentiary powers from the Emperor, but the prestige which he had already gained, and which was increased by the successful outcome of this mission, made it certain that the informal understanding which he achieved with Karl would make the Habsburgs come to terms with the latter's demands.

Apart from the first duke of Buckingham's disastrous forays to Spain and France in the 1620s, Marlborough was the first leading English minister to engage himself in personal diplomacy at the highest level abroad, and mainly in distant continental capitals. He had already made long winter journeys to Berlin, Vienna and Hanover and knew from experience the value of a few hours direct conversation with allied principals, rulers and their chief ministers. Such personal contact could be more effective in resolving difficulties and formulating plans than long sequences of letters. Correspondence was always liable to misinterpretation, but mutual confidence and understanding might follow from personal contact.

Personal diplomacy when added either before or after to the rigours of a campaign significantly increased the stress on

[23] Vault and Pelet, vol. v, pp. 24–5, 297–9.

the physique and stamina of a man nearing the age of sixty. It exposed him to a frightening burden of responsibility; the only man who followed his example in the eighteenth century, Stanhope, was not only a younger man but also chief minister. But the chances of Godolphin or the queen failing to honour the promises made on their behalf were slight; their own credibility would be ruined. Winston Churchill gives these personal missions considerable and illuminating attention: without doubt his study and understanding of the reasons for Marlborough's success was a major factor in leading him to follow a similar diplomatic strategy in World War Two. However, unlike Winston Churchill who was virtually an elected dictator in 1940–5, Marlborough did not have plenipotentiary powers and, unlike Castlereagh who revived the practice of personal diplomacy in 1814–15, he did not have the assistance of formal instructions to serve as a guide: even though Castlereagh drafted his own these were discussed and approved by the cabinet.

No skilled advisers accompanied Marlborough on what in 1707 was literally a person to person mission. The only assistance he received was from the remarkable John Robinson, the chaplain to the mission in Stockholm who had become de facto chargé, and was later to play a leading part in the Utrecht negotiations. In this case everything depended on Marlborough's ability to strike up a good relationship with Karl, whom he had never met or corresponded with but who hero-worshipped him as a great general, second in ability and in fortune to himself. Although several Swedish generals and ministers received 'presents' from allied governments (and often simultaneously from France also) they were powerless to influence major decisions which the king made personally (and often very impulsively).[24]

---

[24] Snyder, vol. II, pp. 747, 752, 760. Murray, vol. III, pp. 313, 315–17. R. Hatton, *Charles XII of Sweden* (1968), p. 224.

Marlborough's task was complicated by the fact that he could not represent or commit any of the allies. The Dutch were suspicious of his mission. As always they feared that Swedish predominance in the Baltic would adversely affect their trade, and traditionally had allied with Denmark while England favoured Sweden as a counter-balance. In 1707 the Dutch also feared that an agreement with Karl would antagonise the Tsar and imperil their increasingly valuable Russian trade. Nor could Marlborough speak (or wish to speak) for the Emperor whose obduracy over Protestant rights in Silesia was precipitating the crisis: he had earlier tried and failed to persuade the Imperial ministers to make concessions which would end the rebellion of the Hungarians, most of whose leaders were Protestant.[25]

When Marlborough arrived at Altranstadt for his meetings with Karl, which took place between the 15th and the 18th of April, the information which Robinson passed to him actually understated the dangers to the allies. Robinson had learnt that French diplomats were urging Karl to insist to the allies that they accept him as mediator in the Spanish Succession War, and that he would then receive inducements to formulate a settlement in favour of France and Philip. In reality the French had developed their approach: they were now also offering to bring about a peace between Karl and Tsar Peter, on terms advantageous to the former, so as to free the Swedish king to intervene in Silesia. Once hostilities began on a local scale the French would quickly manoeuvre him into their camp. But the ultra-sophisticated chicanery of this French diplomatic strategy, which went beyond their support for the partly Protestant Hungarian rebels, contained a fatal flaw. Karl's fervent Protestantism made him distrustful of Louis XIV as the author of the Revocation of the Edict of

<hr/>

[25] Snyder, vol. II, p. 746. T'Hoff, p. 337.

Nantes; the persecution of the Huguenots that followed was far more savage than the discrimination against the Silesian Lutherans by the Emperor.

The confessional issue gave Marlborough a decisive advantage. Karl admired him not only as a victorious general but also because of his commitment to the Protestant religion which he had displayed with such effect in 1688 by defecting from James II. The atmosphere at the meetings was intensely personal; the outcome depended on the impact which Marlborough made on a strange young man. In political terms he concentrated on the argument that the Tsar was, and would remain, Karl's most dangerous enemy and that no patched-up peace with him would give Sweden and his protégés lasting security. Peter must be defeated and preferably dethroned, which would involve installing and maintaining a Swedish puppet ruler in Moscow as well as Warsaw. Karl already believed that it was essential to eliminate Peter, but Marlborough undoubtedly helped to deflect him from a diversion into Silesia that could have escalated rapidly into a ruinous conflict with the Emperor. Marlborough also accomplished another diplomatic task during his meetings, stifling a Swedish project intended to consolidate their influence in Germany by concluding a triple alliance with Prussia and Hanover. This would add to confessional tensions and French propaganda would represent it as an alliance against Catholic princes and their religion.[26]

The Altranstadt meetings went extremely well but they were never intended to produce a formal agreement, and this meant that Marlborough had a good deal of business to conclude afterwards. He visited Berlin and Hanover on his return journey to ensure that the triple alliance project was

[26] Hatton, *Charles XII*, pp. 222–3. Murray, vol. III, pp. 178–9, 476. T'Hoff, pp. 324–5, 328–9, 335–6, 455.

dead. He had given Karl assurances about the rights of the Silesian Lutherans and had to brief allied diplomats to exert pressure in Vienna so as to ensure the Emperor's compliance. He had not been able to avoid giving Karl an undertaking that Anne would recognise Stanislaus, the puppet king of Poland, but it was not until the autumn that the Emperor finally concluded a convention on the question of Silesia.

The objective of deflecting Karl into what proved ultimately to be a fatal invasion of Russia was achieved so that Marlborough could concentrate on another campaign in the Low Countries. It made it possible for him to persuade the rulers of Prussia and Hanover to provide full-size contingents. However by the time Marlborough assumed the command a series of disasters had befallen the allies in other theatres of the war.[27]

The desperate state of French state finances led them to adopt a strategy of extorting money and supplies from enemy territories by sudden raids in great strength: this represented a return to the practices of the Thirty Years War, of war living off war, of armies maintaining themselves by the contributions they could collect themselves, or simply by plundering. Feuquières had devastated southern Germany in the previous war: Villars repeated his raid after breaking through the Stollhoven lines (23 May). His troops ranged as far as Bavaria and Würzburg, living off the country and seizing a large surplus of money for the support of other French armies. Prince Lewis had died in January but Marlborough regarded his successor, the margrave of Bayreuth, as even more irresolute and incompetent. The generals whom he respected and would have liked to see in command had all been passed

[27] Snyder, vol. II, pp. 757–64. Hatton, Charles XII, pp. 224–6. A. E. Stamp, 'The meeting of the Duke of Marlborough and Charles XII at Altranstadt', Transactions of the Royal Historical Society, new series, 12 (1896), 113–14.

over by the Emperor because they were Protestants. Bayreuth's failure to take active counter-measures, and the
devastated state of southern Germany, meant that nothing
could be expected from the Rhine front in 1707.[28]

By the time Marlborough assembled his army he knew that
the allied offensive in Spain had ended in disaster at Almanza
(25 April). Galway in repeating the previous year's advance
into Castile ran into a vastly superior French and Spanish
army, including reinforcements sent from Italy after the
Emperor allowed isolated French garrisons to withdraw. This
was a serious, and time was to show a decisive, defeat. It left
Marlborough at a loss afterwards to know what should be
done to retrieve the situation in which Karl, having lost the
parts of Valencia previously taken, fell back on the defence of
Catalonia. This defeat in the field was all the more serious
because by 1707 it had become apparent that military victory
was the only way in which Karl could gain sovereignty over
all his Spanish kingdoms: all earlier expectations that his
subjects would rally to him, either voluntarily when he
appeared among them or when French forces could no
longer overawe them, had now been exposed as totally
illusory.[29]

Marlborough's own campaign in the Low Countries
proved to be even more inconclusive than the campaigns of
1703 and 1705. Had he been able to start operations earlier he
would have seized the initiative with a major siege, of Mons
or Tournai. Instead it was Vendôme who made the first move,
advancing on Huy and compelling Marlborough to follow
with a numerically inferior army. However Vendôme had
instructions not to risk a general engagement unless he was

[28] Snyder, vol. II, pp. 785, 789. C. C. Sturgill, Marshal Villars and the War of the Spanish
Succession (Lexington, KY, 1965), pp. 71–5. Murray, vol. III, pp. 286, 392, 396,
403–4, 453–4, 499, 651. T'Hoff, pp. 329, 331–2.
[29] Francis, First Peninsular War, pp. 244–50. Murray, vol. III, pp. 360, 367–8, 378.

absolutely certain of the advantages to be gained. Similar cautionary advice had also (as Vendôme knew) been given to the Dutch field deputies. The chances of the French offering battle were reduced to zero when the allied invasion of Provence led to Vendôme being ordered to send a sizeable force to its aid. Marlborough sought to take advantage of this weakening of his opponent, initiating in August a phase of open warfare in which by rapid marching he tried to force Vendôme into fighting. This change of tactics came to nothing. Vendôme skilfully avoided battle; Marlborough seems to have bungled the only chance he had to inflict a minor defeat by cutting off the French rearguard, but in general he was foiled by the weather, incessant rains reducing his ability to manoeuvre. The resultant stalemate favoured the French. Their army improved in condition and morale as the campaign went on.[30]

The attack on Toulon, the other campaign on which Marlborough invested hope of achieving much in 1707, ended in total failure. Its capture was intended to open up the entire Midi to the allies, in the expectation that this would reignite the rebellion of the Huguenots and free those who had been forcibly converted to join their militant coreligionists. In greatly overestimating the readiness of former Huguenots to abandon both their new faith and their submission to Louis, Marlborough and his ministerial colleagues reflected the general opinion in England, which had been largely moulded by Huguenot exiles. The Toulon attack was also aimed at more tangible targets. It would deprive the French navy of its main Mediterranean base and dockyard. When taken, a further attack could be made on Marseilles and a thrust up the

[30] Snyder, vol. II, pp. 776–7, 785, 828, 831, 864–5. T'Hoff, pp. 311–12, 313, 340. Murray, vol. III, pp. 362, 365, 383, 390–1, 448, 513–14, 549, 556, 592. *Historical Manuscripts Commission, Portland*, vol. IV, pp. 440–1, 441–3.

Rhone valley would compel Louis to weaken other fronts in order to form a defensive force.

One of the two allied commanders, Eugène, showed himself unenthusiastic about the plan of campaign which involved an expedition beyond the mountains in a barren country and at the height of summer. He consistently showed himself sceptical about the assurances which he received from the English admiral Shovell that the navy would provide all the necessary supplies and ammunition – no Habsburg army had recent experience of combined operations and the sixteenth-century precedents of Charles V's maritime expeditions reinforced his doubts. He also had political reasons for scepticism and defeatism. He and the ministers at Vienna became suspicious about the reasons for the great enthusiasm shown for the operation by the other commander, the duke of Savoy. They interpreted this as showing that the duke would do anything to gain English backing, in order to play off England against the Emperor. Indeed Marlborough had helped to create this impression during the past two years: he had pressed giving maximum support for Savoy and criticised Imperial shortcomings in Italy. Most relevantly the project of an attack on Toulon originated in an agreement between Marlborough and the duke, with pressure being subsequently exerted by the former to which the Emperor and Eugène reluctantly acceded.

The expedition failed miserably. The English fleet fulfilled all Shovell's promises, landing supplies and by bombardments forcing the French to abandon outlying defences. But Eugène hesitated before launching an immediate assault while the French were weak. The topography prevented a complete siege being established, so that French reinforcements poured in. Eugène dismissed the duke of Savoy's arguments for persisting as 'complaisance for England', as no more than an attempt to ingratiate himself so as to secure

English backing for his claims in the eventual peace settlement, claims which ran counter to those of the Emperor and Karl. On 21 August the allied army decamped and retreated.[31]

The stalemate provoked very different conclusions from Marlborough and Godolphin. Marlborough remained unshaken in his belief that the war must and could still be decided by achieving victory in Flanders. Indeed with the repulse at Toulon, the defeat in Spain, the French ascendancy established on the Rhine and the cessation of hostilities in northern Italy there was nowhere else that it could be achieved. Like Haig and the 'westerners' in 1914–18 Marlborough was arguing that the enemy must be confronted where he was strongest, and that only by overcoming his main force could final victory be won. The conclusion was that the allied army in Flanders must be augmented for 1708, by the Dutch as well as England. This would put the onus on Godolphin to persuade a Parliament made reluctant by the failures of 1707, despite the vast expenditure incurred, to vote the necessary supply.

Godolphin, like the 'easterners' of 1914–18, believed that the army that remained on the defensive in Flanders possessed decisive and virtually irreducible advantages. Therefore he advocated attacks on the French where they were weak. He argued that by using the Anglo-Dutch fleet to land an army of 10,000 men (detached from Flanders) in a 'descent' on the French coast they would find themselves 500 miles from any sizeable enemy army, could live off the country and 'do what they please'. Marlborough never placed any reliance on descents: their advocates could never specify

[31] Francis, *First Peninsular War*, pp. 250–6. J. H. Owen, *The War at Sea under Queen Anne* (Cambridge, 1938), pp. 158–92. Henderson, *Prince Eugen*, pp. 136–49. Murray, vol. III, pp. 200, 250, 251–3, 255, 268–9, 294, 299, 306–7.

credible, major targets other than naval bases, and their capture would be more significant from a naval rather than military perspective. Any landings on the remote Biscay coast, again in the hypothetical belief that Huguenots would join the invaders in large numbers, would not threaten vital French interests. The one descent actually made during this war, at Sète on the Languedoc coast, proved to be a non-event. The unopposed landing force reembarked within a week having achieved nothing.[32]

The campaigns of 1707 were the most disheartening of the entire war during Marlborough's period of command. The allies achieved nothing. But the French significantly improved their position and a satisfactory peace was now less likely than it had been. Nevertheless Marlborough intensified his efforts to ensure the most vigorous prosecution of the war in 1708. He held a conference of allied representatives at the Hague to make arrangements and travelled to Frankfurt to negotiate with the electors of Hanover and Mainz. He added his voice to those seeking to persuade Eugène to take command in Spain, but found from Wratislaw that the Emperor intended Eugène to serve in Germany. On the negative side he found that the political situation in the Dutch Republic was deteriorating. He now acutely feared that a strong party was emerging in favour of a compromise peace with France, based on a partition of the Spanish territories, which he knew would be unacceptable to the Whigs at home on whom the Godolphin administration had come to depend. The serious implications of this development made it all the more important to achieve major victories in 1708.[33]

---

[32] Snyder, vol. II, p. 914; vol. III, pp. 1581, 1586. Murray, vol. III, p. 652.
[33] Snyder, vol. II, pp. 912, 923, 930, 933. T'Hoff, pp. 359–60. Murray, vol. III, pp. 621, 622, 636, 639, 650–2.

The almost total inactivity of large and expensive allied armies in the Low Countries during 1707 led many English politicians to argue that a complete change of strategy was needed. Until the first months of 1708 questions of grand strategy and diplomacy were worked out in personal meetings during the winter between Marlborough, Godolphin and secretary Harley, and by correspondence during the rest of the year. Marlborough occupied the key position because the other two remained in England, whereas he met Heinsius and allied diplomatic representatives and generals at the Hague each autumn before he returned to London, and again each spring, when he would learn what resources the allies would actually provide, with (usually overoptimistic) forecasts of when they would become available. By contrast Godolphin and Harley were constantly beset by domestic matters, particularly in preparation for, and during, parliamentary sessions. During 1707 Marlborough had tended to omit consultations with Harley, but he was obliged to work with Godolphin although his advice on strategy was increasingly influenced by political considerations.

As relations with Harley went sour, and even more after his dismissal (11 February 1708), Godolphin became dependent on Whig support and had to take into account their ideas about war strategy. Memoranda to Godolphin survive from Cowper, reputedly the least partisan of the Whig chiefs, outlining suggestions for the 1708 campaign.[34] His alternative strategy was determined by the Whig party commitment to 'no peace without Spain', the expulsion of Philip V from all Spanish territories. Cowper asserted flatly that since Marlborough had achieved nothing during 1707 in the Low

---

[34] H. L. Snyder, 'The formulation of foreign and domestic policy in the reign of queen Anne: memoranda by lord chancellor Cowper of conversations with lord treasurer Godolphin', *Historical Journal*, 11 (1968), 144–60.

Countries 'the people' were now convinced that nothing could be done there. He added that if the army there was maintained at its previous strength this would be interpreted and attacked as showing that the administration was putting Marlborough's personal prestige and interests before the best interests of the nation – a clear threat was intended here of the violently critical line the Whigs would take. This warning, and there were certainly others couched in more extreme forms, explains why Godolphin was so reluctant to allow Marlborough to leave early for the Hague, and probably why he was so eager to go as soon as possible.

Cowper advocated standing on the defensive in all theatres of war except Spain, to which large forces should be transferred from Germany and Italy, with units being sent from the Low Countries to replace them. If possible Eugène should be persuaded to take the command in Spain. These were suggestions characteristic of a politician, whose strategy was influenced largely by what he thought public opinion wanted – in practice that of the politico-economic interest groups aligned with the Whigs. This certainly explains why he also proposed sending reinforcements to wage offensive war in the West Indies on a larger scale than before. Godolphin as a minister on the defensive felt obliged to let Cowper's ideas be given serious consideration. The scheme of concentrating on an offensive in Spain was refined, with forces in overwhelming strength being put into the field: no consideration seems to have been given to the crucial question of how they were to be supplied and fed once they moved into the interior. Eugène with one army should advance from Barcelona, Marlborough with another from Lisbon. They would converge on Madrid in what was essentially a repetition of the failed strategy of 1706, and there was no solution suggested as to how they should maintain themselves there, if they ever arrived, or how logistical support could be provided.[35]

Marlborough adhered to his belief that Spain was to be won by defeating France in the Low Countries. He did not take the alternative strategy seriously, and was also sceptical about a scheme for a three-pronged offensive away from the Low Countries. This involved the duke of Savoy crossing the Alps to invade Dauphiné, another army from the upper Rhine invading Franche Comté, and Eugène advancing up the Moselle. His scepticism, shared by Heinsius, centred on the scheme's dependence on Imperial and German princely contingents assembling in time and sufficient strength to ensure success.[36] He also resisted pressure from Godolphin to hold himself in readiness to return to London at short notice in order to prevent the administration from collapsing. He could not agree with Godolphin's pessimistic prediction that no military victory in the field could materially assist the administration to overcome its domestic political difficulties. Politicians beset by domestic difficulties that impinged on them every day necessarily thought in terms of policies that were, or might be made to appear to be, what the public wanted, that is with what would please people of influence, taxpayers and the electorate. They left out of their calculations the likely reactions and attitudes of Britain's allies and, equally inexcusably, they assumed that the French would continue to remain on the defensive.[37]

When Marlborough met Eugène and Heinsius at the Hague, on 12 April, for detailed planning of the campaign all previous proposals had been made irrelevant by strong indications that the French were adopting an offensive

---

[35] Francis, *First Peninsular War*, pp. 259–64.
[36] Snyder, vol. II, pp. 946–7, 948–9. T'Hoff, p. 364.
[37] Snyder, vol. II, pp. 983–4, 987.

attitude. It had been known since January that Louis would mount a diversionary invasion of Scotland, and the administration in London had information about Jacobite activities, but the obvious precautionary counter-moves had already been taken. While the French had 6,000 men at Dunkirk ready to embark, Marlborough sent ten battalions to Ostend ready to follow them. In the event bad weather and Jacobite incompetence foiled a landing, but allied command of the sea meant that the danger of the Pretender establishing himself and bringing into existence a new war front was limited.[38]

A more dangerous and unexpected development quickly emerged in Flanders. The French put into the field a numerically superior army, and the appointment of the duke of Burgundy to command it jointly with Vendôme confirmed intelligence reports of plans for offensive action. Initially these were indeed extremely bold, envisaging attacks on Huy and Liège, leading to one on Maastricht.[39] Advanced indications of such revived aggressiveness caused the abandonment of the initial allied plan, which included an offensive up the Moselle by Eugène, with backing from the German forces on the Rhine. However this decision was not communicated to elector George of Hanover when Eugène and Marlborough met him in April, although he was to command these Rhine forces. Eugène and Marlborough feared that the knowledge that he would now be expected to do no more than conduct a holding operation would make George, and the German princes generally, even more leisurely in completing their preparations. Nevertheless this deceit hurt George bitterly, and he never fully regained confidence in Marlborough.[40] Under the revised plan, of

[38] Murray, vol. III, pp. 679–80, 689. T'Hoff, p. 377. Owen, *War at Sea under Queen Anne*, pp. 238–70. *Historical Manuscripts Commission*, 15th Report, appendix 4, p. 466.
[39] Vault and Pelet, vol. VIII, p. 6.
[40] Snyder, vol. II, pp. 1087, 1112. T'Hoff, p. 397. R. Hatton, *George I Elector and King* (1978), pp. 102–3.

which he was kept in ignorance, Eugène was to make a show of strength on the Moselle but be ready to move to Flanders to assist Marlborough.

The objective which Louis set his generals in 1708 was to improve his bargaining position in future negotiations for what would at best be a compromise peace. This could best be done in Flanders. By having had to agree a convention with the Emperor under which French troops were withdrawn from Italy and hostilities there ceased, Louis could not exert decisive pressure on the Emperor. But the way of strengthening his hand for negotiations with Britain and even more the Dutch was by recovering parts of the Spanish Netherlands, and especially cities which featured in the Barrier demanded by the Dutch. He expected his extremely large army to fight at least a drawn battle with the allies, to prove to them that they could not win decisively in the Low Countries. And the retaking of cities and fortresses would show the Dutch – whom French diplomats continued to rate as the weak link among the allies – that a continuation of the war could only reduce, not improve, their chances of gaining a full and effective Barrier.

Initially Marlborough thought that Ath, the most advanced and exposed allied fortress, was to be the French target. Although he calculated that without Eugène's troops his army would be insufficiently strong to prevent it being invested he made the decision to engage the enemy if any opportunity could be created. When the French moved forward it was to threaten Brussels, but Marlborough had no difficulty in blocking them. However his inferiority in cavalry prevented him making a bold forward move himself: June therefore proved to be a lost month, with nothing positive achieved. Only on the 29th had sufficient troops assembled at Koblenz for Eugène to begin his march to join Marlborough, and only when he arrived could the allies impose themselves on the enemy. Marlborough proposed to begin with a siege of Charleroi, on the Sambre, in order to confront the French with some difficult decisions. If they declined to give battle in order to relieve Charleroi he would then be in a position to follow with another siege, either Mons to the west, or Namur to the east: the capture of these three fortresses, or any two of them, would prise open an invasion route into France.[41]

However it was Marlborough who had to react to moves by his opponents, which began at a time when Eugène's infantry were still several days march away, but the general himself had joined him. The daring French initiative took the allies completely by surprise. It was worked out only a few days before it began, by Burgundy and Vendôme in the field, acting on the discretionary powers given them by Louis, and largely as a result of the promptings of Bergeyck, Philip's chief minister in the Spanish Netherlands.[42] The main French army broke camp late in the evening of 4 July: Marlborough followed in pursuit the next morning but he did not overtake them. Not only did the French enjoy a ten-hour start but their organisation of the march showed a marked improvement over their performance in earlier campaigns. They moved quickly north, keeping out of Marlborough's reach whereas in previous periods of forced marches he had usually been able to capture numbers of stragglers.

Marlborough at first concluded that this was yet another move to threaten Brussels, but he quickly became aware that he faced a new and much greater challenge. As he marched in pursuit a separate French army coming from the west appeared before Bruges and was immediately admitted into the city. A second force escorted Bergeyck to Ghent which

[41] Snyder, vol. II, pp. 986, 1014. T'Hoff, pp. 387–8.
[42] Vault and Pelet, vol. VIII, pp. 10, 24.

was promptly surrendered to him by his network of associates. By their march north the main French forces were able to cover both cities, and the way both had fallen without resistance made Marlborough fear, with reason, that there were similarly subversive groups in all the other major cities: Bergeyck's associates who opened the gates to the French were officers in garrison units who had come over to the allies after Ramillies and accepted Karl's sovereignty, but the townspeople had actively supported their action. As Marlborough told Heinsius, 'we have lost the hearts of all the people', and consequently he was deprived of the option of reinforcing his army by drawing on men from existing garrisons: these had to remain on full alert against internal subversion.[43]

Unless quickly rectified these defections threatened to sour Anglo-Dutch relations. Contemporary English politicians, whose harsh judgements have generally been echoed by British historians, blamed Dutch extortion and cupidity for the alienation of the local elites and the urban populations. The reasons were more complex. The provinces and cities had had no alternative in 1700–1 but to accept Philip V, but they soon became aware that though his administration might appear to follow traditional forms it was being worked in the French fashion. As he showed in Spain throughout his reign Philip aimed at centralising control over administration, overriding provincial and urban privileges. In June 1702, as the war began, he instituted a royal council for the Spanish Netherlands which instituted new taxes and conscripted men, animals and supplies. Those who protested were repressed as allied sympathisers. The government also gratuitously imitated Louis's crusade against the Jansenists. By 1706 Philip's government had made itself detested, and

43 Ibid., vol. VIII, p. 24. Snyder, vol. II, pp. 990, 1022–4. T'Hoff, p. 395. *Historical Manuscripts Commission, Portland*, vol. IX, pp. 216–17.

Marlborough recognised its errors when he promised that the allies and Karl would confirm and respect their privileges. But although Marlborough repeatedly drew the attention of the Dutch deputies charged with supervising the local administration to his guarantees, the increasing necessities of war prevented their being meticulously observed. By 1708 the Dutch were nearing the exhaustion of their own resources and this led the deputies to try to offload as much as they could of the costs of operations on to Brabant and Flanders. They spent as little as possible locally, whereas the British pumped money back into the economy in purchasing supplies and services. Furthermore the Dutch war aim of a Barrier, which included control over the administration of its fortresses, created a prospect that the Dutch would remain as a permanent occupying power.[44]

Militarily the defection of Ghent and Bruges put the allied army in a difficult situation. These cities stood across its lines of communication with Ostend, which became dangerously isolated. Supplies from England would have again to travel via Rotterdam, Willemstadt or Antwerp. Allied river transport could no longer use the Scheldt or Lys. The most westerly conquests of 1706 – Menen, Kortrijk and Oudenarde – now formed a vulnerable salient. By contrast the French occupied a strong defensive line with good communications, and could now threaten Brussels from the north. On 9 July they seemed to be taking the first step towards exploiting their advantages by sending detachments forward as a preliminary to an investment of Oudenarde, most of which lies on the north bank of the Scheldt, so as to consolidate their defences.

Marlborough stationed his army in a covering position at

[44] J. Lefevre, 'De Zuidelijke Nederlanden 1700–1748', in *Algemene Geschiedenis der Nederlanden* (12 vols., 1954), vol. VII, pp. 164–9.

Asse, having wrongly thought that the French threat was to Brussels. He was ill on the 8th, probably an instance of the stress-induced or psychosomatic disability which affected him when things were going wrong. He quickly recovered: all his decisions and movements in the following days were purposeful and decisive, in contrast to the leisurely way in which the French commanders acted after their coup. Marlborough ordered Cadogan to cross the Dender at Lessines on the 9th, a first move into the territory between that river and the Scheldt: the French were in the same area, but further north. Since Cadogan might be attacked by them Marlborough ordered him to fortify a bridgehead, but the French did not move and seem to have failed to see that Marlborough might be about to move his main army across the Dender, which would make any attempt to invest Oudenarde impracticable. Instead on the 10th the French army moved to Gavere and camped, ready to cross to the west bank of the Scheldt on the following day. Burgundy's intention was to observe Oudenarde from high ground to the north while an advance guard continued westwards to initiate a siege of Menen, closer to the main French bases and magazines.[45]

Marlborough now saw a chance to force the French to give battle. Nothing in his entire career illustrates more clearly his central military principle, that wars can only be won by forcing decisive set-piece battles, than the rapidly executed moves that enabled him to precipitate a general engagement at Oudenarde on 11 July 1708. First his plan involved marching his army more than sixteen miles before they could engage, whereas the distance from the French camp at Gavere to the likely field of battle was only just over six. This made

---

[45] Vault and Pelet, vol. VIII, pp. 28–9, 31. Snyder, vol. II, p. 1023.

him despatch Cadogan with the advance guard at 0100 hours, which meant a day of twenty hours marching and then fighting. The whole army followed in column along ways which had in places first to be made passable: there was (and is) no direct road and the middle section is hilly and tortuous. At the end of the main march bridges had to be thrown across the Scheldt; the pontoons had to be provided. There were two bridges in Oudenarde itself, but the town and its gates would act as a bottle-neck for marching troops, and one of them collapsed during the day. The five pontoon bridges were not complete until noon, just in time for the main units to cross. The French had also to build pontoon bridges to cross the Scheldt downstream at Gavere, but they did this without any sense of urgency and the main army did not start to move until 1000 hours: on a day when everything depended on the clock Marlborough could not have depended on being given this advantage.

Nor could Marlborough have counted on the dissensions and indecision that marked the French leadership on the day, and were to persist during the remainder of the campaign. Had the French advanced briskly early in the day, as soon as they knew that allied units were crossing the river in strength, it must be doubtful whether they could have been deployed in formation in time to withstand an attack. With a river at their backs the first units to arrive could find themselves in a precarious situation; an orderly retirement would not have been easy with only pontoon bridges and the gates of the town available.

The French were gravely weakened by the incompatibility of their two commanding generals. Vendôme was a crude and abusive fighting man, an inspiration to hard-pressed soldiers but overconfident and impetuous. The fact that he was coupled with Burgundy was a reflection of the prestige and glory which were now attached to their opponents,

Marlborough and Eugène. In his last two wars Louis, who never went into action except in semi-symbolic fashion during the concluding stages of sieges in 1666–7, saw the need to involve princes of the blood in order to embody and uphold the honour and glory of the House of Bourbon. Originally the purpose was to counter the greater honour and respect which William III had earned from even his French opponents. After 1702 it was to counter the prestige won by Marlborough, Eugène and Karl XII. The Dauphin, little more than an idle slob, was no use for this purpose, but his eldest son Burgundy had an outstanding personality and many at Versailles were beginning to pin on him their hopes for the future. He had been nominally in command, but really under the tutorship of Boufflers, in 1702. Now his determination to play more than a nominal role led him to dispute decisions with Vendôme, despite the latter's great experience. Junior staff officers, seeing in Burgundy their future sovereign and his grandfather's favourite grandson, followed his lead for the sake of their future careers.

Burgundy had serious defects as a field commander. He had a violent temper and excessive confidence in his own abilities. His sense of his own importance naturally followed from the place which God had given him as heir but one to the throne of France. To compromise, as Marlborough, like William before him, had to do frequently, went against his sense of personal honour and dignity. He would not admit to weaknesses or mistakes. These greatly facilitated Marlborough's task. Burgundy had already rejected Vendôme's proposal for a lightning attack on Oudenarde. He failed to reconnoitre the ground on which the battle would be fought, and had not monitored Marlborough's movements or the strength of his forces. As he moved on to the high ground north of the town he seems to have had no idea of the rapid, hourly approach of the whole of the allied army. Worse was to come during the battle. At its crisis point he failed, and this may have been a refusal, to respond to Vendôme's urgent call to launch a general attack in order to relieve allied pressure on the French centre-left. This led to disaster. And when the battle was going badly wrong Burgundy, supported by all the other generals present, rejected all of a succession of proposals made by Vendôme to try to retrieve the situation. By the end of the day the frustrated if fearless Vendôme was openly subjecting the colleague who might become his future sovereign to obscene insults.[46]

A minor disadvantage for the French was the presence on Burgundy's staff of a hostage to fortune, James III, the Old Pretender. He was there for no particular reason, except for the possibility that some prestige might trickle down to him, but his death or, even worse, capture would have deprived Louis of a valuable bargaining counter. Burgundy's younger brother Berri was also present at what proved to be a major defeat. Consequently an English woodcut was able derisively to depict the three royals in an ignominious light, first sheltering from the fight in a church tower, and then fleeing for their lives. Even though French propaganda concealed the full extent of the defeat, Oudenarde did not increase the prestige of the Bourbons.

Vendôme made two critical early mistakes. Not realising that Marlborough intended to move his whole army across the Scheldt, he did not intervene when a staff officer on the spot countermanded his initial orders that the first allied troops to deploy should be attacked immediately by the French advance guard. Then he did not try to persuade Burgundy to depart from the route to the north of Oudenarde along which it had earlier been agreed that they should deploy. This positioned them over a mile from the line along

---

[46] Vault and Pelet, vol. VIII, pp. 34–5. Snyder, vol. II, p. 1067.

which the allied units deployed, that is too far away for them to interfere or disrupt the process. Some of Burgundy's units were to remain there throughout and did no more than observe the battle that developed.[47]

The fact that the battle was not really joined until as late as 1500 hours is further evidence of Marlborough's determination not to neglect any opportunity to make the French face him in battle, but even at this late time much (perhaps as much as a half) of his army had not yet crossed the Scheldt. First Cadogan with the advance guard attacked on the far allied right, virtually annihilating the most forward enemy forces, mostly Swiss in French service. Then the Hanoverian cavalry charged, broke and dispersed Biron's cavalry who threatened to counter-attack Cadogan: among those participating was the future king George II, then electoral prince, who had a horse shot under him. These initial successes significantly retarded the exertion of pressure on the allied right, the most vulnerable sector because nearest to the point at which French reinforcements were arriving all the time.

There then ensued what can best be described as an encounter battle, with units on both sides being thrown into the conflict as they arrived. The allied success depended largely on Marlborough's judgement in distributing new units as they arrived across the pontoon bridges or via Oudenarde to the points at which they were most needed. He had in a constantly changing situation to balance the entirely different needs of the two sectors into which the allied army effectively divided. On the allied right, where Eugène commanded, the task was to hold back Vendôme's superior numbers, constantly reinforced as they were by freshly arrived reinforcements. On the allied left, where Overkirk

[47] Snyder, vol. II, p. 1024. Churchill, *Marlborough*, vol. III, pp. 405–32. Chandler (ed.), *Military Memoirs*, pp. 72–5.

commanded, Marlborough beyond keeping up pressure on the French opposite was intent on building up a strike force in maximum strength. As always aiming at the destruction of the enemy army his tactic was to out-flank the whole enemy position on the allied left, and then move in to encircle the enemy centre as well.

Marlborough had the advantage of being able through his staff officers to control and distribute the flow of units, but he could not overcome the difficulty that those crossing the Scheldt by the two Oudenarde bridges (and one then collapsed) moved much more slowly. In addition the men who had marched sixteen miles and had another one to go before they reached the front were fatigued, while the French infantry had had comparatively short distances to cover. As Vendôme received fresh troops Marlborough faced a recurring danger that the French would establish a numerical superiority sufficient to push back the allied centre and right. Some extremely fierce hand to hand fighting ensued, with Eugène only barely able to hold his own. That he did was partly due to a 'death charge' by the Prussian cavalry under Natzmer. They suffered virtual annihilation in an attack against heavy odds, but unlike similar charges such as those by the French at Reichshoffen and Sedan in 1870 this one achieved its objective and justified the sacrifice of men. It disorganised the main French cavalry force, preventing it from joining effectively in the mass attack on the allied right for which Vendôme called.

Vendôme's attempt to launch all French units present into an overpowering, concerted assault provoked the central crisis of the battle. By then all French forces had reached the battlefield, or its immediate vicinity, but allied units were continuing to arrive, and some were only approaching the bridges. The French response to Vendôme's call was fatally mixed. While a ferocious mêlée developed on the right and right-centre of the allied line, which almost broke in places, Burgundy would not participate in the assault, for no known or even conjectured reason. It was equally damaging that he did not inform Vendôme that this would be so, and once the mêlée became extended along the front the latter became personally involved in the struggle and lost contact with the other generals.

The danger of the French defeating the allied centre forced Marlborough to make a major modification in his planned dispositions. He had to send twenty battalions, under Lottum, to its aid, units that he had originally intended to form the bulk of the force which was to out-flank the enemy on the extreme left. The detachment of this substantial force and the approach of darkness made Marlborough scale down this out-flanking manoeuvre. He sent in a relatively small force of eight battalions, under Week, to carry out a much less wide-ranging movement, but one that contributed to the general confusion which affected the enemy as it became apparent that the assault on the allied centre had not succeeded. The French had now no alternative but to retreat as best they could and in the gathering dusk the generals lost all control over their units. Later Vendôme claimed that if his colleagues had supported him he could have held his ground in order to renew the battle on the next day, but in the last hours of the engagement he did not have the ability to command any units except those in his personal vicinity.

Although Marlborough had to scale down his out-flanking movement only the darkness saved the French right and part of their centre from annihilation. Their casualties were heavy: they left behind about as many (7,000) killed and wounded as the allies lost, but also about as many extra in prisoners. The effects in morale were very considerable: the allies regained all their former triumphant confidence, the French infantry so obviously flinched from the prospect of another battle of this intensity that their generals feared they could not be relied upon. Marlborough commented with satisfaction on 'the terror that is in their army', and among the French generals dissensions continued to rage.[48]

Marlborough received unhelpful advice from Godolphin as to how the victory should be followed up. He suggested that the attack on Toulon should be repeated, that a siege of Dunkirk should be organised, or that Marlborough should invest Lille while Eugène besieged Douai. None of these suggestions were practicable. An attack on Toulon could not be improvised and autumn was not an appropriate season with no grass for the horses: the Emperor and the duke of Savoy would have to be consulted and approve. Dunkirk, as Marlborough explained, was covered by Nieuport and Ypres and its approaches could be inundated. Nor was the allied army sufficiently strong to undertake two major sieges simultaneously.[49]

Only one of Godolphin's suggestions resulted in action being taken. However his idea of an invasion of northern France from the sea has received more serious consideration from Winston Churchill and other historians than it did from Marlborough at the time. The advantage of the plan was that all the major French fortresses would be by-passed: the campaign would become one of movement over open country and the fact that the battlefields of Agincourt and Crécy lay in this area showed the practicality of this part of the scheme. Another advantage was that although the infantry, artillery and supplies would be landed from the fleet it would not be necessary to undertake the difficult and time-consuming task of providing horse transports: cavalry would be provided from Marlborough's army who would come

---

[48] Snyder, vol. II, pp. 1026, 1027, 1037.   [49] Ibid., vol. II, pp. 1028, 1029, 1037.

overland in a body through French-held territory, no difficult operation. The centre-point of the plan, the seizure and fortification of a port to act as base, presented difficulties. English medieval armies had the use of Calais with its accessible harbour and magazines, but both Calais and Boulogne were strongly fortified and would require a prolonged siege. Consequently the weakest aspect of the scheme was its reliance on using the small harbour of St Valery-sur-Somme for the landing of supplies, with magazines being established in Abbeville, twelve miles inland.

There was no chance of attempting a large-scale combined operation. Not surprisingly, in view of his reluctance to attack Toulon in 1707, Eugène was opposed. The Dutch were anxious about any move which would weaken the security of their frontiers – and the French still held Bruges and Ghent. Marlborough's attitudes showed that he did not see the invasion project as the key to unlocking the defences of northern France, although it must be added that when in 1710 a new project promised to give the allies Calais, without resistance, he became enthusiastic. However by then the allies had made serious inroads into the French fortress defences.

Marlborough's reservations were confirmed by the abject failure of the attempted descent. He expressed doubts when it was decided in London to go ahead on a small scale, landing eight battalions to take Abbeville and being joined there by cavalry riding through the French lines. On reconsideration he decided that he could not spare the cavalry and ordered cancellation of the operation. His orders came too late to prevent an attempt being made but the operation ended in total fiasco. As should have been known the Somme estuary, with a narrow, tortuous navigable channel, was unsuitable and the pilots refused to enter tidal waters. Subsequently the fleet and transports staged an ineffective demonstration along the Normandy coast. Marlborough commented acidly that if the commanders were deterred from landing anywhere by French militia then descents would achieve nothing. Fortunately he was able to secure the return of the infantry to Ostend, to play a vital role in the rest of the campaign.[50]

In the view of both contemporary critics and many historians the main exploitation of the victory at Oudenarde took a depressingly conventional form, a major, prolonged and extremely expensive siege of Lille. It began on 13 August, with the city surrendering on 22 October, but the citadel held out until 9 December. Throughout these months the allied armies were pinned down: while one force prosecuted the siege another had the task of holding off the main French army which tried to relieve the defenders, and also protect long and vulnerable lines of communication.

The siege of Lille proved to be the most hard-fought and complex of all set-piece actions during the war, and the most expensive in terms of human lives with the possible exception of Malplaquet.[51] Its horrors and heavy casualties provoked contemporary criticism, and twentieth-century historians have been influenced by its strong resemblances to the similarly expensive offensives of 1915–18 on the western front. Marlborough and Eugène were concentrating their power against what was probably the strongest fortress in the world, the masterpiece of Vauban's military architecture, commanded by Boufflers the veteran specialist in fortress defence, and garrisoned by an exceptionally strong force of 16,000 men, few of whom had shared in the demoralising experience of Oudenarde.

For most of the time the siege was directed by Eugène, but

[50] Ibid., vol. II, pp. 1040–1, 1049 and note, 1050–1, 1058, 1066, 1068, 1086, 1089.
[51] Ibid., vol. II, pp. 1037, 1058 passim. Churchill, Marlborough, vol. III, pp. 483–501, 518–19, 528–9.

when he was wounded the work had to be taken over by Marlborough, the first time he had taken responsibility for the detailed prosecution of a major siege. During the first phase Eugène concentrated on the circumvallation and assault work, that is looking inwards towards the defences, while Marlborough had charge of the contravallation, the outward-facing defences against repeated French attempts at relief and reprovisioning. These latter enemy efforts posed very great problems for Marlborough. Immediately after Oudenarde Louis ordered Burgundy to hold on to Ghent but not to risk another battle, but when Berwick's forces joined up with him the French again enjoyed considerable superiority in numbers. As the pressure on Lille increased Louis gave Burgundy authority to engage, and French cavalry incursions began to threaten the allied lines of supply. By holding Ghent the French denied Marlborough the use of the rivers leading to the neighbourhood of Lille. Consequently all the supplies that usually went by barge – artillery, powder in bulk, flour, timber for the siege works – had to come overland in long slow-moving convoys. The organisational effort this required was immense: the siege train of guns and mortars, with powder and shot, needed 16,000 horses and covered over fifteen miles of road. Convoys offered the French vulnerable targets. In the first phase protection could be given by the main armies, but once the siege began Marlborough had a series of difficult decisions to make about the size of the detachments he could afford to allocate to convoy escort, and the minimum force which was needed to prevent Burgundy relieving Lille.[52]

The logistical problems were aggravated by the initially low stocks which the besieging army possessed, and the extremely high level of expenditure of powder by the

[52] Snyder, vol. II, pp. 1033–4, 1042, 1058, 1140.

artillery. Throughout the siege the allies' supplies were sufficient for only a few days more, so that the loss or even delay of a convoy would have caused a critical hiatus in the siege or even necessitated its being lifted. In late September supplies had to be sent direct from England, via Ostend, although the route from there to Lille was even more vulnerable than the ordinary way from Brussels. The French made a major effort to intercept the convoy, whose escort consisted of the infantry that had earlier been embarked for the descent: they were commanded by major-general Webb who was not a member of the inner group of Marlborough's military associates. To increase the escort Marlborough sent troops under Cadogan, who was probably the officer most in his confidence. The French made a clumsy attack in great strength only to be totally routed by Webb (Wijnendale, 28 September), and the convoy got through unscathed. This brilliant victory had a damaging and ominous sequel. The first despatch announcing the victory appeared to give the credit to Cadogan. Webb was bitterly resentful and his cause was taken up by a number of other generals and colonels who were beginning to feel neglected. A rancorous dispute followed (echoed in Thackeray's *Henry Esmond*) which provided an early indication of the jealousies and factionalism that were developing in the army. In addition Webb became the Tory hero and with their encouragement his intransigence increased.[53]

Marlborough had one very considerable but hidden advantage in performing the vital task of covering the main French army: the low morale of the French infantry which greatly discouraged their generals and added to the endless disputes and dissensions between them. Berwick's arrival actually aggravated these tensions: he consistently disagreed

[53] *Ibid.*, vol. II, pp. 1104, 1106, 1116, 1175. Churchill, *Marlborough*, vol. III, pp. 502–19. J. J. Cartwright, *The Wentworth Papers* (1883), p. 69.

with Vendôme and, subject to conflicting advice, Burgundy hesitated before committing his army. Once his artillery arrived he moved to within five miles of the siege works and into direct confrontation with Marlborough's covering force. Between 5 and 11 September the two armies faced each other and although initially reluctant to entrench his troops in the presence of the enemy – something he had never done before – Marlborough had to compensate for his inferiority in numbers. He therefore constructed field works for his centre, while deliberately and demonstratively he left the ground open on each flank so as to give himself space in which to counter-attack. With artillery in place these defences became increasingly formidable as the French generals discussed whether an attack was practicable. Marlborough's show of confidence was not a bluff: he later confided to his wife that he would have inflicted a decisive defeat if the French had attacked, despite their outnumbering him by two to one.

The French were deterred. They had to decide whether to attack a general and an army that had defeated them three times in four years, and on ground entirely of Marlborough's choosing. They had too many generals who gave Burgundy varied and discordant advice. He was perhaps understandably reluctant to take a decision that could lead to the destruction of the army, the loss of Lille and an ignominious end to the war on allied terms. He therefore referred the issue back to Louis at Versailles. The king renewed his instructions to attack Marlborough, but as an insurance and in case the situation had changed sent Chamillart, the minister of war, to take the orders and see the situation for himself. Seeing how strongly entrenched was Marlborough's position, and how divided the French leadership, Chamillart agreed with Burgundy that an attack would probably fail: he authorised a retirement to Tournai. Consequently the confrontation between Marlborough's section of the allied army and the entire French field force ended without more than a desultory artillery duel. Marlborough had simply checkmated his opponents.[54]

Fortunately for the allies the French retired before Eugène was put out of action by a serious wound. This left Marlborough with responsibility for directing as well as covering the siege. He had to be on constant guard against a succession of enemy enterprises. The most daring prolonged the defence of the city: French cavalry carried 60,000 pounds of powder in their saddle-bags in a dash through the allied lines, although at the cost of heavy casualties. Vendôme moved to threaten the allied lines of communication, but had to withdraw when his colleagues declined to stand to fight a major battle (3 October). A more elaborate set of manoeuvres in the last week of that month collapsed: the elector of Bavaria appeared before Brussels on 22 October, with a siege train. Marlborough's intelligence system had warned him of the move, enabling him to plan counter-measures effectively. Vendôme was intended to block the line of the Scheldt, to prevent Marlborough marching to relieve Brussels, but he had already selected four points at which the allies could force their way across. They drove off and dispersed Vendôme's detachments, and then moved rapidly to the relief of Brussels. When Marlborough's first units came up the elector decamped hastily, leaving behind his artillery and abandoning his wounded.[55]

Although Marlborough's foresight and detailed staff work enabled him to overcome his difficulties, political animosities at home now reached such venomous extremes that opponents of the administration gloated over exaggerated reports of his problems. One of Harley's intimates described

Marlborough as 'our distressed general', and prophesied that either his army would be surrounded and destroyed, or that at least he would be forced to raise the siege. Privately Marlborough found much to criticise in the conduct of the siege by the engineers, but the unavoidable difficulty was that the siege of Lille, like that of Tournai in 1709, saw what was probably the most brutally intensive fighting of the entire eighteenth century. The comparatively small number of British units that were directly involved lost 30% of their effectives. As in the Flanders fighting of 1917 daily progress could be measured in yards and at fearful cost.

The French defence, ably directed by Boufflers, received valuable assistance from the townspeople and their militia, who had been wrongly expected by the allies to be prepared to welcome liberation from French rule, which had lasted since 1668. At one stage when faced with pessimistic reports from his engineers Marlborough feared that he might have to order a general assault to storm the city. Not only would this have meant heavy losses, but there would be a strong likelihood that maddened by their casualties the soldiers would go berserk (as Wellington's did in Badajoz) and indulge in a sack recalling the atrocities of the Thirty Years War. The length of the operation until the city fell on 22 October, and the citadel on 9 December, imposed greater strains on Marlborough personally than any other campaign, because he was under constant, daily pressure. The strains showed in tensions with Dutch colleagues, some of whom he suspected of embezzling stores and so causing delays, and in deteriorating relations with some of his own officers.[56]

Marlborough, though, had the resilience to insist that the surrender of the citadel did not mean the end of the

---

[56] Snyder, vol. II, pp. 1137–47, 1152. Historical Manuscripts Commission, Portland, vol. IV, pp. 503, 505–6, 508–9.

campaign. He was determined to recover Ghent and Bruges, 'let it cost what it will', although it was already far later in the year than the usual time to go into winter quarters. This decision was a surprise to the French who had exaggerated Marlborough's losses at Oudenarde and Lille, and thought Ghent and Bruges safe for the winter.

A winter campaign demanded careful planning. The cavalry and all draught animals would be entirely dependent on dry forage provided for them. Sharp falls in temperature in mid-December threatened to freeze the rivers and canals immobilising all barges, and make it virtually impossible to dig trenches and earthworks for batteries, whereas the defenders would have existing masonry fortifications, and housing in cities. Marlborough's soldiers could not be expected to survive in bivouacs; he began building huts for them. But it would turn into a real test of endurance if, as expected, the sieges lasted into the spring meaning that the campaign would run without a pause for rest and reorganisation for an entire year. It was agreed that Marlborough should continue to command through January and February, with Eugène taking over for March and April to enable him to make a brief visit to London.

Superior logistical skills and organisation enabled the allies to overcome their difficulties, whereas growing French weaknesses rendered abortive a number of projects (such as a lightning strike at Lille, whose defences were of course in ruins). By 30 December the batteries were ready to fire on Ghent. Although he had orders to defend it to the last the irresolute French commanding officer, la Motte, who had lost the battle of Wijnendale, then agreed to surrender on 2 January unless relieved before then, and he knew that the French army could not even attempt this. His surrender led to a simultaneous evacuation of Bruges. This collapse can be attributed to general demoralisation in the French ranks: the defences were still intact and the garrisons had sufficient supplies.[57]

For the French there was far, far worse to come. This series of defeats was followed by a natural catastrophe. The onset in mid-January of probably the coldest winter weather in Europe during modern times, which would have forced Marlborough to abandon the sieges and put his army in great difficulties, devastated the French nation. It brought famine, disorganisation and despair to most of Louis's subjects. The prolonged arctic cold caused a rising tide of deaths and conditions were at their worst in the northern provinces, the rear areas of the French armies where the billeting of troops and the exactions of the combatants had exhausted supplies of foodstuffs. France suffered far more severely than neighbouring countries, largely because of the stresses and poverty caused by years of merciless levying of taxes, and Louis could not evade responsibility for imposing intolerable burdens on his people. By the time a sadly belated spring in 1709 permitted the renewal of campaigning it seemed possible not only that French military resistance could be finally overcome, but that the French state could be pushed to the point of collapse.

Ironically the bitter winter and the famine which it caused, bringing the French economy and society to the brink of collapse, proved to be the main factor that prevented Marlborough and Eugène from waging the continuously aggressive campaign that was necessary in 1709 if Louis was to be forced to capitulate. This campaign is remembered for Malplaquet, the biggest, bloodiest and most controversial of all Marlborough's battles. But Malplaquet was fought as late as 11 September, and even if allied losses had been less

---

[57] Vault and Pelet, vol. VIII, pp. 153, 155, 157–8, 159. Snyder, vol. II, pp. 1159, 1164, 1165–6, 1167–8, 1170, 1174, 1176, 1180, 1181–2, 1184–5.

crippling it is doubtful that their logistical problems could have been sufficiently overcome to support a full-scale invasion of France that autumn.[58]

The campaign of 1709 was the least characteristic of all Marlborough's campaigns. It unavoidably started very late, and with a major, prolonged siege, that of Tournai. This was forced on him by the aftermath of the arctic weather of the previous winter. Stores of provisions were below normal. Even the harshest requisitioning and exaction of contributions from enemy territories could not be expected to produce much at a time when, as Marlborough himself observed, half the population of the villages had died from starvation or its effects. In addition the French *intendants* had ordered people from the indefensible countryside to move into the fortified towns (with their animals, if any still lived). Throughout the Low Countries and northern France the new grass, seared by the abnormally severe and prolonged frosts, grew slowly and there would be insufficient grazing to support cavalry and draught horses. If the army was launched into a penetrative invasion of northern France it would have to carry its own provisions and most of its forage with it.[59]

As in previous years the French initially possessed numerical superiority, partly because desertion rates during the harsh winter had been far lower than usual: winter quarters had at least ensured survival whereas going off on one's own meant a risk of death from cold or starvation, and few people still had much to steal and loot. It was in many ways a ragged army, like the Confederate army in 1864–5. Defects and losses in equipment had not been rectified, partly because Louis did not have the money to pay contractors. Marlborough quickly realised its weaknesses but he and

---

[58] Pierre Goubert, *Louis XIV and Twenty Million Frenchmen* (1970), pp. 256–61. Francois Bluche, *Louis XIV* (Paris, 1986), pp. 787–93.
[59] Snyder, vol. III, pp. 1268, 1272–3, 1278. T'Hoff, pp. 435, 437.

Eugène had to rule out a major battle until the late summer. Although commanded by Villars and Boufflers, notably aggressive generals, the French remained on the defensive behind a series of carefully prepared lines.[60]

The outcome was an allied decision to begin the campaign with a siege or sieges, in the full realisation that the taking of two or three fortresses would be insufficient to persuade Louis to agree to peace on allied terms. This was because of the excessive harshness of the conditions which the Dutch, acting on behalf of the other allies, were now demanding – including the clause (xxxvii) by which Louis would be obliged to expel Philip by force of arms if he refused to give up Spain and all its possessions. Privately Marlborough, and even Eugène, disapproved of the totally intransigent way in which the allied negotiators had handled the terms. The former said that if he was in Louis's place he would certainly refuse to expel his grandson.[61]

The French rejections of the terms, and both the Emperor and the Whigs were certain to continue to insist on clause xxxvii, meant that peace could now be achieved only if Villars's army was destroyed. But the effects of the winter weather forced a postponement of the pursuit of an aggressive strategy specifically designed to produce the kind of set-piece battle, on the largest scale, which was essential to coerce Louis into conceding the full allied demands. Most of the summer had to be spent in what in strategic terms was a form of marking time until conditions were (literally) ripe for the precipitation of what hopefully would be the decisive battle to end the war.

Marlborough's own preference was for a siege of Ypres, a place then (as in 1914–18) of great strategic significance. However this aroused Dutch jealousies. They feared it would

[60] Snyder, vol. III, pp. 1266, 1280, 1291. T'Hoff, pp. 434, 437. Sturgill, *Villars*, pp. 89–91.   [61] T'Hoff, pp. 439, 445.

be followed by an attack on Dunkirk, which Godolphin had advocated in 1708, and that the port would be permanently retained as a British possession (as in 1658–62), to act as a counter-weight to the Dutch Barrier. For political reasons, then, Marlborough agreed to Eugène's preference for Tournai as the target. This was probably a mistake: after the capture of Lille its strategic value was reduced. However, in preliminary manoeuvres Marlborough made a feint towards Ypres, deceiving the French into reinforcing the garrison whereas the defenders of Tournai were under strength when the investment began on 27 June. However they made a ferocious and prolonged resistance; the town surrendered on 29 July but the citadel held out until 5 September, and the allies suffered heavy losses, particularly in the underground warfare of tunnels and mining. Constant rain also impeded the progress of the siege, in which previous roles were reversed. This time Marlborough directed the siege, while Eugène commanded the covering force: this interchange of functions testified to the strength of their partnership and the mutual confidence between them.[62]

Having lost so much time in the siege of Tournai the allied generals were eager to force the issue, moving quickly – apparently to invest Mons, but in the hope really of precipitating a final, decisive battle. Villars and Boufflers were now equally prepared to fight. During the summer Villars had uncharacteristically but wisely restricted himself to a defensive strategy, building and manning virtually unassailable lines. During the summer he had restored the morale and efficiency of his officers and men to the point where a defensive battle could be ventured with the aim of proving that France was not defeated.[63]

[62] Snyder, vol. III, pp. 1285–6, 1307, 1310, 1322–3, 1331, 1351.
[63] Sturgill, *Villars*, pp. 81–9.

The failure of Marlborough and Eugène to achieve at Malplaquet a final and decisive victory has been used to query the validity of their strategy, but on balance a battle-seeking strategy was still valid and achievable. First there is the objection that it was too late in the year to fight a major engagement. But the experience of 1708 showed that exploitation of a victory could continue into the winter: good organisation could support the successful siege of sufficient fortresses to create an irreparable gap in the essential defences covering France, so that Louis would have to see that an invasion in 1710 could not be resisted effectively.

Secondly a set-piece action against Villars in a defensive position was bound to be expensive in casualties, and critics then and since emphasise the fact that Malplaquet was by far the bloodiest battle of the entire eighteenth century. But the allies knew this and were prepared to pay a heavy cost in casualties in order to destroy the French army. Heavy losses among the enemy's officer corps could not now, after so many defeats, be fully recovered. Conscription provided raw recruits in great numbers every year, but without exper-ienced officers and NCOs an army capable of fighting another set-piece battle in 1710 could not be reconstituted. In this sense the army commanded by Villars was the last army of France, like that of MacMahon at Sedan in 1870, the last professional or regular force able to defend the country and ultimately Paris itself. As a last resort, in the event of the army being defeated, Louis considered putting himself at the head of whatever forces could be collected in order to bar the allied advance, but an army consisting mostly of militia would have been as militarily ineffective as Gambetta's levies in 1870−1.[64]

---

[64] Snyder, vol. III, p. 1282. T'Hoff, p. 441.

Marlborough and Eugène in imposing a battle at Malplaquet did not expect to produce a final victory in 1709 – it was
too late in the campaigning season – but to convince Louis
that he must make peace during the winter on allied terms
because he would have lost the capacity to resist an allied
invasion in 1710. However signs that allied demands were
likely to increase was one reason why in fact Louis was
determined to go on fighting even if Villars had been totally
defeated. The integrity of France itself was coming into
question. Some allied ministers were talking of recovering
Alsace or of restoring the frontiers of 1659 or even 1648.
Whigs favoured a restoration of Huguenot privileges with
external guarantors. There was even a suggestion of converting France into a pacific state by reducing its sovereign to
dependence on the States General and the Parlements, a move
that was being canvassed by some critics of Louis. It should be
noted that such sweeping war aims were not unique at that
time. Major sieges and set-piece battles had entirely reversed
the power relationship between the Ottoman Empire and the
House of Austria. Like Marlborough and Eugène Karl XII also
followed a strategy based on forcing and winning major
battles, in order to achieve grandiose aims – the subjection of
Poland and Russia by the installation of puppet rulers in
Warsaw and Moscow.[65]

On both sides it was recognised at the time that a set-piece
battle in September 1709 would form a climax to the war. The
allies were confident of victory. By this stage of the campaign
their superiority in numbers included a massive superiority
in cavalry which made them hopeful of out-manoeuvring the
French once they began to move into more open country.
This prospect made it advantageous for Villars actually to

---

[65] Snyder, vol. III, pp. 1264–6, 1270.

challenge a battle immediately, and on ground of his choosing, before the allies advanced beyond the wooded country between Mons and Valenciennes, which offered him several good defensive positions. But Villars could not take the risk of an attack: he did not try to exploit a possible opportunity on 9 September, when he found Marlborough's section of the army camped separately and at some distance from Eugène's.[66]

Essentially it was faults in the execution of the allied battle plan that prevented Marlborough and Eugène achieving a total victory.[67] The most open question among the controversies concerning their behaviour relates to the decision, on 9 September, not to launch a general attack the next day, but to wait until the last section of the allied army arrived. This consisted of a substantial force of nineteen battalions under Withers that had been engaged at Tournai. By this postponement they gave Villars a whole extra day in which to improve his defences substantially. Such a question, whether to attack before all one's forces are ready but while the enemy's defences are incomplete, or to wait until additional forces arrive, admits of no general answer: each case depends on local circumstances and on the tactical doctrine that is being followed. The view that Marlborough and Eugène made an error is based on the fact that the troops commanded by Withers did not play an important part in the battle, when it was joined on the 11th. Originally intended to reinforce the mass assault on the French right they were switched to the other wing, to carry out an out-flanking movement around the French left but this had little effect. With the advantage of hindsight it looks as though the allies should have attacked on the 10th, but although this would probably have reduced their casualties, this is not to say that the French army could

[66] Sturgill, *Villars*, p. 93.
[67] Ibid., pp. 94–8. Churchill, *Marlborough*, vol. IV, pp. 142–78.

have been annihilated, and that was what the overall war situation demanded.

The second criticism relates to the mass attack by the Dutch infantry, at this time generally rated the best in Europe, on the exceptionally strong French position on their right. This was intended to pin down enemy forces, including elite units, and to suck in reserves from the centre – the sector in which Marlborough planned to make his decisive charge. This was the tactic that had been used with success at Blenheim and Ramillies, but the sector which the French were defending was more strongly fortified, was narrower, and above all was commanded by enfilading fire from their artillery. It was the losses in this sector, particularly, which made allied casualties so high. However yet another inevitably futile attack would have been made but for Marlborough's veto, which seems to show that his original battle plan was based on a serious underestimate of the strength of the French right.

Marlborough's problem was how to create the opportunity to make decisive use of his massive quantitative and qualitative superiority in cavalry in a battle that would have to be fought on an extremely narrow front. Unlike Blenheim and Ramillies, where the battlefield extended over several miles, the physical lay-out at Malplaquet restricted easy movement. There was a one-and-a-half-mile gap between dense woods, but this gap was bisected by a small wood and fortified the whole way across, with prepared defences extending into the bordering thickets. Marlborough and Eugène worked out a plan to mount attacks on both flanks, although they knew that there would be great difficulties in pressing them home. But these attacks were essentially subsidiary, intended to bring the enemy under pressure, cause Villars to switch troops from the centre to aid those under the initial attacks and threaten to cut off these units from the main body in the centre. But Villars would not weaken his centre unless the attacks on the flanks were made with real determination, regardless of at least their initial losses.

As at the Schellenberg, Blenheim and Ramillies Marlborough (and the plan bears the stamp of his tactical methods) accepted the certainty of heavy losses on the flanks as the price for creating a decisive local superiority in the centre. There he relied on tactical movements which had served him well in past victories. First the allied infantry would drive a hopefully weakened enemy back from his defences, which would then be dismantled. The way would then be open for the second phase, the mass attack by the cavalry. As at Blenheim this was intended to punch a hole through the enemy line, take in the rear the strongest sector of the defences (on the allied right) and push back in a disorganised mass the main body of French cavalry. In addition a very wide out-flanking move was initiated on the allied right, with cavalry sent to circle round the wood of Taisnières to appear well to the rear of the French defences. The long distance this force had to cover meant that it would arrive only some time after the enemy centre had been broken, or was breaking, so its function was clearly to pursue retreating forces and ensure a rout.

Eugène commanded the allied right, Marlborough and the prince of Orange the left. Orange had the smallest of the three forces, to undertake the hardest task: thirty-two battalions against forty-six French occupying very formidable positions. His Dutch troops attacked on a narrow front in a dense mass and were simply slaughtered. A second and equally costly assault made a few inroads, but lost them to counter-attacks. Orange wished to try a third time but Marlborough vetoed this. The French were unbroken and this part of the allied battle plan had miscarried. The allied right also suffered heavy casualties as it advanced very slowly through the wood of Taisnières, but it at least partially fulfilled its part in the overall plan. Its leading units fought their way through to the west side of the wood in sufficient strength for Villars to have to draw back men from the centre in order to prepare a counter-attack. But he had to wait until more infantry could be assembled because Eugène's men had manhandled artillery forward as they advanced through the wood. Then, just as the counter-attack was about to go in, both Villars and Albergotti, commander of this French sector, were incapacitated by serious wounds, and by the time effective command was regained the allies had become too strong to be driven back. The French left could do no more than hold back the allies from converging on the centre.

The French centre, having been weakened by the detachment of infantry to their left, and with their cavalry being retained in reserve, was overrun with relatively light allied losses. Marlborough's infantry began to dismantle the physical defences of trenches and barricades to allow the cavalry to move through and form up in rapidly increasing strength. But their first attacks beyond the former French positions were driven back by the French as far as those positions. This apparently minor success was probably crucial. It delayed the main mass of the allied cavalry, an enormous force of nearly 30,000 horse, preventing them from deploying in formation on relatively open ground until the French were ready to meet them. Instead of the kind of irresistible charge that had proved so decisive at Blenheim and Ramillies a vast mêlée ensued, very like a large-scale confrontation between masses of pikemen in the warfare of an earlier generation. Inevitably in the end sheer, literal weight of superior numbers told, and the French had to go back, but they were not broken. In addition their slow retirement gave time for both the French wings to retire in relatively good order.[68]

This fighting retreat frustrated the allied plans; although their outlines had actually been followed it had been at a literally crippling cost that prevented a systematic or ruthless attempt at pursuit – although several hours of daylight remained. Allied casualties were far heavier, both in actual numbers and as a percentage of the total strength of the army, than in any other major battle of the entire eighteenth century. Figures given at the time were approximations, but the allies were thought to have had 24,000 killed and wounded, the French something under 15,000, but only 500 prisoners. Even in an age when armies were not yet seen as embodiments of the nations, being composed mostly of foreign mercenaries and con-scripts drawn from the surplus poor of the rural areas, and the cadres of officers and NCOs came mainly from socially and economically more backward areas, these losses shocked opinion in Britain and the Dutch Republic. Though in fact British units lost less than German and Dutch ones, Marlborough's critics at home stepped up the charges that had been made during the siege of Lille, that he would willingly sacrifice lives in order to keep the war going so as to produce greater fame and more wealth for his family.[69]

On the day of Malplaquet Marlborough wrote to Godol-phin that 'if Holland pleases it is now in our power to have what peace we please'.[70] No judgement could have been more incorrect. Marlborough's army was never

---

[68] Snyder, vol. III, pp. 1377, 1381.
[69] *Historical Manuscripts Commission, Portland*, vol. IV, pp. 526–7.
[70] Snyder, vol. III, p. 1360.

again the same cohesive, confident, united and all-conquering force that he had led since 1702. Contrary to the view of his critics he felt deep personal sorrow at the deaths of officers and men who had served with him for years; he did not have the imperturbable insensitivity of Napoleon or Grant. The loss of many veterans at regimental level reduced the army's efficiency, and in the campaign of 1710 it was noticeable that many of the senior officers began to criticise his conduct of operations, and military factions began to form and make known their antagonistic opinions.

In the widest perspective it cannot be denied that Marlborough failed at Malplaquet. The French army by surviving the maximum battle that he had constantly tried to force on it, assuming that its total destruction could be achieved, made it unrealistic to persist in trying to coerce Louis into accepting the full allied peace terms. Significantly Marlborough in the course of his last two campaigns, in 1710 and 1711, did not choose to attack the opposing army on the occasions when he faced it in strongly prepared positions, and he failed to out-manoeuvre the French into having to give battle on ground of his choosing.

The last phase of the 1709 campaign can be characterised as no more than a mopping-up operation. Mons was besieged, with Eugène and Marlborough again reversing roles: the former conducted the siege while the latter commanded the covering force. Marlborough would have preferred a more aggressive move, to attack Maubeuge, further south and a portal opening up an invasion route into France. Louis clearly regarded it as more valuable, since he authorised Boufflers to risk a battle if it was attacked: this order also reveals the revival of French confidence after their achievement in surviving the allies' mass onslaught at Malplaquet. But after Mons fell, on 20 October, the campaign spluttered out, with the allied armies going into winter quarters over two months earlier than in the previous year.[71]

[71] Ibid., vol. III, pp. 1381, 1385, 1396. T'Hoff, p. 471.

Chapter 4

Power ebbs away

After Malplaquet the strategy which Marlborough and Eugène had followed lost its validity, and as a result the campaigns of 1710 and 1711 in France and the Low Countries were bound to be inconclusive. The allies after Marlborough's three victories and Eugène's expulsion of the French from Italy had concentrated on forcing the enemy to fight a major set-piece battle which they confidently expected would result in the final destruction of the main French army, and so compel Louis to accept peace on allied terms. The survival of Villars's army disproved this belief, something that Marlborough, but not Eugène, came to realise. From the autumn of 1709 it was the defensive strategy adopted by the French that became valid: Villars had only to avoid defeat in a major battle for a compromise peace settlement to become inevitable, and he had already demonstrated his ability – on the Moselle in 1705 – to checkmate the allies without having to risk one.

In the campaigns of 1710 and 1711 Marlborough executed a succession of brilliant manoeuvres to out-flank French defensive lines, and he covered a number of sieges deep in enemy territory, but he did not succeed in pinning Villars down and forcing him to fight under unfavourable conditions. When Marlborough did find himself with an option to fight a battle it was only when Villars faced him from behind defences as strong as those at Malplaquet, and no assault was attempted. Yet Villars was an aggressive general, as he was to show in the campaign of 1712 when Eugène went over to an unlimited offensive only to suffer a crushing defeat.[1]

Marlborough's failure to engage in a battle when circumstances did not favour him represented a tacit admission that he could not afford another Malplaquet and its casualties. In the early summer of 1710 it would have brought down the already crumbling Godolphin administration; after the ministerial changes of the late summer those who were now (as he knew) his political masters would not permit any risky moves, and would punish him for a bloody and inconclusive battle with instant dismissal. However during the course of the whole of 1710 there seemed to be a good (and new) reason for avoiding risks in the campaign in northern France; a renewed likelihood that the war might now be won by a new offensive campaign in Spain itself. The sticking point in the peace discussions at Geertruidenberg had been reached over the allied demands that if Philip refused to abandon his Spanish kingdom Louis should forcibly expel him. However the initial success of the allied campaign seemed to be making this demand redundant. Advancing out of Catalonia, defeating Philip first at Almenara (28 July) and then heavily before Saragossa (19 August), the generals persuaded Karl to advance on and occupy Madrid. But although this proved to be a major political and military error, as few Castilians rallied to him and the army's communications quickly became precarious, the overoptimistic view prevailed that Karl was now established in his capital.[2]

---

[1] C. C. Sturgill, *Marshal Villars and the War of the Spanish Succession* (Lexington, KY, 1965), pp. 101–5, 106–9.

[2] David Francis, *The First Peninsular War 1702–1713* (1975), pp. 306–22.

While the allies advanced in Spain Marlborough's essential task was to maintain pressure on the French so as to prevent Louis sending reinforcements to help Philip. Implicitly this for the first time made Marlborough's the subsidiary campaign. There was no further talk of winning Spain in Flanders and Picardy, and a decline in his confidence and dynamic energy can be detected. In 1710 Marlborough reached the age of sixty, and he admitted that his physical and mental stamina were diminishing, but not the stresses to which he was subject. During earlier campaigns he had tried consciously to insulate himself from the bitter political in-fighting of home politics, although he knew that this could never be done completely. But in 1710, with Anne now totally alienated and the Godolphin administration running into terminal difficulties, he became depressed by the mounting evidence that his colleagues could no longer shield him from the malice and criticism of his domestic enemies. It is noticeable that he was eager to make the most of any and every success, for example magnifying the importance of his capture of Douai (29 June) by despatches which tried to equate it with Blenheim or Ramillies.[3]

Marlborough's plan for the 1710 campaign was first to besiege Douai and then Arras: the capture of the latter would open up the way to the Channel coast, isolating and putting Boulogne and Calais within his reach. Godolphin warmed to this scheme, reviving projects for a descent, a combined operation to take the ports. This was because of the propaganda advantages; such an operation would be popular in Britain and specifically would restore the 'drooping Whigs' on whom his ministry depended.

The allied army made an early start, completing the

[3] Murray, vol. V, pp. 11, 19, 35, 39, 58, 59, 61. *Historical Manuscripts Commission, Portland*, vol. IX, pp. 229–30, 231.

investment of Douai on 28 April. But the siege took a month longer than Marlborough expected, and proved to be very expensive in casualties. Villars observed the siege from a close distance, but considered that his army was insufficiently strong to attempt its relief. On his side Marlborough's caution was reflected in the care with which he fortified his camp during the siege, something he did in all future sieges. When Douai fell he found his way to Arras blocked by Villars, who had received considerable reinforcements and occupied a formidable defensive position. Earlier Marlborough had alarmed Godolphin by writing of his hopes to bring about a new and decisive battle, but only on ground that gave him advantages, but judging that Villars was too strong to be attacked he turned instead to invest Béthune, which controlled strategically important waterways. After it fell (29 August) the allied army undertook two simultaneous sieges of the fortresses of St Venant and Aire, which were six miles apart and so could be covered by a single force. St Venant fell on 30 September, giving Marlborough a theoretical opportunity to attack Villars in the nearby position which he had occupied in order to exploit any opportunities to interfere with the siege work. He did not attack: as he frankly admitted he would not neglect any opportunity that the French gave him, but he would not take risks.[4]

Sensitive to the malicious but well-received attacks being made against his alleged arrogance and covetousness in pamphlets and news-sheets at home, Marlborough knew that politicians would load him with blame in order to justify his removal from command if operations went badly. He therefore erred on the side of caution. For example he did not commit himself to the project for an attack on Calais and Boulogne by the main army, leaving behind them such

[4] Murray, vol. v, pp. 69, 72, 83, 96, 105, 116–17, 131–2, 135, 193, 205, 221. T'Hoff, pp. 506, 519, 524.

fortresses as Arras still in French hands. The plan was for the army to be kept supplied from the sea, but this would only be possible with good weather since until one of the two ports was taken all supplies would have to be landed on open beaches or at fishing villages.[5]

The prolonged resistance by the small garrison of Aire, which fell as late as 9 November and absorbed what was left of the campaigning season, caused the abandonment of the Calais project. Consequently the achievements of the army for the year were limited to four successful sieges, Douai, Béthune, St Venant and Aire, which amounted to little more than a denting of the French defences. Marlborough could do little to speed up siege operations. The British army still did not have the organisation and personnel with the experience and technical expertise to carry out a major siege on its own, but had to rely on Dutch engineers. They were nothing if not methodical, meticulously following conventional methods. As Marlborough explained to Heinsius this systematic approach had the advantage that taking a strong place usually took only a little longer than taking a relatively weak one, but it had the disadvantage that every siege took up a significant amount of time, invariably exceeding Marlborough's calculations. The campaign of 1710 provided the clearest example of this.[6]

There is clear evidence that from the time of his return to France in the spring of 1710, that is long before the Godolphin administration began to crumble, Marlborough sought to reduce his responsibilities in order to concentrate on his military command. He greatly alarmed Godolphin by revealing his intention of ceasing to correspond personally

[5] Snyder, vol. III, pp. 1465, 1469, 1489, 1503–4, 1507, 1583, 1587, 1600, 1642, 1645, 1651.
[6] Ibid., vol. III, pp. 1567, 1644, 1648, 1655. T'Hoff, p. 513. On siege warfare see David Chandler, *The Art of Warfare in the Age of Marlborough* (1976), pp. 234–82.

and directly with allied sovereigns and their ministers, in the process winning their confidence and understanding. The reason was only partly a desire to reduce the burden of work; it was also a growing disenchantment with virtually all the allies. He was made uneasy by increasing Dutch war-weariness and driven to fury by their continuing international banking operations, which he had earlier tried to sabotage; these included the extension of credit to Louis, enabling him repeatedly to rebuild and then to sustain his armies. He was weary of the annual uncertainties of the negotiations with Prussia and the German princes for the provision of the military contingents on which he depended. Whereas earlier in the war Marlborough consistently championed the interests of Savoy, and this had paid off in the duke's active lead in the Toulon expedition of 1707, he now came to think that efforts to stimulate him into renewed activity were futile. His relations with Eugène remained excellent but continuing difficulties with the Imperial Court convinced him that nothing could be done to persuade the Emperor and his ministers to subordinate their own narrow interests to those of the 'common cause'.[7]

Godolphin's dismissal, of which he learnt on 28 August, concentrated Marlborough's mind on the effect that the political changes occurring at home would have on his position. He now gave first priority to the single question of how he could retain his command. The manner in which the ministerial changes were made, one by one and over a long span of time from Kent in April to Sunderland in June and Godolphin in August, put Marlborough on the rack. Contrary to Harley's expectations he never had any intention of resigning, although he expressed himself (admittedly to Godolphin) as 'sick and weary of everything' because of the

---

[7] Snyder, vol. III, pp. 1508–9.

'folly and ingratitude' of Anne. However he was buoyed up by the support of Heinsius and the elector of Hanover who both urged him not to do anything that might lead to his dismissal. The support of the latter was absolutely crucial: he was the prime candidate to replace Marlborough in his command, and Harley had decided to offer it to him in the event of Godolphin's dismissal leading to the resignation of his colleague.[8]

Harley was greatly relieved when he realised that Marlborough would not resign and went to a great deal of trouble to persuade him to continue serving in 1711. The two men detested each other but recognised that each depended on the other, at least for the time being. Marlborough's first reaction to the ministerial changes was to fight back politically: he does not seem to have appreciated how weak the credit of the ex-ministers and Whigs had become. As late as early October, while conducting the siege of Aire which had the unforeseen advantage of postponing his return to England, he assured the duchess and Godolphin that he would allow his conduct on returning to be determined by the advice of Godolphin and the Whigs. Further, he urged them to communicate their recommended line of policy to him, so that he could obtain the agreement of Eugène, Heinsius and George to it during the usual post-campaign meeting at the Hague. This would have been disastrous for all concerned. It is doubtful whether any one of the allies would have committed themselves, but even the attempt to obtain their consent (which would certainly have leaked) would have been construed as a totally inadmissible intervention in British affairs. It would certainly have provoked Marlborough's disgrace, probably an impeachment in the new

---

[8] Ibid., vol. III, pp. 1598–9, 1609, 1614. J. J. Cartwright, *The Wentworth Papers* (1883), p. 127. Historical Manuscripts Commission, Portland, vol. II, p. 339. B.W. Hill, *Robert Harley* (1988), pp. 129–30.

Parliament, infuriated the Tories into breaking the alliance and even brought the Protestant succession into question.[9]

Despite the eagerness of the Tory rank and file to sweep all Godolphin's associates out of office, Harley knew that he needed both Marlborough and the allies in order to keep France under pressure. The agents whom he employed to approach the allies and (at first) Marlborough proved to be inept. The crass Rivers made the Dutch anxious when, expressing his own prejudices rather than the immediate intentions of the new ministers, he gave the impression that Marlborough would soon be dismissed for his past 'insolences' to Anne. He then went on to Hanover, where a first agent (Southesk) had failed to reassure the elector, and made a most unfavourable impression with his arrogance and rudeness.[10]

A first, inept approach to Marlborough, in August at a time when the ministerial changes were not complete, produced no response at all. Marlborough did not want to commit himself until he could see the final outcome, and indeed by remaining abroad during the general election in October and the first weeks of the new Parliament in November, he avoided becoming entangled in party warfare. But he could not indefinitely postpone a decision whether he could come to terms with ministers whom he hated and distrusted, as was essential if he was to retain his command. This was made clear to him by the obscure but remarkable confidential agent employed by Harley. Drummond, a Scottish merchant and financier resident in Rotterdam gave Marlborough, who still appeared to be the greatest man in all Europe, some very plain-spoken advice. In late November Drummond warned him that it was essential for him to come to terms with

[9] Snyder, vol. III, p. 1638.
[10] Ibid., vol. III, pp. 1613–14. T'Hoff, p. 521. Cartwright, *Wentworth Papers*, p. 154. *Historical Manuscripts Commission, Portland*, vol. IV, pp. 580, 582.

Harley. Humiliating as it might be the duke had no choice but to accept these blunt warnings from an obscure Scotsman. When Marlborough tried to excuse himself, arguing that after being insulted by Tory MPs and journalists he could not be expected to make the first move, Drummond gave him the lie direct. He told Marlborough that it was essential for him not to be drawn into party heats by those who wanted to exploit him: to which the duke responded huffily, 'you mean my wife and those I must live with', meaning particularly his son-in-law the doctrinaire Whig Sunderland. But in the end he came to terms, promising not to engage in 'the heats of party debates', and to give support to all measures connected with the prosecution of the war.[11]

Although Tory abuse of Marlborough was both venomous and indiscriminate, and so could be easily answered, the officially inspired journalism sponsored by Harley was extremely clever and hard to counter. It was selective, designed to indicate to Marlborough that the ministers possessed the material to destroy his reputation for good as well as justify his dismissal. The line taken by Jonathan Swift in *The Examiner* was to draw attention to negative aspects of his conduct so as to demonstrate the absolute necessity of bringing him under the control of the civil authorities. Swift hinted that if Marlborough accepted in future legal limits on his power – which allegedly Godolphin had scandalously failed to enforce – there would be no danger in allowing him to continue in command.

During the winter of 1710–11 Swift reserved his choicest invective for the Whigs, above all his personal enemy Wharton, but he gave his readers – including Marlborough himself – some notion of the devastating charges that could be advanced against him if he caused political trouble. For

[11] Ibid., vol. IV, pp. 619–22, 622–5, 634–7, 655, 663, 690.

example Swift accused the 'late ministers' of deliberately prolonging the war for their personal advantage: implicitly this excluded Marlborough, but everyone knew that he was vulnerable to the same charge if the new ministers chose to make an extension. In order to cut him down to the size of a mere servant of the Crown, to warn him about his future behaviour and to justify putting limits on his powers, Swift very cleverly and effectively exercised self-restraint in his comments on Marlborough. In his criticisms he concentrated on defects that were already common knowledge, in particular Marlborough's avarice, but in ways that hinted at further and much more serious faults. A Whig politician like Wharton could simply be covered with vituperative abuse, but in Marlborough's case it was first necessary to disabuse the public of the prevailing impression that he was a great man, a Titan or hero, the greatest man in all of Europe. By comparison a great deal of Tory propaganda failed to make more than a fleeting impression because it was too obviously the work of little men (and Mrs Manley), Lilliputians eaten up by envy and personal resentments. Of course Swift was being briefed by the new ministers on their continuing (but hopefully temporary) need for Marlborough's services. His criticisms led to the conclusion that Marlborough must recognise that his defects would no longer be passed over by the administration: this warned him that he would be disgraced as well as dismissed if he turned against it, but left open the possibility that all could now go well after he had been 'taken out of ill Hands and put into better'.[12]

Characteristically Marlborough, alone among the major members and supporters of the former Godolphin

---

[12] H. Davis (ed.), *The Prose Works of Jonathan Swift* (13 vols., 1939–59), vol. III, pp. 4, 19–24, 40–6, 80–5. The first of these references was on 2 November (*Examiner* number 13), the last on 8 February 1711 (number 27) when Marlborough's reappointment was secure.

administration, agreed to work with Harley in order to retain his office. His prudent, circumspect but essentially self-interested behaviour, achieved through some unimaginable exertion of self-restraint and dissimulation went even further: Sarah was persuaded to resign all her household appointments as a condition for her husband's retention of the command. Given his thoroughly uncomfortable situation in domestic politics, and the coolness of his relations with former colleagues, it is not surprising that Marlborough returned to the Low Countries as soon as he could, in February 1711, long before his presence was really necessary.[13]

During this last campaign Marlborough's duties and powers were more limited than they had been in previous years. He no longer had any diplomatic responsibilities. Although he continued to correspond with Heinsius he made it clear that he could no longer commit his government. His exchanges with other allies were similarly limited by his being in ignorance of the intentions of his masters, Harley and St John, but also by changes which occurred after his early departure from England. In particular the sudden death of the Emperor Joseph, on 17 April, and the uncertainties created by the need for a new Imperial election, delayed the effective start of the campaign and diverted Eugène with a sizeable force to the Rhineland. When a conference was held at the Hague in June to discuss future strategy in the light of these changes Marlborough was excluded from it, and must have found particularly galling his being kept in ignorance of papers submitted to it, including a memorandum from the States General whose contents he did not know until St John graciously sent him a copy. In reality the conference was very much a non-event; it was too late in the season to make

[13] Frances Harris, *A Passion for Government: The Life of Sarah Duchess of Marlborough* (Oxford, 1991), pp. 176–8. Murray, vol. v, pp. 255, 256, 260.

changes in strategy. It discussed a long-promised but always postponed Savoyard invasion of Dauphiné; an Imperial offensive on the Rhine; a descent on the French coast – replaced by St John's scheme for an expedition to take Quebec; yet another allied revival in Spain. But inevitably the main allied effort would have to be made in northern France.[14]

Militarily the campaign of 1711 saw Marlborough at his most skilful. A close parallel can be drawn between his display of brilliant military virtuosity and Napoleon's meteoric 'Six Days' Campaign' of February 1814. Both out-manoeuvred their more numerous opponents and after long years of war and success still had the intellectual resilience to adopt new techniques that they had not had to use before – Napoleon on the defensive making limited, lightning attacks on each of the armies closing in on him, Marlborough in thwarting Villars by constructing defensive works to cover the siege of Bouchain and protect his communications. There is also a more negative resemblance. Neither of these campaigns had, or could have had, any significant impact on the outcome of the war. Napoleon had already lost his last chance of obtaining a favourable peace; Marlborough got no nearer to being able to compel Louis to agree to a peace on allied terms.

In 1711 Marlborough faced a formidable defence system, the *Ne Plus Ultra* lines, backed up by Villars's army which could move along short routes behind it to cover any potential danger of attack. In early August Marlborough took up a position west of Arras as if to attack the lines at that point; naturally Villars manned the defences opposite him. This initial move was a feint; Marlborough deceived Villars (and indeed his own army) by the thoroughness of his preparations, going so far as to carry out a personal

[14] Murray, vol. v, pp. 354–5.

reconnaissance of the defences. However after dark on 4 August the army began a forced march to the east, the artillery having been secretly sent on before, joined with other units sent direct from Douai, and broke through at a point some forty miles from Arras on the 5th. The following day some generals including several Dutch, which was surprising considering their defensive mentalities in earlier campaigns, advocated making an immediate attack on Villars now that he no longer had defences to protect him. However most generals supported Marlborough's judgement that broken ground presented considerable difficulties for an attack to be mounted in uniform strength along the whole of the enemy's front. Instead he adhered to his original plan of investing Bouchain, one of the anchor fortresses holding the *Ne Plus Ultra* lines together.[15]

In Wolfe's famous phrase war is an option of difficulties. An attack on Villars could have gone wrong, but the French no longer had a superiority in numbers and the allied army was elated by the breaking of the lines. Before Malplaquet, when all Marlborough's strategic moves had as their objective the bringing of the main French army to battle, the opportunity would probably have been taken despite some unfavourable ground. He could have relied on his powers of observation and quickness in making decisions to work out a tactical plan, or even to improvise one and communicate it clearly to his subordinates in the heat of the battle. But after the casualties of Malplaquet, and in view of the altered administration at home and the rabid Tory majority in the Commons, he could no longer afford to take what would once have been acceptable risks. There was also the simple fact that he was getting old and losing his earlier dynamism.

The option he chose, to besiege Bouchain, certainly

---

[15] Ibid., vol. v, pp. 428–9, 432–3. T'Hoff, p. 558.

proved to be full of serious difficulties. Once the siege began the French army became numerically superior to the covering force allocated to holding it at a safe distance. In fact the local topography was such that it could only be held at a relatively short distance, about two or three miles from the actual siege works. At times the siege forces were themselves under bombardment from both the town defences and the forces trying to relieve it. Equally serious was the vulnerability of Marlborough's communications. He had to rely on overland routes for his supplies since the Scheldt was controlled downstream by the French. Large enemy forces, and not just raiding parties, posed a constant threat to these routes. Consequently it was not sufficient to provide escorts for convoys of carts: Marlborough constructed entrenchments which set up and protected a corridor down which supplies could come safely from Marchiennes on the Scarpe, some ten miles from the camp. It was a failure to follow these precautions and man the defences protecting his communications that led to Eugène's disastrous failure in the offensive campaign of 1712 in the same area.

The surrender of the garrison on 12 September represented a humiliation for Villars and his army, who remained for most of the time within cannon range of the siege but were unable to force Marlborough to raise it. However Villars could survive this, and lived to wipe out any slur by his crushing victory the next year at Denain. Marlborough celebrated this last triumph by commissioning the splendid set of Bouchain tapestries, and panegyrists made the most of its capture. But Bouchain was only a minor fortress held by a small garrison of 3,000. Its capture did not open the way for an invasion into the heart of France: the major fortress of Cambrai blocked the way.[16]

[16] Murray, vol. v, pp. 437, 440–1, 445, 450, 452–3, 462, 466–7, 474–5, 486, 488. Historical Manuscripts Commission, 14th Report, appendix 9, p. 233.

Marlborough used his success at Bouchain to urge the ministers and the allies to adopt a new project, to winter the armies in the captured fortresses on the French frontier. This would ensure the earliest possible start to the next campaign, but it would also be expensive especially for the Dutch, who showed no enthusiasm. Marlborough's sponsorship shows that he was still hoping for a final and decisive campaign and that he expected to continue in command. It was not until October that he became fully aware of the intention of the British government to make a preliminary agreement with France that would lead to peace, regardless of the attitudes, interests and protests of the allies. It had always been Marlborough's guiding principle that the allies must maintain unity, for the disintegration of the alliance would in his view restore to the French the predominant European position and influence that it had been formed to contain and reduce. Such dominance or the new danger which was now emerging, of a partnership between France and the Tory administration to force peace on the allies, would also endanger the other cause to which he had committed himself, the Protestant succession. Consequently on his return to London he changed his political stance, lending all the assistance he could to the concerted attempt in Parliament to wreck the peace negotiations, in the full knowledge that if this failed the ministers would dismiss and attempt to disgrace him.[17]

Marlborough's confidence in expecting at the end of the campaign that he would continue in command during 1712 is all the more remarkable because he had faced significant challenges within the army to his authority during 1711. Marlborough raised the issue of insubordination by senior officers in his discussions with Drummond in November

[17] Murray, vol. v, pp. 506, 514, 516, 518, 538, 553.

1710, complaining that the then new ministers were showing favour to officers who had been 'lessening' him. By this he meant criticising him openly and repeating their criticisms in correspondence with politicians at home. He named the earl of Orrery, who had been promoted to major-general. His complaint was ignored, for the very good reason that St John, who retained close knowledge of army affairs from his time as secretary at war (up to 1708), expressly intended to use appointments and promotions to 'break the Marlborough faction' among the senior officers. What he meant by telling Harley that this could be done without mortifying Marlborough is unclear.[18]

Dissident officers like Orrery had in fact been corresponding with Harley as well as St John about their growing dissatisfaction with Marlborough since before the ministerial changes in the summer of 1710. They alleged that he ignored their claims to recognition and promotion in order to concentrate his favour on a coterie of protégés and dependants. The first openly critical general, Webb, who never forgave Marlborough for diverting the credit for his victory at Wijnendale (1708), was given a home appointment. Argyle and Orkney who had for years served loyally posed a more serious threat because as Scottish peers they possessed considerable political influence in their own right: Orkney's wife, formerly William III's mistress, ably fostered her husband's interests while he served abroad.

Argyle despised Marlborough's overreaching ambition; the break began with the latter's attempt to become captain-general for life. He made no attempt to conceal an intense antipathy to Marlborough who responded with the comment 'I cannot have a worse opinion of anybody than of the Duke of Argyle.' More seriously the dissident officers criticised the

18 Historical Manuscripts Commission, Portland, vol. IV, pp. 575–6, 656.

conduct of the 1710 campaign, deploring the heavy loss of lives in the sieges. Consequently St John knew that the proposals which he made to take promotions and appointments out of Marlborough's hands, and which followed closely suggestions made by Orrery, would encourage the anti-Marlborough faction whose sniping continued during 1711. By then Marlborough realised that it was his old auxiliary, St John, who was behind the undermining of his authority, but an appeal to Harley for 'visible' support from ministers as evidence of Anne's continuing 'protection' received no effective response.[19]

The growth of military factions was an ominous development, not just for Marlborough but for the nation. The process of politicisation initiated by the senior officers in dissociating themselves from their commander, and the encouragement they received from the ministers, could eventually have led to civil war. Ironically by 1714 it was Argyle who protested against the blatant remodelling of the army being carried out by Bolingbroke (formerly St John), which he suspected was aimed at facilitating a Jacobite Restoration. And by then those officers who had formed Marlborough's military faction were organising themselves to resist any Jacobite coup, and asked him to return from voluntary exile to assume their leadership.

Marlborough's physical and intellectual stamina and resilience enabled him to withstand the pressures imposed by domestic politics on top of the demands made by his military, diplomatic and administrative duties. Like William III whose annual involvement in the continental campaigns made him the first absentee sovereign since Henry V,

---

[19] Ibid., vol. IV, pp. 544, 548, 554, 605, 619–22, 623–5. Cartwright, *Wentworth Papers*, p. 104.

Marlborough could only devote part of his time and energies to domestic issues, but knew that errors by his colleagues and subordinates at home could undermine his influence and entire position in Europe. Frequently the letters from Godolphin and Sarah which informed him of difficulties at home reached him too late for even his advice to have any relevance, and however full and frequent these letters could never adequately prepare him for the part they expected him to play when he did return. He had to take a plunge into domestic politics and since the parliamentary session had usually already begun he was confronted on several occasions by unexpected problems and questions.

Marlborough's annual reentry into domestic politics came after activities that would have exhausted most younger men, and which had eventually killed William. Arduous campaigns, one of which was protracted until January (1709) and several into wet and cold autumn weather, were followed invariably by intensive discussions at the Hague and on occasion by long journeys to Berlin, Vienna and Hanover. Early winter sea-crossings often proved to be an ordeal. On his return Marlborough tried to reserve a little time to recover and take stock. But he never appears to have had any difficulty in resuming instantly a harmonious working relationship with Godolphin, and in contributing to the work of the Council. It was as a councillor that he excelled, rather than as a parliamentarian. He does not seem to have had the temperament and attributes to sway debates in the Lords. His early career had not required him to develop the art of rhetorical eloquence or taught him how to manipulate parliamentary procedures. Marlborough did not set out to rally or inspire a following of devoted political adherents, and still less did he excel at the art (of which Godolphin was a master) of political management and the fixing of individuals – as distinct of course from the related art of controlling military patronage. In short he was never a party man. Rather he saw himself as primarily the servant of the queen and he explicitly detested the way in which both parties – the Tories in 1702–5, the Whigs in 1706–9 – deliberately brought such pressure on the administration as to threaten the effective prosecution of the war.[20]

The administration of which Marlborough was a member from 1702 until 1710, headed by Godolphin as lord treasurer, and with Robert Harley as junior triumvir until 1708, represents the last attempt to govern and legislate through a non-party ministry. That is, the chief ministers did not see themselves as either Whigs or Tories, and tried consciously to avoid becoming dependent on support from either of the parties, which would have to be purchased by appointing party nominees and accepting partisan policies. Ultimately the attempt failed – between 1708 and 1710 Godolphin and Marlborough became virtual captives of the Whigs – but in the early years they remained in command although the composition of the ministry was subject to frequent changes. By contrast during the 1690s the parties had alternated in control of government; a repetition of this pattern would have made Marlborough's position untenable since the Tory leaders fundamentally disagreed with his continental strategy. Ministerial colleagues did often try to persuade him to change his strategy. Nottingham provoked Marlborough's resentment by urging large-scale transfers of his troops to Spain. Godolphin repeatedly pressed for 'descents' on the French coast which, like Pitt's in 1758–62, would have little more than propaganda value. Any major failures would be exploited for party advantage; in 1704 Seymour was poised

[20] The best studies of party politics during Anne's reign include Geoffrey Holmes, *British Politics in the Age of Anne* (1967); B. W. Hill, *Robert Harley; Speaker, Secretary of State and Prime Minister* (1988); and B. W. Hill, *The Growth of Parliamentary Parties, 1689–1742* (1976).

to impeach Marlborough, expecting the Danube campaign to misfire; in 1708 associates of the ousted Harley gleefully anticipated exploiting what they hoped would be disaster during the siege of Lille. From that year Marlborough became too closely associated with the Whigs, and all subsequent successes were disparaged for purely party reasons by the Tories.[21]

Marlborough's military victories were his main contribution to the success and longevity of the Godolphin administration. In the first years his influence at Court, as the person most in Anne's confidence and with Sarah established as her intimate friend, played an important part but it diminished with his absences overseas for half of every year and his consequent inability to restrain Sarah. By incessantly correcting the queen, pressing her for offices, rewards and recognition for relations and associates she soon began to tire Anne and then to alienate her. Relentlessly Sarah poured out her partisan opinions on every subject, revealing that unlike her husband she held strong Whig views, and she expressed them in strident and hectoring language. From as early as 1704 relations between Anne and Sarah were becoming uneasy. The latter was now too grand to perform some of the physical and comparatively menial services on which Anne's comfort and health increasingly depended. Although, like her husband, a sincere Anglican Sarah did not share Anne's total devotion to the Church, and this became apparent when the ministers (under Whig pressure) tried to force Anne to promote clerics of whom she disapproved.[22]

The administration depended on control over royal patronage in order to construct a bloc of peers and MPs, but their number always fell short of providing even a working

[21] Henry Horwitz, Revolution Politicks (Cambridge, 1968), pp. 167–8, 174–7. Historical Manuscripts Commission, Portland, vol. IV, pp. 506, 507, 508–9.
[22] Harris, Passion for Government, p. 44, G. V. Bennett, 'Robert Harley, the Godolphin ministry and the bishoprics' crisis of 1707', English Historical Review, 82 (1967), 726–46.

majority in Parliament. In order to function and remain independent of the party leaderships it was necessary to attract and retain moderate men, 'the gentlemen of England' as Harley called them, beholden to nobody and averse to being transformed into dependants. Such men needed constant attention, but as 'reasonable men' they judged issues on the merits. Instinctively Marlborough identified himself with them, relying on their sharing his own detestation for 'angry men', for those who like Seymour and Rochester judged everything according to considerations of personal and party advantage, and were consumed by prejudices and personal rancour. He expected independent peers and MPs to help in keeping the queen and the government out of the hands of party leaders, and to cooperate with other reasonable men, even if they were of a different party from themselves.

For Godolphin and Marlborough to succeed they had to detach a significant number of peers and MPs from their partisan chiefs. This was always easier to do in the case of Tories, who in organisational terms were a loose confederation, than with the more tightly disciplined Whigs. In the first years Marlborough had to disrupt the influence exercised by the Tory chiefs, Rochester, Nottingham and Seymour because they contended that all campaigns in the Low Countries would be as futile as William's had been. Therefore England should confine itself to an auxiliary and defensive role there, and concentrate on attacks on Spain and its colonies. Anticipating such attitudes, and distrusting Rochester as a politician who judged everything and everybody from a narrow party perspective, Marlborough created the essential preconditions for his achievements as a general by persuading Anne, at the start of the reign, to prefer Godolphin to Rochester in the key office of lord treasurer.[23]

[23] Snyder, vol. I, pp. 86, 99.

Marlborough persisted in distrusting the Tory leaders because they consistently gave priority to domestic issues over measures to support the war-effort. They demonstrated this by their attempts to force through an Occasional Conformity bill, whose aim was to disqualify dissenters from holding public office: ostensibly this would secure the Church, but it would certainly enfeeble the Whigs. Although its effects would be deeply divisive Marlborough and Godolphin could not openly oppose the bill, which was lost in the session of 1702–3 when the Houses failed to agree on amendments initiated in the Lords. They voted again for a second bill in December 1703, which was rejected by the Lords, but Tories believed that underhand they had encouraged peers to throw it out. They therefore took reprisals by opposing the Recruiting bill on which Marlborough's army depended for replacements. They also spoke of 'tacking' a third Occasional Conformity bill to the Land Tax, so as to get round the Lords' veto, and this was attempted in the session of 1704–5. Unless the administration gave way this would undermine the entire war-effort. Consequently ministers had to organise intensively to defeat it, inserting in the queen's speech a plea for union and lobbying MPs and peers.[24]

The struggle over the Tack was exploited by the Whigs; they put up John Smith against a tacker for Speaker of the newly elected Commons in 1705 and when the ministers felt constrained to support him most Tories were alienated. The Tory leaders had already left the administration, Rochester in 1703, Seymour and Jersey were dismissed in April 1704 and Nottingham subsequently resigned. Sarah denounced them

---

[24] *Parliamentary History*, ed. William Cobbett (36 vols., 1806–20), vol. VI, p. 361: General Cutts (an MP) said the Tack would reverse the effects of the victory at Blenheim.

to Anne as Jacobites; Marlborough condemned them for more subtle and valid reasons. He thought that they did not see the likely consequences of their policies which, if implemented, would make the allies, and particularly the Dutch whom they constantly criticised, conclude that they could not depend on English support. The result would be separate peace settlements with France.[25]

The elections of 1705 gave the Whigs greater numbers in the Commons, and with many Tory MPs waging guerrilla war on the administration the ministers became increasingly aware of the narrowing basis of its parliamentary position. The Whig leaders began to exert pressure to force on the queen the appointment of a succession of their number, starting with the tactically shrewd choice of Sunderland, Marlborough's son-in-law. The ways in which pressure was applied proved to be extremely damaging. By obstructing business the Whigs made Godolphin desperate and Marlborough, being overseas for over half of each year, could not help. Unfortunately Godolphin had to make use of Sarah in giving a reluctant Anne advice to make concessions, but she had no wish to become as much the captive of the Whigs as she saw that Godolphin was becoming. Anne resented Sarah's abrasive manner. She objected not only to being compelled to appoint party nominees but also to the character of most of the leading Whigs.

Marlborough enjoyed immunity from the worst of the constant Whig pressure thanks to his absence on campaign, but Godolphin bombarded him with letters complaining about his predicament, and Sarah about her difficulties with Anne. Sunderland's appointment as secretary of state in December 1706 did prove to be an irrevocable step. It rightly

---

[25] Snyder, vol. I, pp. 149, 156, 198 and note, 202, 224–5, 274–5, 453. Horwitz, *Revolution Politicks*, p. 180. *Historical Manuscripts Commission, Egmont*, vol. II, p. 220.

alarmed Harley who saw that the Whigs were planning to drive him out of office. Marlborough tried to reassure him, but Harley knew that it was Godolphin who counted in terms of domestic politics and that under pressure he would give way. To preserve his position he began to rally support among independent politicians and to redouble his very promising moves to win Anne's confidence and to strengthen her distrust of the Whigs. He began to develop a scheme for a changed administration, in which there would naturally be no place for Godolphin but Marlborough would be retained (as he was to be in 1710) in order to maintain pressure on France to ensure a satisfactory peace.[26]

The essential difference between Marlborough and Harley lay in their relationship with, and attitude to, the Tories. For Harley the Whigs were enemies whereas he believed that he could enlist most of the independent country gentlemen who called themselves Tories, but not their leaders. In contrast Marlborough thought – wrongly, as events were to show – that the Whigs could be accommodated in the administration without becoming able to dominate it. More erroneously, as he told Anne in July 1707, the Whigs would be the more easily 'governed' by her – that is they would not try to bring her under pressure. This is another example of his blind spot, a failure to realise how devotedly committed Anne was to the Church and therefore how probable clashes were on ecclesiastical matters with the Whigs.

Whig harassment of Godolphin continued during 1707, intensifying during the autumn. Marlborough had a new complication with which to cope, Sarah's increasing alarm that her former protégée, Abigail Masham (née Hill) was supplanting her in Anne's favour, and her claims that Abigail was being manipulated by Harley. Outwardly Harley's

---

[26] Snyder, vol. II, pp. 636, 638, 656, 659, 670, 675, 683, 699, 717. *Historical Manuscripts Commission, Bath*, vol. I, pp. 107, 110–11, 121.

position seemed to be worsening; Whigs joined Tories in attacking him for the disastrous summer's campaign in Spain, which he made little effort to defend – to Godolphin's fury. One of his office staff was found to have betrayed state secrets to France, and the Whig leaders tried to extort evidence that would incriminate Harley. But Harley had secured full backing from Anne, and once this became apparent he was confident he could secure sufficient Tory support to carry on the administration once Godolphin had been dismissed. Harley was also confident of Marlborough's support, for when Anne told him it might be necessary to replace Godolphin he replied that he would willingly continue as general. This assured his office whatever the outcome. But when the crunch came on 8 February 1708, before all Harley's preparations were complete, he saw that Godolphin was still indispensable and therefore stood by him. The triumvirate finally came to an end with Harley's resignation on 11 February.[27]

During 1708 Marlborough left Godolphin to face mounting Whig pressure, knowing that the queen had been willing to discard him. There were good reasons for Marlborough to leave England early, with French preparations far advanced, and he declined to make a flying visit to London to help Godolphin in his difficulties such as he made the following year. He does not seem to have been distressed when the campaign proved to be the longest yet: he did not return until February 1709. In correspondence he failed to persuade Anne that her own interest (and that of the administration) coincided with the Whigs' in that they were committed to the vigorous prosecution of the war. He also failed to convince Sarah that Anne's resistance to the admission of Whig leaders into the Cabinet Council was not wholly

[27] Snyder, vol. II, pp. 843, 907. Hill, *Robert Harley*, pp. 101–17.

attributable to the influence of Abigail, with whom Sarah was becoming totally obsessed. From a safe distance he offered her the wise advice that Abigail might certainly be vexatious, a nuisance, but that she was a minor personage, incapable of more than mischief-making. Sarah took no notice. By the end of 1708, after an absurd and very public upbraiding of Anne on the steps of St Paul's, before and after the thanksgiving for Oudenarde, she had become a personal and political liability for Marlborough.[28]

The elections of May 1708 strengthened the Whigs in the Commons, so that they now held Godolphin at their mercy. Anne greatly resented the final bout of pressure which he had to bring on her in favour of more Whig appointments, particularly because this coincided with the terminal illness of her husband George. After his death in October 1708 Marlborough remained as the only minister on reasonable terms with her, as she came to identify Godolphin with her Whig persecutors. Even though he was absent for long periods each year she still valued his remaining as a minister, but as the political difficulties mounted Marlborough indicated that although he was committed to staying on as general for the duration of the war he did not intend to continue as a minister once peace was made.[29]

After the successes of the 1708 campaign – Oudenarde, Lille and the recovery of Ghent and Bruges – Marlborough expected an early peace. At the negotiations with Torcy at the Hague, in which he participated, he and Eugène were determined to reduce France to a condition which would make it impossible for Louis and his successors to 'give the law' to Europe, that is to determine all issues according to the

---

[28] Harris, *Passion for Government*, pp. 141, 143–4, 145–9.
[29] Somers became lord president of the Council and Wharton lord lieutenant of Ireland in November 1708. The queen described the dominance of the Whigs as 'the tyranny of the five lords'; Snyder, vol. II, pp. 1054, 1064–5, 1085.

interests of France and the Bourbon dynasty. This objective necessitated ousting Louis's grandson from the Spanish throne, and by 1709 Marlborough disapproved of the Dutch for being prepared to concede to Philip modest compensation as the price of an immediate and general peace. The territories which the Dutch itemised – Naples and Sicily – were most unlikely to be given up by the Emperor. Consequently, Marlborough feared, Torcy would have a new opportunity to disrupt the alliance and seduce the Dutch into a separate peace.[30]

Marlborough profoundly mistrusted Torcy, the French foreign minister, and all other enemy diplomats because after successive military defeats they had become the main instrument of power at the disposal of Louis, and at this stage seemed to provide him with the only means of obtaining a satisfactory outcome from the war. His own dealings with French diplomacy went back to 1679. He had ample and varied experience of the skill, sophistication and total lack of scruple of French diplomats and ministers. He could not forget recent and blatant French breaches of undertakings, not least Louis's repudiation of the Partition Treaty and his recognition of James III.[31]

As recognisably the most important person in the allied camp Marlborough became wary of involvement in the many unofficial approaches made privately by individuals who had no official 'character' but claimed authorisation by Louis. His reserve proved to be fully justified. The French targeted him, as they did Dutch politicians belonging to the peace tendency, judging him to be open to offers artfully designed to play on his susceptibilities. The baits were money and flattery. D'Alègre in 1705 offered him the enormous sum of 2

[30] Ibid., vol. III, pp. 1237–8, 1426, 1435–6, 1438.
[31] Mark Thomson, 'Louis XIV and the Grand Alliance', in R. Hatton and J. S. Bromley (eds.), William III and Louis XIV (Liverpool, 1968), pp. 190–212.

211

million livres (admittedly in instalments) as a sweetener to peace terms absurdly favourable to France. Marlborough failed to respond but later used the bribe to disconcert the French, when they wanted serious negotiations in 1708, by asserting that the offer still bound them and he would expect payment.[32]

In 1706 an agent acting on behalf of the elector of Bavaria made an approach that relied on flattery. This came in the proposal that a direct personal negotiation between Marlborough and the elector could produce an immediate peace – relying on the specious parallel with the Portland–Boufflers negotiations of 1697 which had cut through the obstructions that were deadlocking the Rijswijk conference. Specious because in 1697 the Emperor had regarded himself as betrayed and in 1706 Marlborough could certainly not have satisfied both the Emperor and the Dutch. Indeed William had wondered retrospectively whether the methods used in 1697 had been wise, because other allies might in future be tempted to seek separate deals with Louis. Consequently Marlborough took great care to keep all the allies informed and made it clear that he was trying to use the negotiations to detach the elector from his alliance with Louis.[33]

The French approaches in 1706 were mere manoeuvres, not serious attempts to obtain a basis for peace, and in 1707 with a deadlock in the Low Countries, and allied failures in Spain and before Toulon, Louis had no motive to renew them. By the time he renewed approaches in the autumn of 1708, after Oudenarde, the allies had agreed procedures to deal with them. Earlier Louis used unofficial emissaries carrying deceptively varying offers; the allies now insisted

[32] Winston S. Churchill, *Marlborough: His Life and Times* (4 vols., 1933–8), vol. III, pp. 69–72; vol. IV, pp. 24, 26.
[33] Murray vol. III, pp. 187–8, 191, 193–5, 222. Snyder, vol. I, p. 566; vol. II, pp. 633, 713. P. Grimblot, *Letters of William III and Louis XIV* (2 vols., 1848), vol. I, pp. 91–2, 124–5.

that he must submit proposals in writing and Marlborough made it clear that there must be no cessation of hostilities during negotiations, lest the allies lose momentum and the advantages won in 1708. By the beginning of 1709 he was convinced that it was now no longer a question of whether to make peace, but on what terms it should be made. One difference between the allies remained that could cause a rift: the Emperor's insistence that the whole Spanish Empire belonged to his brother by right was now accompanied by the commitment of the Godolphin administration to 'no peace without Spain' by the parliamentary resolutions of 22 December 1707, but the Dutch were not so committed and it was essential to tie them down well in advance of a peace conference. This was achieved by an additional clause in the Barrier Treaty negotiated by Townshend: Marlborough had to be kept out of the negotiations because the offer of the Governor-Generalship from Karl had made him suspect as an interested party.[34]

There were several reasons why the allies insisted that Philip must give up the entire Spanish Empire. The Habsburgs, being as wedded as Louis to the principles of divine right would risk losing the entire Spanish Empire rather than allow Philip, as a man without any legitimate claim, any portions as compensation. Marlborough's reasons were pragmatic, not ideological. The detached territories suggested as compensation – up to 1708 the Spanish Netherlands; Naples and Sicily; Milan – were all of the greatest strategic importance and would enable France to renew its aggressions in the future. For British commercial interests Philip's acquisition of Naples and Sicily would give France

---

[34] The Barrier Treaty is printed as Appendix E to R. Geikie and I. A. Montgomery, *The Dutch Barrier* (Cambridge, 1930), pp. 377–86. Thomson, 'Louis XIV and the Grand Alliance', pp. 195–205. *Lords Journals*, vol. 18, p. 400. *Commons Journals*, vol. XV, pp. 481–2. *Historical Manuscripts Commission*, *Egmont*, vol. II, pp. 219–21.

commercial advantages. The Whigs in the short term had no interest in an early peace which might deprive them of the leverage they exercised on the ministry, and in the longer term they needed a peace that would be a total triumph, and give them a continuing domination of Parliament.

However the main attraction of the demand for the entire Spanish Empire was that it was simple and clear-cut, and would give Louis's brilliant foreign minister Torcy no opportunity to confuse the issues and divide the allies – as of course he tried. The processes through which peace was to be attained reflect a deep distrust of Louis. Marlborough and his contemporaries remembered that Louis had arbitrarily broken the terms of the Nijmegen, Rijswijk and Partition Treaties. They knew that the concessions which he offered ran counter to the essential principle of his concept of monarchy, legitimacy or divine right which had made him repudiate the Partition Treaty, recognise James III and reserve the right of Philip to ascend the French throne. For Marlborough no peace could be satisfactory unless Louis recognised Anne and the Protestant succession, and was deprived of the power to intervene to overthrow either. In exasperation at Louis's rejection of the first set of preliminaries, in June 1709, Marlborough went so far as to suggest to Godolphin that the only way that complete security against French aggression could be obtained was to change its form of government. If kings of France became 'again' dependent on the Estates they would cease to be able to disturb the peace of Christendom. Godolphin also reacted belligerently; peace would now have to be signed on a drumhead and reduce France to the frontiers of 1659.[35]

Marlborough was named as first British plenipotentiary for the peace conference, but all essential issues would have to be

---

[35] Snyder, vol. III, pp. 1263, 1265–6, 1270. Churchill, *Marlborough*, vol. III, pp. 71–2.

settled beforehand in preliminary articles which the main parties must ratify, so that there could be no going back on them. Actual negotiation of the preliminaries was entrusted exclusively in 1709 and 1710 to the Dutch, so as to prevent the French having an opportunity to divide the allies, and to saddle the Dutch with the responsibility of agreeing terms from which they could not later recede. Marlborough and his colleagues were not greatly concerned by the breakdown of the 1709 negotiations at Moerdijk, assuming that the position and power of France would continue to deteriorate so that Louis would have to come back with improved offers – and indeed he did in 1710 at Geertruidenberg. Secondly, Marlborough continued to fear that if the British administration showed any sign of accepting a compromise, the Dutch would press for an immediate peace on still more lenient terms. Therefore he showed himself publicly obdurate on the crucial article xxxvii which obliged Louis to ensure that Philip abandoned Spain, if necessary by expelling him forcibly. Privately he conceded that if he were Louis he would never accept such a dishonourable course, but the public interest required it. All experience of the war in the Peninsula indicated that if the allies had to expel Philip the other powers would leave Britain to bear the main burden.[36]

Although Marlborough was only an observer, not a participant, the failure of the negotiations on the preliminaries eventually damaged his reputation severely. It gave general credence to what had previously been a partisan opinion, that he did not want peace because a prolongation of the war would perpetuate his greatness and make him richer with each year that it continued. However in 1710 allegations that the administration in general was unnecessarily prolonging

---

[36] Snyder, vol. III, pp. 1257, 1263, 1268. T'Hoff, pp. 437, 444–5. *Historical Manuscripts Commission*, 14th *Report*, appendix 9, p. 348.

the war played only a contributory part in bringing about its dismantlement, and Marlborough was the only leading figure to survive in office. The Godolphin administration collapsed and its Whig auxiliaries were defeated in the autumn elections because its domestic policies had become discredited, rather than because of the unpopularity of the war. And Marlborough had to be retained as general because there was no alternative general able to carry on an active campaign, and this continued until November when all the ministerial changes had been made. Harley did offer the command for the next campaign, that of 1711, to the elector of Hanover, but he declined.

This outcome, with Marlborough the sole survivor in office at the end of 1710, could not have been predicted at the beginning of the year. On his return in November 1709 he had just received a major rebuff from Anne who rejected his petition to be appointed captain-general for life.[37] Although he did not know that Somers and other leading Whigs had opposed the proposal, he became aware of their unwillingness to back him in a sudden crisis which blew up on the death of Essex, who was Constable of the Tower and colonel of a dragoon regiment (January 1710). Marlborough discovered that Anne had already decided on replacements, and feared that this visible loss of influence would weaken his authority in the army. The new men appointed were provocative choices and he reacted violently. Although Marlborough had refused to recommend him Rivers received the command of the Tower; the regiment was to go to none other than Abigail Masham's brother, Jack Hill. This drove Sarah almost literally mad with fury, while Marlborough

---

[37] H. L. Snyder, 'The Duke of Marlborough's request of his Captain-Generalcy for life: a re-examination', *Journal of the Society for Army Historical Research*, 45 (1967), 67–83. William Coxe, *Memoirs of John, Duke of Marlborough* (3 vols., 1818–19), vol. III, pp. 6–20.

treated the appointment as a trial of strength. Having failed to persuade Anne to alter her decision, in two extremely fraught meetings, he withdrew from London and called on his ministerial colleagues to aid him in forcing Anne to give way on the appointments and, a more unattainable aim, to discard Abigail from her service. Otherwise he would resign. Disconcertingly he received little ministerial support. The Whigs disagreed among themselves. One group under Sunderland's influence went so far as to propose a parliamentary address calling on Anne to remove Abigail, an infringement of what she saw as her prerogative right, and she indicated clearly her extreme repugnance. Marlborough retreated from his own intransigent position by dissociating himself from Sunderland. Other Whigs sat on the fence. Anne also climbed down; Jack Hill was not given the regiment and had to wait a few months for promotion. But when Marlborough tried to smooth over the quarrel by writing an apologetic letter Anne failed to reply.[38]

The damage done to Marlborough's general standing and to his relationship with Anne was substantial because it was so visible. The ministers considered that their interests would be best served by packing him off to the continent as soon as possible before his erratic behaviour, attributable to Sarah's influence, did further harm. He left England on 19 February, which meant that he did not take part in what was to become, from the administration's angle, the fatal impeachment of Dr Sacheverell. When the case was first discussed Marlborough seems to have favoured an ordinary criminal prosecution rather than an impeachment but, like his colleagues, he should have seen that the case would give the Tories the issue of the 'Church in danger' on which they could mobilise the

---

[38] Geoffrey Holmes, *The Trial of Doctor Sacheverell* (1973), pp. 114–16. Cartwright, *Wentworth Papers*, pp. 103–4.

clergy, the mob and eventually the electorate against the administration's policies.

The administration crumbled over a period of months, from Kent's replacement in April, Sunderland's on 14 June, Godolphin's on 8 August and Somers's and Cowper's in late September. At no time did Marlborough seriously consider either resigning or threatening to resign in solidarity with his colleagues. Their failures to support him over the life-term captain-generalcy and Rivers's appointment served as a justification for inaction, although he had the lowest possible opinion of two of those who aspired to replace Godolphin – Somerset and Harley – and did not trust the third, Shrewsbury. He did write that he would do nothing except in concert with Godolphin and his Whig colleagues, but he honoured these pledges only in so far as he did very little: when Sunderland came under threat he limited himself to asking that he should be retained until the campaign ended. His caution increased when he saw that the other Whigs did not rally to support Sunderland: only Sarah did – inevitably in a counter-productive way – firing off a letter full of recrimination to Anne, denouncing Godolphin's inaction and calling on all ministers to resign en bloc. After a sharp reply from Anne to Sarah Marlborough advised his wife not to write again.[39]

The siege of Aire kept Marlborough in the field until 13 November, but wisely he did not hurry home, arriving only on 27 November. The delay contributed largely to his success in retaining his command for another campaign. Since the remaining Whig chiefs had resigned he could disregard his promises to work with them. Harley needed him as general to maintain pressure on Louis. However Marlborough had to humble himself and pay the price of Sarah resigning her

[39] Snyder, vol. II, p. 1031; vol. III, pp. 1488, 1522, 1530.

Court appointments. He knew that he was vulnerable to personal attacks or even criminal charges, if the new ministers chose to press them. The *Examiner* hinted at them with ministerial approval when it refuted charges of ministerial and national ingratitude to the victorious general. The Commons authorised investigations into alleged frauds in the military accounts for Spain and Portugal, but Flanders could be added. A committee of general officers was set up at the Horse Guards to oversee military patronage, but his old colleague St John made it ineffective in practice. Privately St John, Harley and other ministers spoke disparagingly of Marlborough, but in public his position seemed surprisingly intact.[40]

This outcome was surprising because Marlborough had allowed himself to be used by foreign governments in making representations – a resolution from the States General, letters from the Emperor – about matters that exclusively concerned the prerogative: ministerial changes and the dissolution of Parliament. They had no effect, but this failure did not deter Marlborough from placing great reliance on foreign intervention in the last weeks of 1711 when the final contest of strength came.

Oxford no longer needed him once the preliminaries of peace had been unilaterally agreed with France. Marlborough sincerely regarded the terms, and the separate negotiation, as disastrous. He staked everything on a concerted attempt to wreck the peace. A political storm had been created before his return by publication of the preliminary terms on 13 October, leaked to the Whig *Daily Courant* by the Imperial envoy Gallas. Marlborough arrived in London in company with the Hanoverian envoy Bothmar, who had instructions

---

[40] Davis (ed.), *The Prose Works of Jonathan Swift*, vol. III, pp. 19–23. Snyder, vol. III, pp. 1639, 1644, 1649, 1653.

to act in concert with him: the *Daily Courant* had a second scoop when it published the elector's memorandum to the government, denouncing the preliminaries. A further foreign reinforcement was arranged, a personal visit by Eugène. In one sense the Hanoverian memorandum had a decisive effect: it forced the Whig leaders, who had been secretly negotiating with Oxford for a remodelling of the administration to include themselves, to join Marlborough wholeheartedly in the attack on the preliminaries. They had been prepared to abandon their opposition to another Occasional Conformity bill to accommodate Oxford; now they promised the same concession to his Tory rival Nottingham. Marlborough easily went along with them.[41]

This coalition of Marlborough, Nottingham and the Whigs threatened the administration because of its strength in the Lords. But the foreign support which it received was skilfully turned against it by Tory propaganda. Jonathan Swift's vitriolic pamphlet, *The Conduct of the Allies and of the Late Ministry in Beginning and Carrying on the Present War*, had an unrivalled effect: it was published on 27 November; a second edition appeared two days later, the fourth on 3 December. By the end of January over 11,000 copies had been sold and its arguments totally captured both parliamentary and public opinion.[42]

Swift's lethal denigration of an undefeated general who had destroyed French predominance and made Britain a great European power was based on a well-chosen set of linkages between Marlborough and pernicious processes of change that were affecting the clergy and the more conservative

---

[41] Hill, *Robert Harley*, pp. 167–71. N. Henderson, *Prince Eugen of Savoy* (1964), pp. 187–201.

[42] Jonathan Swift, *Political Tracts, 1711–1713*, in Davis (ed.), *The Prose Works of Jonathan Swift*, vol. VI, pp. viii–xi. For a general account, Michael Foot, *The Pen and the Sword* (1958).

landowners. First he was associated with perfidious and selfish allies whom he allowed to exploit Britain: it was the Dutch whom Swift singled out, because they were long-standing and familiar rivals, rather than the more blame-worthy Habsburgs. Secondly Marlborough was depicted as actuated primarily by his greed for wealth on a previously unknown scale; Swift had earlier estimated his fortune at £540,000 – all acquired during the war. Swift travestied Marlborough's continental strategy as being designed to bring him and corrupt associates immense wealth whereas the alternative Tory-backed colonial and naval strategy would have brought profit to the entire nation. Nearly all this fortune had been invested in government stock, not land, and the national debt which his strategy had required would lie as a burden on future generations. The profiteers would be Marlborough and the financiers and contractors (many of them immigrants and some Jews) of the hated 'monied interest'. This rank xenophobia, masquerading as patriotism, was reinforced by appeals to social envy and resentment; Marlborough and the men of money were 'upstarts', new men with new forms of wealth establishing a new social order based on wealth, nearly all of it derived from the public purse.

Marlborough's Whig associates provoked even greater resentment in Swift's heart because they championed the dissenters, the voluntary separatists who divided the nation and defied the traditional hierarchical order. For all those sections of the political nation with acute grievances he confirmed what they had always suspected, that the entire war had been a conspiracy against the landed interest. The war as Marlborough had fought it had been deliberately intended to bring about 'the ruin of the public interest, and the Advancement of a Private, increase the Wealth and Grandeur of a particular Family, to enrich Usurers and

Stock-jobbers, cultivate the pernicious Designs of a Faction by destroying the Landed-Interest'.[43]

The administration had decided to dismiss Marlborough before he voted for Nottingham's motion on 7 December, that no peace was safe if Philip retained Spain and the West Indies. On 31 December Marlborough was dismissed – by a letter from Anne, as Godolphin had been. Marlborough burnt the letter. On the next day the ministry acquired a majority in the Lords by the creation of twelve new peers, and during January the Commons committee of accounts assembled evidence to charge Marlborough with fraudulent practices on the intelligence funds and bread contract. But Oxford indicated privately that no further action would be instituted. Nevertheless despite the implied condition of good behaviour Marlborough did join in attacks on the orders sent to his successor Ormonde, restraining him from cooperating with the allies, and against the terms proposed for the peace. All such efforts proved futile. After attending Godolphin's funeral on 7 October, he and Sarah went into voluntary exile on 1 December 1712.[44]

[43] Swift, 'Conduct of the Allies', in Davis (ed.) The Prose Works of Jonathan Swift, vol. VI, p. 59.
[44] Parliamentary History, ed. Cobbett, vol. VI, pp. 1037–8, 1095, 1137, 1146.

Conclusion: Marlborough's reputation

For all effective purposes Marlborough's dismissal by Anne ended his active career. He spent his period in exile in almost continuous but futile and unproductive intrigue, aimed at bringing down the Tory administration at almost any cost. But that ministry self-destructed in Anne's very last days, and Marlborough (who was travelling back and arrived in England on the day after she died) contributed little to the smooth and unopposed accession of George I. George restored him to the office of captain-general, and he did supervise the suppression of the Jacobite rebellion of 1715, but his former assistant Cadogan actually directed the operations. In May 1716 Marlborough suffered a disabling stroke, with a second in November. After this he lived in retirement, becoming increasingly isolated by the incessant and bitter quarrels that Sarah provoked with almost everyone near to them – surviving daughters, sons-in-law, former army and political colleagues and, not least, John Vanbrugh the architect of Blenheim Palace – until he died on 16 June 1722.

It has been said that the careers of almost all great public servants end in failure because they do not know when to retire gracefully but cling on to the power and influence which they have come to love as they acquire and use it, and after they have outlived their usefulness. This was particularly true of Marlborough's contemporaries. William III died unmourned in England. Godolphin had become a discredited captive of the Whigs when he lost office. Harley (Oxford) and St John (Bolingbroke), absorbed entirely by their mutual enmity, antagonised the dying queen, forfeited all confidence and effectively wrecked the Tory administration in 1714. Even the supremely realistic Walpole was reluctant to acknowledge by resignation that his power had irretrievably ebbed away.

Marlborough's career, like that of his descendant Winston Churchill, exemplifies this statement. After 1708 he was set on a line of national policy, and a military strategy, that he could no longer hope to achieve. He does not seem to have realised this himself, perhaps because it was inveterate and committed enemies who kept pointing this conclusion out, especially in vicious and slanderous pamphlets whose grotesque exaggerations made it easy for him to ignore the substance of the criticisms. In addition his whole upbringing, within the royal Court at Whitehall and St James's Palace, made him very largely immune to considerations of popularity and unpopularity. He and Sarah (also largely a product of a Court upbringing) attributed the attacks on his conduct of the war and his influence on politics to personal malice and covetousness for office and perquisites: the exaggerated influence they attributed to Mrs Masham is a clear indication of this distorted judgement.

Marlborough's dismissal was seen at the time as not just the fall of a minister but as that of a royal favourite. As a prodigiously successful courtier he could be compared with Elizabeth's Leicester or James I's Buckingham. But this conclusion would be a travesty of the truth: John Churchill's ascent had been far from easy or effortless, and his early formative experiences within the royal Court left a lasting mark on his character. He and his sister Arabella knew that their father's influence was exhausted once he had placed them in royal household positions. Thereafter everything depended on them. Churchill as a poor youth saw how much depended on money and never lost an extremely hard-headed and avaricious appetite for it. This would by courtly standards have been excusable if he had indulged in lavish expenditure, but his miserly meanness was well known, and generally regarded as a major blemish and a reason for denying that he could ever be a truly great man.

The assistance that Marlborough received from feminine influences was also held against him. This was almost always exaggerated. Arabella as James's mistress could help him in the earliest years, but it was as an army officer and confidential servant that Churchill became a valued member of James's household. Sarah's companionship consolidated the Churchills' influence with Anne as heir presumptive, but after she became queen friction soon developed with Sarah because of her hectoring attempts at dictation. Absent for most of each year on campaign Marlborough could do little more than offer futile advice calling on his wife to behave in more tactful and diplomatic ways.

The late Stuart Court always resembled a jungle whose inhabitants competed ruthlessly with each other, predators stalked the weak or weakening and there were no rules or safe refuges. It formed a small world in which everyone eyed each other: inevitably the art of dissimulation, of concealing one's own thoughts and even feelings, had to be practised; at this Marlborough excelled. He became noted from an early age for his amiability and even temper, his unfailing polite manners and his ability to persuade and manage others. Even in the years of his greatness he never behaved arrogantly and he never failed to establish an easy rapport with almost everyone he had encounters with – sovereigns, generals (including enemy ones on such matters as exchanges of prisoners), junior officers, Catholic as well as Anglican clergy, even suspicious Jacobite agents. But such control over oneself and the presentation to the world of a mask of civility and politeness were the distinguishing marks of the courtier, part of the personal equipment which Churchill used in his ascent from obscurity to greatness and wealth.

In one important respect Churchill fulfilled a very traditional kind of ambition: he set out – like several of his contemporaries – to found a new family dynasty, to establish it as one of the small number of family-based connections that would continue into the indefinite future to play a leading part in the public life of the country. The death of his only surviving son, while still an undergraduate at Cambridge, disappointed his highest hopes and formed the central tragedy of his life but it did not prevent a dynasty being formed in the female line – although it was not to be until the mid-nineteenth century that it achieved national, as distinct from regional, prominence. But in his own lifetime Marlborough soared over all his rivals: he not only rose from being a plain, poor young gentleman to become a duke and the richest of all subjects, but he also achieved the unique eminence of the most important and powerful person in Europe. Indeed no other individual ever wielded such great and wide powers until Napoleon Bonaparte.

Marlborough's great European influence and reputation did not recommend him to all his fellow countrymen. Few of them realised the extent of the threat to their security and national independence posed by Louis XIV after 1700, when he installed his grandson on the throne of Spain. Most members of the English political nation were far too absorbed in the political warfare between Whig and Tory – which Marlborough himself regarded as a major national weakness, and one in which he never immersed himself (unlike his wife). His first and most decisive victories, Blenheim and Ramillies, received applause from all but the Jacobites but his later successes had a diminishing impact and as Marlborough became a great European figure the suspicion spread that he was subordinating national interests to the selfish ambitions of the allies, the theme which Swift was to develop with lethal effect. Nor did it help Marlborough's reputation with his fellow countrymen that he became a Prince of the Empire, being granted the principality of Mindelheim out of the conquered Bavarian territories as recognition for Blenheim. His cosmopolitanism got under the skin of the stay-at-home, quasi-isolationist English gentleman. There is a telling contrast with Sir Robert Walpole who artfully concealed his immense power in terms of domestic politics by adopting a pose as a simple, fox-hunting, drunken, randy Norfolk squire who could boast famously in a year of European war that no Englishman had been killed in the senseless struggle.

Marlborough's achievement in holding together the alliance against France, made possible by his victories and constant attention to the representations made by the allies, can hardly be overestimated in importance. Whereas Castlereagh held the coalition against Napoleon together for a year, Marlborough maintained allied unity for eight, at first against French military superiority and then despite intense French diplomatic efforts to split the allies. For Marlborough the greatest problems were created by the Habsburgs, especially after he had removed the military threat by his joint victory with Eugène at Blenheim. Then the Imperial Court created difficulties for him by concentrating resources on the suppression of the Hungarian rebellion and on the conquest of territories in Italy, while expecting England (and the

Dutch) to carry the main burden of the war in Spain to install
the Habsburg claimant as king. But the most constant
problems were posed by the Dutch.

Apart from the restrictions placed on Marlborough's
conduct of operations by having to consult and have the
approval of the Dutch field deputies, particularly in 1702–3
and 1705, their policies were (as always throughout the
seventeenth and eighteenth centuries) determined by commercial considerations. Their practice of trading with the
enemy in wartime, which went back to the early years of
their revolt against Spain, and the even more damaging
practice of making finance available to Louis XIV through
Frankfurt and Geneva, survived all his attempts to stop them
through intense diplomatic pressure. In addition he – and
even more the ministers at home – became exasperated at the
increasingly frequent Dutch failures to meet their quotas in
money for allied contingents, ships and men, which reflected
their own economic and financial decline.

The behaviour of the Dutch field deputies and generals
infuriated Winston Churchill to the point where his account
of their frustration of Marlborough's attempts to take the
offensive loses all sight of the context for their defensive
mentality. Like his illustrious ancestor, whom he was
concerned to vindicate from all criticisms and alleged
misrepresentations made of him, Winston Churchill had later
to hold together another heterogeneous coalition against a
powerful enemy. But from 1941 onwards he was to find
himself increasingly in the same position that the Dutch had
occupied in 1702–13, that of a formerly great power now
rapidly approaching the exhaustion of its resources and out-
matched by its allies. His own severe reservations about the
invasion of France, for fear that it might entail a bloodbath
comparable to Gallipoli and the Somme in World War One,
exactly parallel in their assumptions and thinking those of

Marlborough's Dutch colleagues. If he had written his biography after, not before, his experiences in 1940–5 his historical account might have been more sympathetic but his diplomatic activity during World War Two might have been less effective.

Another central aspect of Marlborough's career in which Winston Churchill was motivated by the need – almost an obsession – to vindicate him from particularly Macaulay's condemnatory strictures concerned alleged Jacobite connections. His apologetic arguments on the detail of Marlborough's Jacobite links are unconvincing, and because he denies that they ever had any real importance he is inhibited from offering any coherent or rational explanation for his behaviour in giving the exiled Court at Saint-Germain assurances of his readiness to assist a new restoration of the legitimate king. While James II lived this represented a simple form of life insurance: Marlborough did not want a Jacobite restoration but he had to reckon that one could be brought about by a combined French invasion and domestic rebellion. As conqueror (even by proxy) James would have the nation at his mercy, but prudence and French advice – in order to reduce the amount of support they would be required to provide to keep him on the throne – would favour highly selective punishment. But Marlborough as a prime traitor in 1688 would be on any list of those who were to receive the same treatment as the regicides after the Restoration of 1660. Moreover his dismissal by William in 1692 gave his assurances considerable credibility, although he would only have to honour them if a French army established itself in the heart of England.

After the failure of James's plot to assassinate William (1696) there was really no further danger of a violent restoration, and once James III became the Jacobite pretender a savage proscription and hunt for scapegoats became increasingly unlikely. Marlborough's purpose in maintaining more tenuous connections with Jacobites, including his nephew the duke of Berwick, was to protect himself against a less dire possibility, that he would forfeit not his life but his estates. A Jacobite restoration by negotiation would certainly produce a Parliament venomously hostile to himself. The recent resumption of William's grants of Irish lands to his closest servants had set a precedent, and all the wealth which he had accumulated since 1702 came from the Crown.

Marlborough's conduct was not noble, but he had lived through changeable times and another complete reversal of the wheel of fortune could not be ruled out: there is a close parallel with the behaviour of several Napoleonic marshals, whose comparable prudence was entirely justified by the return of the Bourbons (unimaginable in 1811) before and after Waterloo. Certainly equivocal and expedient, and extremely general or nebulous, promises to Berwick and Saint-Germain cannot be taken as showing that Marlborough's assertions of his concern to preserve the liberties and religion of the English nation were insincere.

Napoleon's refusal to include Marlborough in his short-list of the greatest generals can be defended with the argument that he won many battles but failed to end the War of the Spanish Succession with a final, decisive defeat of the French. In this respect he differed from Wellington who is the most obviously comparable British general (and whom Napoleon slighted as a 'sepoy' general). But there can be little dispute about the fact that Marlborough far excelled any other general of his own time.

Marlborough's first quality was confidence in his own abilities to defeat an enemy who had not suffered a major defeat since the 1640s. From the first weeks of his first campaign he sought to commit his allied colleagues to an offensive strategy based on the principle that the French should be forced to engage in battle with their main force. Yet he had never commanded a large army or planned a campaign.

Marlborough placed great emphasis on his army's mobility, which enabled him to force battle on the French, to manoeuvre them out of prepared defensive positions and to disrupt their attempts to raise sieges. Strategically the supreme example is of course the 1704 march to the Danube; tactically the dawn starts and forced marches of more than twenty miles before the Schellenberg (1704) and Oudenarde (1708). Their success depended on logistical efficiency in providing food, forage, money for pay and subsistence, remounts, even new boots and clothing. This contrasted with the French practice of living off the country, and had the added advantage of ensuring cooperation from the civilian population whom the enemy usually terrorised.

By imposing a pattern of mobile warfare on the enemy in the campaigns from 1702 to 1708 Marlborough was able to turn to his advantage two military attributes in which he personally had a great measure of superiority over any of the generals on the enemy side. First he analysed and used his intelligence information skilfully to form appreciations of enemy intentions as well as the strength and location of their units. By contrast before Blenheim Marsin, Tallard and Maximilian did not know where the allies were and complacently ignored the possibility that they might attack. Secondly, like Wellington in Spain, he never neglected topography. He always tried to reconnoitre the ground personally; when covering the sieges of Lille and Douai he rode into the country to mark out the physical features of ground on which a battle might be fought against an enemy seeking to relieve the besieged garrison. His powers of observation enabled him at Ramillies to move cavalry from their initial positions to concentrate for an attack in massive strength without the enemy realising what he was doing, by using dead ground in the form of a very slight declivity.

In his set-piece actions Marlborough never shirked ordering attacks which he knew would certainly result in heavy casualties, but this was always to achieve a specific result – at Blenheim deceiving the enemy into weakening the sectors in which he intended to make the main attack, at Ramillies on the enemy left for the same purpose. These were the most extended battles of the eighteenth century, but they were fought on fronts only a few miles wide. A general, or generals when Marlborough and Eugène were joint commanders, had to be able to cover all developments, to move to where he was most needed, to scent where critical situations were occurring, to intervene when necessary but not to interfere. Like Wellington Marlborough excelled at his command of the battleground, and like him ran appalling risks in doing so: at Ramillies Marlborough was unhorsed, at Elixhem run down. By contrast at Blenheim all three enemy generals remained static too long and none was available to rally their threatened centre, while at Oudenarde Burgundy simply kept himself aloof, virtually abandoning Vendôme.

The one totally disastrous episode in all Marlborough's battles occurred when he had delegated a difficult task to a trusted subordinate, but then had his attention caught by difficulties elsewhere. He does not seem to have realised that the prince of Orange's troops attacking the French right at Malplaquet had been repulsed twice with appalling losses: he learnt only just in time to prevent a third and suicidal attempt being made. In this pyrrhic victory he and Eugène also seriously underestimated the time that units ordered to outflank the enemy would take to traverse difficult ground. Significantly after 1709 Marlborough did not succeed in provoking a major set-piece battle and there is cumulative evidence that at the age of sixty and after nearly a decade of stress and responsibility he was losing his mental sharpness and, not surprisingly, his physical stamina was declining. Although his political opponents at home alleged that he was deliberately prolonging the war for his own benefit, Marlborough was genuinely saddened by the heavy casualties of Malplaquet and by the failure of the peace negotiations of 1709–10 to bring an end to the war.

In the last analysis all Marlborough's victories depended on his being able to instil in his officers and men the confidence he possessed in the army's ability to defeat the French. He never convinced prince Lewis, and Dutch generals never entirely lost their scepticism or reservations. In fact the claim made for him that, unlike his colleague Eugène, he never lost a battle or had to abandon a siege conceals the full reality. Three of his campaigns – those of 1703, 1705 and 1707 – achieved little in military terms. More seriously it is clear that Marlborough's strategy after Malplaquet had lost its validity. He could never expect to extort the total capitulation which was what the allies were now demanding from Louis by virtuoso manoeuvres and sieges. From 1709 the war was becoming a war of attrition as the chances of ending it by one great victory steadily receded.

By committing himself to the continuation of a war that could not now be ended on allied terms Marlborough revealed his limitations as a politician. It was one thing to try and preserve the independence of the administration from control by either the Whig or the Tory party leaders, but he tended to ignore the need to ensure that its measures were in accord with the interests of the most important sections of the political nation. Immersed in the affairs of Europe, acting as arbiter in inter-allied differences, he lost contact with the minds and prejudiced feelings of ordinary electors; there

233

is an obvious parallel here with Winston Churchill in 1945.

Neither Wellington nor Marlborough feature in the national consciousness as great heroic figures largely because Britain has never possessed the need for a military tradition as a bond to hold the nation together. Marlborough suffers from another disadvantage in that his courtier characteristics – dissimulation, politeness, self-control – conceal his personality from us, and he was the last authentically important person to rise to greatness by the route of Court favour. Nevertheless his achievement is clear enough. He and Tsar Peter were the two men who determined the shape of the European state system for eighty years, until the French Revolution. He completed William's work in converting Britain from a peripheral and quasi-isolationist kingdom of little influence into a great power. He defeated the French bid to establish hegemony, which if successful would have included the restoration of the dependent Jacobite pretender to the thrones of England, Scotland and Ireland, in the process dismantling the union between the first two.

Finally, if a little fancifully, it can be claimed that he and his achievement lived on in the career of Winston Churchill. Naturally he was predisposed in Marlborough's favour, but by studying his career and the reasons for his success Winston Churchill equipped himself for the supreme tests which he was to have to endure after 10 May 1940.

Further reading

The four-volume biography by Winston Churchill, *Marlborough: His Life and Times* (1933–8) is still indispensable, although its rhetorical style and apologetic arguments are now somewhat dated. The more recent studies by Correlli Barnett, *Marlborough* (1974), I. F. Burton, *The Captain-General* (1968), G. M. Thomson, *The First Churchill* (1979), and David Chandler, *Marlborough as Military Commander* (1973), all contain valuable insights. Chandler's *The Art of Warfare in the Age of Marlborough* (1976) is an essential storehouse of information. Frances Harris, *A Passion for Government* (1991), is certain to become the definitive study of Sarah Churchill.

Virtually all the essential military and diplomatic correspondence concerned with Marlborough's direction of the war between 1702 and 1711 are now accessible in print: Henry L. Snyder, *The Marlborough–Godolphin Correspondence* (3 vols., Oxford, 1975), and B. Van T'Hoff, *The Correspondence 1701–1711 of John Churchill, First Duke of Marlborough, and Anthonie Heinsius Grand Pensionary of Holland* (the Hague, 1951), supersede the older, partial material published by William Coxe. However, George Murray, *The Letters and Dispatches of John Churchill, First Duke of Marlborough, from 1702 to 1712* (5 vols., 1845), is still essential, particularly for Marlborough's relations with allied states.

Index

Index

Index

Index

Index

Index

Index

Index

Orkney, earl of: role at Ramillies, 120–2; dissatisfied, 200
Ormonde, second duke of: rival to JC, 58; fails before Cadiz, 67–8; JC denounces, 222
Orrery, earl of, 200–1
Ossian, 7
Ostend, 19–20, 69–70, 165; taken, 126; and Barrier, 132; isolated, 155; supply link, 167
Oudenarde: battle, 87, 135, 156–63, 231; town submits, 126; threatened, 155, 165
Overkirk, Hendrik van Nassau, 56, 62, 68–9, 104, 107, 108
Oxford, earl of, see Harley
Oxford parliament, 23

Paget, John, 3
Palatine: elector, 69; troops late, 103; JC meets, 113
Parnell, Arthur, 51
Partition Treaties, 55, 211, 214
Peter, Tsar, 140, 141, 234
Peterborough, Charles Mordaunt, earl of, 56
Peterborough, Henry Mordaunt, earl of, 19n, 24
Petre, father Edward, 19n, 25, 31
Philip V, king of Spain, 58, 116, 175, 186, 211, 213, 222
Pitt, William, 203
Portland, Hans Willem Bentinck, earl of, 47, 54, 212
Portsmouth: Berwick governor of, 31–2; court-martial at, 32–3
Portugal, alliance with, 74, 80, 129
Prussia: troops from, 60, 74; king and allied command, 62; troops needed for Italy, 99; troops late, 103; bad relations with Dutch, 112; JC tries to reconcile, 113; holds back troops, 118; JC encourages, 124; and Sweden, 137; and a Triple Alliance, 141; to provide more soldiers, 142; JC weary with, 190

Quebec, 196

Ramillies, battle, 101, 120–3, 232
Regensburg, 79
Rijswijk, Treaty of, 58, 212, 214
Rivers, earl, 192, 216, 218
Robinson, John, at Altranstadt, 139–41
Rochester, Laurence Hyde, earl of, 23, 24, 42, 53, 61; blue water strategy, 68; opposes continental campaigning, 205, 206
Roermond, 66
Rommel, field-marshal, 122
Roosevelt, F. D., 5
Rotterdam, 155
Russell, lady Rachel, 13n

Saarlouis, 102–3
Sacheverell, Dr Henry, 7; JC absent from impeachment of, 217–18
Sackville, Edward, 50–2
St John, Henry, earl of Bolingbroke, 195, 200–1, 219; commits political suicide, 224
Saint-Simon, duke of, 95
St Valery-sur-Somme, 164
St Venant, 188–9
Sandwich, Edward Montagu, earl of, 10
Saragossa, 186
Savoy, Victor Amedeo, duke of, 80; JC concerned to rescue, 99, 115–17; presses Toulon attack, 145–6; JC disillusioned with, 190
Scheldt, river, 155, 198
Schellenberg, battle, 86–8, 231
Schomberg, duke of, 35, 42
Scipio Africanus, 7
Sedgemoor, battle, 27
Sedley, Catherine, 24
Sète, landing at, 147
Seymour, Sir Edward, 203–4, 205–6
Shovell, Sir Cloudesley, 145–6
Sicily, 111, 116, 211, 213
Sidney, Henry, earl of Romney, 22, 30, 39
Sierck, 103, 107
Silesia, dispute over Protestants in, 137